LR Parsing

LR PARSING
Theory and Practice

NIGEL P. CHAPMAN

Department of Computer Science, University College London

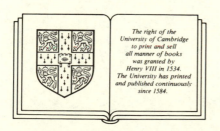

The right of the
University of Cambridge
to print and sell
all manner of books
was granted by
Henry VIII in 1534.
The University has printed
and published continuously
since 1584.

CAMBRIDGE UNIVERSITY PRESS

Cambridge

New York   New Rochelle

Melbourne   Sydney

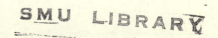

Published by the Press Syndicate of the University of Cambridge
The Pitt Building, Trumpington Street, Cambridge CB2 1RP
32 East 57th Street, New York, NY 10022, USA
10 Stamford Road, Oakleigh, Melbourne 3166, Australia

First published 1987

Printed in Great Britain at the University Press, Cambridge

British Library cataloguing in publication data

Chapman, N. P.
LR parsing : theory and practice.
1. Linguistics – Data Processing
I. Title
418   P98

Library of Congress data available

ISBN 0 521 30413 X

Contents

Preface   vii

1   Introduction   1

1.1   Syntax Analysis and its Applications   1
1.2   Historical Notes on LR Parsing   4
1.3   Presentation of Algorithms   6

2   Languages, Grammars and Recognizers   9

2.1   Languages and Grammars   9
2.2   Bottom Up Parsing   19
2.3   Recognizers   23

3   Simple LR Parsing   33

3.1   LR(0) Parsers   33
3.2   The Item Set Construction   40
3.3   Inadequate States and the Use of Lookahead   46
3.4   Augmented Grammars   54

4   Introduction to LR Theory   56

4.1   LR(k) Parsers and Grammars   56
4.2   Parser Construction   62
4.3   Relationships among Grammars and Languages   69
4.4   Complexity Results   75

5   Practical LR Parser Construction   78

5.1   LALR(k) Grammars and Parsers   78
5.2   Practical LALR Constructor Algorithms   87
5.3   A Practical General Method   94

6   Implementation of LR Parsers   98

6.1   Data Structures and Code   98
6.2   Language Dependent Implementations   112
6.3   Optimizing the Parser Tables   120

7   Using LR Parsers   135

7.1   Supplying the Input   135
7.2   Including Semantic Actions   140
7.3   Attribute Grammars   149

8   Errors   158

8.1   Detection, Diagnosis and Correction of Errors   158
8.2   Recovery from errors   163

9   Extending the Technique   175

9.1   Use with non-LR grammars   175
9.2   Regular Right Part Grammars   180

10   LR Parser Generators   191

10.1   Some Examples   191
10.2   Using LR Parser Generators   204
10.3   Conclusion   209

Appendix
Relations and the Computation of Reflexive Transitive
Closure   211

Bibliography   219
Index   225

Preface

LR parsing has become a widely used method of syntax analysis; this
is largely due to the availability of parser generators and compiler-
compilers based on LR techniques. However, the readily available accounts of the theory of these techniques are either superficial or are
weighed down with tedious mathematical detail of a merely technical
nature. At the same time, much of the knowledge of practical matters
concerning the implementation and use of LR parsers is scattered in
journals or known only through experience. This book has been written
to bring together an accessible account of LR theory and a description
of the implementation techniques used in conjunction with LR parsers.
It is aimed primarily at users of LR parsers who believe that it is undesirable to use complex tools without understanding how they work.

The book does not quite fall neatly into two parts called 'Theory' and
'Practice', but most of the theory is to be found in Chapters 2 to 5,
while Chapters 6 to 10 are mainly concerned with practical matters.
Chapter 4 contains the theoretical core, and is based on Heilbrunner's
account of LR theory, which uses parsing automata and item grammars
to prove that LR parsers do indeed work, and that the widely used parser
construction techniques are correct. In addition, the theory allows the
class of grammars which can be parsed by LR techniques to be related to
other interesting grammar classes, and certain complexity results to be
derived in a straightforward way. This approach to the theory provides
an account of LR parsers more closely in line with the informal notion of
a bottom up parser using lookahead to make its parsing decisions, than
a more traditional method based on 'valid items' and 'viable prefixes'.

The elements of formal language and automata theory required for an
understanding of LR theory are introduced in Chapter 2, and there is an
appendix on relations and reflexive transitive closure computations. No
prior familiarity with this material is assumed, but some mathematical
ability and a little knowledge of set theory and its notation is required.
Detailed proofs of most of the important results are included, but these
may be omitted on a first reading, if necessary.

The practical chapters deal with data structures and code sequences used to implement LR parsers as computer programs, and with the ways in which a parser may interact with other parts of a software system such as a compiler. One chapter is devoted to methods of dealing with syntax errors, and there is a chapter describing some ways in which the LR parsing technique may be usefully extended. The final chapter contains a survey of a few existing systems and includes practical hints on their use. A familiarity with the rudiments of data structures is assumed in these chapters.

As well as material directly referenced in the text, the bibliography includes extra references to relevant papers. It is not, however, exhaustive; the bibliography [BuJa81] can be consulted for additional references prior to 1981.

Acknowledgements: It is a pleasure to express my thanks to Stephan Heilbrunner for carefully reading the draft of this book and for making many corrections and suggestions for improvement. I am also grateful to John Washbrook for comments that have led to improvements in the presentation, especially of some algorithms, and to Simon Peyton-Jones for advice on functional languages. Finally, acknowledgement is due to Donald E. Knuth, who first described LR grammars and parsers, and also attribute grammars, which form an important subsidiary topic of this book. Professor Knuth is also the designer of TEX, the typesetting system which made it possible for me to prepare this book without exhausting the patience of a typist.

1

Introduction

1.1 Syntax Analysis and its Applications

Syntax is the structure of language. In natural languages, such as English or French, it is concerned with word order and the relationships and connections that expresses between, for example, a verb, its subject and its object. The rules defining permissible word orders are part of the grammar of the language. Syntax *analysis* is the process of determining the syntactical structure of a sentence according to the grammatical rules which define the forms of all permitted sentences. This process will be familiar, at least to older readers, as being similar to 'identifying the parts of speech': given a sentence, say which class of word (noun, verb, etc.) each of its constituent words belongs to. This process is extended to identify larger constituents of the sentence, such as noun phrase, subject, and so on. The end result is often displayed in the form of a diagram.

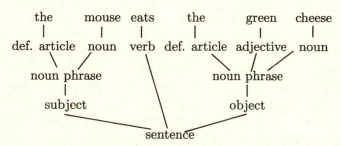

The diagram shows that 'the mouse eats the green cheese' has the structure of a simple sentence, consisting of a subject, verb and object, where the subject is a noun phrase itself consisting of a definite article (the) followed by a noun (mouse). In itself, it says nothing about the meaning of the sentence, but only shows how the words are functioning within it: 'the cheese eats the green mouse' has an identical syntactical structure and is perfectly well formed according to the rules of English syntax. It is nonsense because of the meaning of the words and our experience of the habits of mice and cheese.

A similar analysis can be carried out on 'sentences' written in a computer programming language. In this context, 'sentences' are usually called 'programs', the rules corresponding to natural language grammatical rules are those which express restrictions such as 'the keyword **begin** must be matched by a corresponding **end**', 'two arithmetic operators may not appear next to each other' and so on. The grammar of a programming language also expresses rules such as 'the multiplication operator is more binding than addition'. An analysis made according to such rules will show that the expression $a + b * c$ in an Algol-like language requires c to be multiplied only by b and not by the sum $a + b$. This is clearly important if the expression is to be evaluated correctly in accordance with the intention of the programmer, by a computer. In a similar way, it is conjectured that a syntactical analysis of a spoken or written sentence in a natural language is a prerequisite to understanding it.

It will be apparent that syntax analysis is an algorithmic process: a syntax analyser implements an algorithm, that is, a procedure for determining syntactical structure. Such procedures are commonly referred to as *parsing algorithms* or simply *parsers*.

In summary, the purpose of syntax analysis is to discover the structure of a sentence. This makes the important assumption that the sentence has a structure; that is that the sequence of words to be analysed is truly a sentence, properly formed in accordance with the rules of the language. It is not possible, using the generally accepted rules of English grammar, to construct a diagram such as the one above, for the sequence of words 'green the the eats mouse cheese'. Any algorithm for performing syntax analysis will fail if presented with an ill-formed sentence, or, in the context of programming languages, a program containing syntax errors. It is usual therefore to describe syntax analysis as having a dual purpose: to determine whether its input is a correctly formed sentence in a particular language, and, if it is, to determine its syntactical structure.

For certain languages, in particular for contemporary programming languages, this process can be carried out on a computer. More importantly, it can be carried out systematically, using provably correct algorithms which can be applied to a large class of languages. Programs to perform the analysis can themselves be constructed automatically from a description of the grammatical rules. This is because most of the syntax of programming languages can be modelled by formal structures known as context free languages which can be defined by sets of rules known as context free grammars (these will be described in detail in Chapter 2). Context free languages and their definitions can be precisely mathematically defined and analysed in such a way that parsers may be generated.

A number of different parsing algorithms based on this theory have been developed and put into use. A classification of these can be made on the basis of whether they build up the structure by starting with the symbols of the input and collecting them together into successively larger units in a *bottom up* fashion, or by starting with the largest unit ('sentence' or 'program') and breaking it up into smaller units until a structure is produced that matches the input. This second approach is called *top down* analysis; nearly all parsing algorithms of practical interest fall into one of the two categories. LR parsers, the subject of this book, are a very useful class of bottom up parsers which can be generated for a large subset of the context free languages, operate in linear time (i.e., the time taken to parse an input is directly proportional to its length) and have good error detecting properties. In a sense to be made precise in later chapters, they are the best bottom up parsers.

The most successful application of syntax analysis techniques derived from the theory of context free languages has been in compilers for programming languages. This is true of LR parsers as much as any others and it is a result of a number of factors. In order to generate machine code which is equivalent to a program in a high level language a compiler must first of all determine the structure of the source program, making sure that it contains no syntax errors. Therefore, all compilers must perform syntax analysis in some way. *Ad hoc* techniques suffer from the disadvantage of being unreliable and difficult to generalize, whereas systematic techniques based on theory can be proved correct and applied to many languages, since they result from general properties of all context free languages and not from the properties of any particular language. LR techniques are especially successful because of the wide range of languages to which they can be applied and because they are suitable for automatic parser generation.

It is unfortunate though that syntax analysis has been largely considered of concern only to compiler writers, since it can fruitfully be applied elsewhere. Structure editors for programming languages [Cele78, MoSc81] provide a good example of a useful application in software engineering. It should be obvious that any program whose input possesses grammatical structure could make use of syntax analysis techniques to process it. Examples here include database query languages, text processors and operating system command line interpreters. The languages involved in such applications correspond to the usual notion of a language as a system of writing using symbols, but structural systems of many different kinds may be described as languages, in a formal sense, and it may then be meaningful to perform syntax analysis. Examples arise in pattern recognition, where parsing algorithms have been used to analyse the structure of such things as chromosomes, bubble chamber photographs and handwritten characters [Fu82]. In the area of human-computer interaction work has been done using a linguistic approach; the symbols of the language are the possible user actions and computer system responses, the syntax specifies which sequences form legitimate human-computer dialogues [LaBS78, Reis81].

One area in which these techniques have not been much used is in the analysis of natural language, whether for purposes of translation, textual analysis or man-machine communication. This is because context free languages do not seem to provide an adequate model for natural languages, which are widely thought to require a second level 'deep structure' description. However, recently interest in context free analysis of natural language has revived somewhat (see, for example [JoLe82]) and it is possible that techniques devised for analysis of computer languages may be adapted, at least for modest tasks.

1.2   Historical Notes on LR Parsing

Early attempts to perform syntax analysis using computers concentrated on the parsing of arithmetic expressions. The major problem here is to take account of the different binding power of operators used in ordinary mathematical notation. The very earliest algorithms described for this process needed to work on the entire formula to be analysed, but this was improved as early as 1952 by the invention of a sequential algorithm that only needed to read the formula from left to right, performing the parsing as it went. By 1959, a number of algorithms, many of which made use of a stack to hold partially parsed subformulas, had been proposed for the analysis of arithmetic expressions and for the analysis of the structure of computer programs written in some high level language, which had become recognized as a more general instance of the same problem. (The first Fortran compiler was completed in 1956 [Back57].) Bauer [Baue76] remarks that, with one apparent exception, all the algorithms described by that date operated in bottom up fashion.

In 1957, Chomsky published a description of context free grammars and languages, and their usefulness as a descriptive notation for the syntax of programming languages was soon recognized. Their use in this way became widely known with the publication of the revised report on Algol 60 in 1963, where the syntax of the language was defined using *Backus Naur Form (BNF)*, a notation derived from context free grammars. Work on the problem of mechanically producing an analyser from such a description dates from around this time.

In the previous section, it was explained that a bottom up parser works by collecting together symbols and combining them into larger constituents of a sentence, then combining these larger constituents, and so on. The elements which are to be combined at any step are sometimes referred to as a handle (for a more precise definition of handle, see section 2.2). A bottom up parser obviously needs some way of finding handles. In 1964, the notion of a *bounded context* grammar was developed [Floy64]. In such a grammar, it is possible to determine whether a particular collection of symbols is a handle by looking at a finite number of symbols to each side of it. It became apparent that certain grammars for which it was intuitively reasonable to suppose that it was possible to parse using a bottom up approach were not bounded context. In his 1965 paper [Knu65], Knuth generalized the idea to LR(k) grammars, in which the entire string to the left of the handle is considered, with a finite number (k) of *lookahead* symbols, to its right. (The possibly enigmatic term LR(k) will be explained later.) In this paper, he also gave a parsing algorithm for LR(k) grammars and two methods of testing whether a grammar is LR(k) for some given value of k. One of these methods, at least, provides a basis for an automatic parser constructor for LR(k) grammars. However, as originally described, it was impractical because the parsers produced had large storage requirements and the parser generating process was extremely inefficient, with a running time that increased very rapidly with the size of the grammar. The definition of LR(k) grammar seemed, however, to capture the idea of grammars for which parsing in a single scan of the input using limited lookahead without having to back up or change a parsing decision once it had been made, was possible. Furthermore, the parsers operated in linear time, and although the space occupied by the parser itself was considerable, the working space it used was also linear in the length of the input.

By 1969, a number of practicable algorithms based on Knuth's proposals appeared. Korenjak [Kore69] used a technique of splitting a grammar up into sub-grammars and applying Knuth's algorithm to these separately, combining the resulting sub-parsers into a parser for the whole grammar. DeRemer, in his thesis [DeRe69], was able to define subsets of the LR(k) grammars – so-called SLR(k) and LALR(k) grammars – for which LR-style parsers could be produced efficiently. LaLonde and others ([LaLH72] and [AnEH73]) built practical parser generators for SLR(1) and LALR(1) grammars.

Subsequently, several LALR parser generating algorithms have been devised and used in parser generators which are in daily use. LALR parser generators are widely considered to be valuable software tools. As recently as 1979, however, DeRemer and Pennello could claim (with justification) that '...no-one heretofore has recognized the essential structure of the problem [of LALR(1) parser construction] and provided an algorithm that efficiently exploits that structure' [DePe79]. Thus, the development of optimal and practically useful algorithms from Knuth's original description of LR(k) grammars has been a long and difficult process. It has been helped by the fact that a mathematically rigorous theory of LR(k) grammars has been developed over the same period, so that the practical work on parsing has been supplied with a firm theoretical base.

1.3   Presentation of Algorithms

Throughout the book, algorithms are described in a pseudo-programming language in which notations derived from set theory and those developed in the text are incorporated into the framework of a conventional imperative language. This framework has been chosen, despite good reasons for preferring an applicative language, partly because it is more likely to be familiar to most readers and partly because it is closer to the way in which these algorithms will have to be programmed on a present-day computer. The algorithms should be comprehensible to anyone with a working knowledge of any of the Algol-derived languages. The specific syntax employed is mainly influenced by BCPL[RiWS79] and S-Algol[CoMo82]; the following detailed points are worthy of note.

The expected statement forms such as assignment, conditional, case and loops are present. Compound statements are delimited by { and }, instead of **begin** and **end**; this usage does not conflict with their also being used in the conventional way to delimit sets. Assignments may be combined: $a, b := x, y$ assigns the value of x to a and that of y to b, conceptually in parallel. Declarations are freely mixed with statements; the declaration syntax allows for simultaneous declarations (like the simultaneous assignments just described) and for a limited form of pattern matching in the style of, for example, Sasl[Turn79]. The way in which this works should be obvious from the context. The treatment of types is lax.

Comments, extending from the symbol $\|$ to the end of a line are included. Nevertheless, English text is used to augment the algorithm when it provides a clearer description than the more formal notation.

Because strings are widely featured in the algorithms, the syntax includes a general string slicing operation. If s is a string, $s(i)$ is its ith element, $s(i \ldots j)$ is the substring extending from the ith to the jth element, and $s(i \ldots)$ is the substring from the ith element to the end. These expressions are only allowed on the right of an assignment, it is not possible to assign to the middle of a string.

One construct which may not be familiar to readers who do not know BCPL is the *valof/resultis* expression. This takes the form **valof** { *compound statement* }, where a statement of the form **resultis** *expression* appears somewhere in the compound statement. The compound statement is executed until the resultis is encountered, when the following expression becomes the value of the whole *valof/resultis* expression. This construct thus provides a means of making a compound statement produce a value, without losing the distinction between statements and expressions. It is most commonly used as the body of a function definition.

In Chapter 6, when implementations are considered, several programs are given. These are to be distinguished from algorithms; in particular, objects such as sets are explicitly mapped onto data structures that can be easily implemented. For most of these examples, BCPL has been used, partly out of personal prejudice, but also because a machine-oriented high level language is especially convenient for illustrating the implementation issues that arise on a real computer. Again, readers familiar with an Algol-like language should be able to follow these examples. The main point to understand is that every value in a BCPL program is a *word* and may be used in any way the programmer wishes. (Thus, the language is either typeless or permits an infinite number of types, depending on your viewpoint.) Every word has an address and one of the most important things a word may be used for is to hold an address and thus serve as a pointer. The operator ! de-references such pointers: if x holds the address of y, !x has as its value the contents of y. A vector is a pointer to a contiguous number of words, and by definition v!i = !(v+i) so ! doubles as a subscription operator. Used in conjunction with named constants, declared by *manifest* declarations, the ! operator can also be made to look like a structure field selector. In this way, completely general data structures may be easily built up, but the facility obviously has its pitfalls.

A few points about BCPL syntax: the two way conditional takes the form **Test**...**Then**...**Else** whereas the single branched conditional is **If**...**Do**.[†] A conditional expression in the style of Lisp is provided: *condition* ->*exp1*, *exp2* has value *exp1* if *condition* evaluates to **true**, *exp2* otherwise. **$(** and **$)** are **begin** and **end** respectively. Finally

```
Switchon expression Into
$(
Case constant-1:
     statement
     Endcase
Case constant-2:
     etc
Default:
     statement
$)
```

is the somewhat idiosyncratic syntax used for the case statement. The **Endcase** transfers control out of the whole case statement. In its absence, control drops through to the next case. Since empty statements are allowed, this permits multiple cases to have the same statements associated.

Upper and lower case letters are equivalent, but in this book the convention will be followed that reserved words begin with an upper case letter.

[†] This isn't strictly true, since Do and Then are synonyms, but it is the convention followed here.

2

Languages, Grammars and Recognizers

2.1 Languages and Grammars

For the purposes of syntax analysis it is sufficient to consider text (or programs or whatever it is that is being analysed) purely formally as sequences of symbols into whose meaning, if any, it is unnecessary to enquire. A language comprises those particular sequences of symbols which satisfy certain grammatical constraints which thus define the language. A programming language such as BCPL is, on this view, simply the set of all syntactically valid programs. Many languages, including BCPL, will be infinite, although all use only a finite number of symbols; despite this, it is possible to specify languages in a finite manner. These ideas can be made precise by the introduction of some simple notation and definitions.

An *alphabet* Σ is a finite, non-empty set of indivisible symbols. Examples of alphabets include the sets

$$\Sigma_1 = \{0, 1\} \qquad \Sigma_2 = \{a, b, \ldots, z, A, B, \ldots, Z\}$$
$$\Sigma_3 = \{\text{all BCPL reserved words}\}$$

A *string* over an alphabet Σ is a finite sequence of members of Σ. Some examples of strings over Σ_1 are

$$0 \qquad 1 \qquad 10 \qquad 10110 \qquad 000000$$

Note that the decision as to what constitutes an indivisible symbol is arbitrary, being determined by the particular area of concern. Thus **Endcase** is a symbol in the alphabet Σ_3 but a string over Σ_2.

The *length* of a string s, written $|s|$ is the number of symbols in s; if $s = X_1 X_2 \ldots X_n$, $|s| = n$. There is a string of length 0, the *empty string*, written Λ.

If $x = X_1 X_2 \ldots X_m$ and $y = Y_1 Y_2 \ldots Y_n$ are strings, then their *concatenation* written $x \cdot y$ (or simply xy where context permits) is the string $X_1 X_2 \ldots X_m Y_1 Y_2 \ldots Y_n$ formed in an obvious way. Clearly $|xy| = |x| + |y|$ and, for any string s, $s\Lambda = \Lambda s = s$. Furthermore, the concatenation operation is *associative*, i.e., for strings x, y and z,

$x(yz) = (xy)z$, so either of these may be written as simply xyz. It follows that left and right cancellation are possible: $xz = yz$ if and only if $x = y$ and $zx = zy$ if and only if $x = y$. If $z = xy$, then x is a *prefix* of z and y is a *suffix* of z. If $x \neq \Lambda$ and $x \neq z$, x is a *proper* prefix; y may similarly be a proper suffix.

The concatenation operation can be extended to a cartesian product on sets of strings. If X and Y are sets of strings, then $XY = \{\, xy \mid x \in X \wedge y \in Y \,\}$. This, in turn, permits the use of an exponent notation for such sets by defining $X^0 = \{\Lambda\}$ and $X^i = XX^{i-1}$ for $i \geq 1$. This notation can also be applied to alphabets, considered as strings of length 1; it is easy to see that for an alphabet Σ, Σ^i is the set of all strings of length i over Σ.

Finally, define $\Sigma^* = \bigcup_{i \geq 0} \Sigma^i$ and $\Sigma^+ = \Sigma\Sigma^* = \Sigma^* \setminus \{\Lambda\}$. Σ^* is thus the set of all strings over Σ. [†] In accordance with the remarks at the head of this section, a *language* over Σ is any subset $L \subseteq \Sigma^*$.

Small languages can easily be exhibited. Thus $\{10, 11, 01\}$ is a language over Σ_1. This becomes impractical for large languages and impossible for infinite ones; some other mechanism is required. The mechanism which has proved most successful in computer science is the context free grammar, or CFG, originally proposed by Noam Chomsky as one of the members of a hierarchy of rewriting systems for defining natural languages[Chom59]. CFGs have been used successfully for many years as the basis of the syntax definitions of programming languages.

A CFG is a type of *phrase structure* grammar: it provides a set of rules, known as productions, showing how a string in a language, a sentence, may be built up from its constituent parts, or phrases. Each type of phrase, such as 'noun phrase' or 'subject', is called a *nonterminal*; each production of the grammar shows a possible way of writing some nonterminal as a sequence of other nonterminals and possibly symbols of the alphabet that make up the actual sentences of the language. This can be expressed in a formal definition, as follows.

A *context free grammar* is a 4-tuple (N, T, P, S) where N is a *nonterminal alphabet*, T is a *terminal alphabet* such that $N \cap T = \emptyset$, $P \subseteq N \times (N \cup T)^*$ is a set of *productions* and $S \in N$ is the *start symbol*.

If, for some $A \in N$, $\beta \in (N \cup T)^*$, $(A, \beta) \in P$, it is customary to write the production in the form $A \rightarrow \beta$. A is the *subject*

[†] Technically, Σ^* is the free monoid over Σ generated by the concatenation operator.

of the production, β is its *right hand side*. The productions of the grammar constitute a set of rewriting rules and $A \rightarrow \beta$ may be interpreted as meaning that where the nonterminal A occurs in a string it may be replaced by β. A CFG defines a language by describing how to generate it: the start symbol of the grammar is taken as a starting point and strings are derived from it by successively applying productions to replace nonterminals. The language defined by a CFG comprises the possibly infinite number of strings consisting of nothing but terminals which may be produced by this process; it is thus a language over T. This is captured in the following definitions.

For $\alpha, \beta, \gamma \in (N \cup T)^*, A \in N : \alpha A \gamma \Rightarrow_G \alpha\beta\gamma$ if and only if $A \rightarrow \beta$ is a production of G. The relation $\Rightarrow_G$ is read 'directly derives in G'. If there exist strings $\alpha_i, 0 \leq i \leq m$ such that $\alpha_0 \Rightarrow_G \alpha_1, \alpha_1 \Rightarrow_G \alpha_2, \ldots, \alpha_{m-1} \Rightarrow_G \alpha_m$ then $\alpha_0 \Rightarrow_G^* \alpha_m$. The relation $\Rightarrow_G^*$ is the reflexive transitive closure (RTC) of $\Rightarrow_G$ (see appendix) and is read 'derives in G'. Note the possibility that $m = 0$. If this possibility is excluded, then $\alpha_0 \Rightarrow_G^+ \alpha_m$, meaning that α_m may be derived from α_0 in one or more steps; $\Rightarrow_G^+$ is the transitive closure of $\Rightarrow_G$. From now on, whenever no ambiguity results the subscript G will be dropped from $\Rightarrow_G$, except for emphasis.

The language generated by G is $L(G) = \{ w \in T^* \mid S \Rightarrow_G^* w \}$. The strings in $L(G)$ are called *sentences*; strings that can be derived from S but do not consist entirely of terminals (i.e., strings $\omega \in (N \cup T)^*$ such that $S \Rightarrow_G^* \omega$) are called *sentential forms*.

A language that can be generated by a context free grammar is known as a *context free language*.

Example. Let $G_1 = (\{L, M, E, P\}, \{;, ,, \mathbf{a}, (,)\}, P_1, L)$ where P_1 is

$$
\begin{array}{ll}
L \rightarrow L;E & P \rightarrow \mathbf{a} \\
L \rightarrow E & P \rightarrow (M) \\
E \rightarrow E,P & M \rightarrow \Lambda \\
E \rightarrow P & M \rightarrow L
\end{array}
$$

$L(G_1)$ is a very simple language consisting of lists of **a**s, variously separated by commas and semicolons. Lists may have sublists, enclosed in brackets; the empty list, written as the empty string, must always be enclosed in brackets. Some of the strings in $L(G_1)$ are

$$\mathbf{a} \quad () \quad (\mathbf{a}) \quad \mathbf{a,a;a,a} \quad \mathbf{a,(a,a;a);a}$$

One possible derivation for the string **a,a;a,a** in G is as follows (using

an obvious shorthand)

$$L \Rightarrow L;E \Rightarrow E;E \Rightarrow E,P;E$$
$$\Rightarrow P,P;E \Rightarrow \mathbf{a},P;E \Rightarrow \mathbf{a},\mathbf{a};E$$
$$\Rightarrow \mathbf{a},\mathbf{a};E,P \Rightarrow \mathbf{a},\mathbf{a};P,P \Rightarrow \mathbf{a},\mathbf{a};\mathbf{a};P$$
$$\Rightarrow \mathbf{a},\mathbf{a};\mathbf{a},\mathbf{a}$$

$$(2.1)$$

This is not the only way of deriving this string. For example

$$L \Rightarrow L;E \Rightarrow L;E,P \Rightarrow L;E,\mathbf{a}$$
$$\Rightarrow L;P,\mathbf{a} \Rightarrow L;\mathbf{a},\mathbf{a} \Rightarrow E;\mathbf{a},\mathbf{a}$$
$$\Rightarrow E,P;\mathbf{a},\mathbf{a} \Rightarrow E,\mathbf{a};\mathbf{a},\mathbf{a} \Rightarrow P,\mathbf{a};\mathbf{a},\mathbf{a}$$
$$\Rightarrow \mathbf{a},\mathbf{a};\mathbf{a},\mathbf{a}$$

$$(2.2)$$

And there are many others. Derivations (2.1) and (2.2) have not been chosen entirely at random. In (2.1), at each step in the derivation the leftmost nonterminal has been replaced, whereas in (2.2) it is the rightmost nonterminal which is replaced. These two sorts of derivation provide convenient canonical forms for derivations and, it will be seen later, occupy a special position in syntax analysis. Formally, a *rightmost derivation* is one which consists entirely of steps of the form $\alpha A\gamma \Rightarrow \alpha\beta\gamma$ with $\gamma \in T^*$. Each sentential form in a rightmost derivation is a rightmost sentential form. A *leftmost derivation* consists of similar derivation steps with $\alpha \in T^*$. Its sentential forms are leftmost sentential forms.

Despite their differences, there is a sense in which (2.1) and (2.2) are the same, in that they impose the same structure on the terminal string $\mathbf{a},\mathbf{a};\mathbf{a},\mathbf{a}$. This is not immediately apparent from the derivations themselves, but can be made clear by displaying the progress of the derivation in pictorial form as a sequence of labelled trees.

Figure 2.1.1. Initial Tree

The initial tree (Figure 2.1.1) consists of a single node, labelled with the start symbol. At each step in the derivation the tree grows: the node labelled with the nonterminal being replaced is given descendants labelled with the symbols of the right hand side of the production being

used. Thus derivation (2.1) proceeds as in Figure 2.1.2, carrying on in
a similar way to arrive finally at the tree shown in Figure 2.1.3.

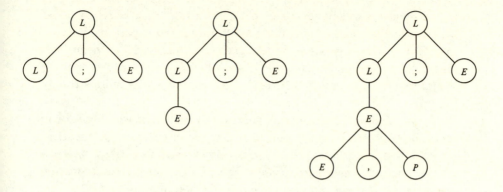

Figure 2.1.2. Steps in the Derivation

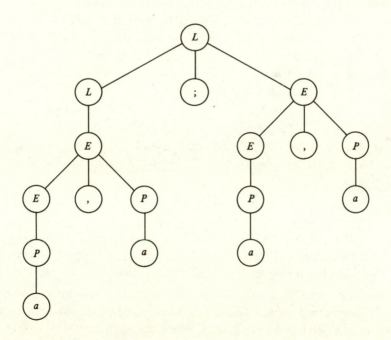

Figure 2.1.3. Completed Tree

The strings formed from the labels of the leaves of these trees read in left to right order (their frontiers) are the sentential forms of the derivation (2.1). The reader should construct the sequence of trees corresponding to derivation (2.2). If this is done correctly, the final tree in the sequence will be identical to Figure 2.1.3. Such a tree is called a *derivation tree* and it illustrates the structure of a particular string in a CFL which is imposed by the grammar being used to define the language. In this particular case, it shows that of the two list forming operators (, and ;) provided in $L(G_1)$ the comma is the more strongly binding.

The two-fold purpose of syntax analysis, to determine whether a given string belongs to a language and, if it does, to discover its grammatical structure can thus be expressed in terms of derivation trees: *given a CFG G and a string s purporting to be in $L(G)$, construct a derivation tree for s or, if this is impossible, announce that s is not in $L(G)$.*

It is worth providing a more precise definition of a derivation tree and examining some of its properties. First some auxiliary definitions are required.

A *labelled tree (of order k) T* for an alphabet Σ consists of
a)   a symbol from $\Sigma \cup \{\Lambda\}$, called the *root* of T, $R(T)$.
b)   zero or more labelled trees, of arbitrary orders, for Σ called the *descendants* of T, $D_1(T), \ldots, D_k(T)$ for $k \geq 0$.
A *leaf* is a labelled tree with no descendants ($k = 0$ in (b) above).
The *frontier* of a labelled tree T is

$$F(T) = \begin{cases} R(T), & \text{if } T \text{ is a leaf} \\ F(D_1(T)) \cdot \ldots \cdot F(D_k(T)) & \text{otherwise} \end{cases}$$

A *partial derivation tree* for a sentence w and nonterminal A in a CFG $G = (N, T, P, S)$ is a labelled tree T_w for $N \cup T$ satisfying the following conditions

a) $R(T_w) = A$
b) $F(T_w) = w$
c)   if $k > 0$ then $R(T_w) \rightarrow R(D_1(T_w)) \cdot \ldots \cdot R(D_k(T_w))$ is a production in P and for $1 \leq i \leq k$ if $R(D_i) \in N$ then D_i is a partial derivation tree for $F(D_i)$ and $R(D_i)$ in G.

A *derivation tree* for w in G is a partial derivation tree for w and S in G. It follows that terminals and Λ may only appear as leaves since the subject of a production is always a nonterminal.

Example. Figure 2.1.4 shows a derivation tree T_2 for the sentence **a;()** in G_1. Notice that there is an explicit Λ-leaf produced by the derivation

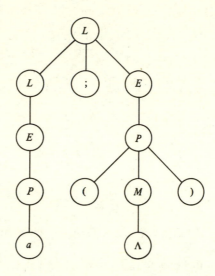

Figure 2.1.4. Example Derivation Tree

step $L;(M) \Rightarrow_R L;()$. Because Λ is the identity for the concatenation operator, though, $F(T_2) = \mathbf{a};()$, as required.

The definition satisfies the fundamental property that one would expect for a derivation tree.

Theorem 2.1. Let $G = (N, T, P, S)$ be a CFG.

(1) $A \Rightarrow^* w$ iff there is a partial derivation tree for A and w in G.

(2) $w \in L(G)$ iff there is a derivation tree for w in G.

Proof. (1) By induction.

If-part. Assume T_w is a partial derivation tree for w and A. Assume T_w has descendants $D_1, D_2, \ldots, D_k$. If $R(D_1) \cdot R(D_2) \cdots \cdot R(D_k) = w$ then $A \to w \in P$, so $A \Rightarrow^* w$. Otherwise, each D_i is either a leaf or has $R(D_i) = A_i$ for some $A_i \in N$ and has frontier α_i. For convenience let $\alpha_i = R(D_i)$ for the leaf descendants. Then $F(T_w) = w = \alpha_1 \alpha_2 \ldots \alpha_k$ (see Figure 2.1.5).

Assume as inductive hypothesis that the theorem holds for any tree with fewer nodes than T_w. Then it surely holds for every descendant, so $A_1 \Rightarrow^*_G \alpha_1$ and since $A \to R(D_1) \cdot \ldots \cdot R(D_k)$ it follows that $A \Rightarrow^* \alpha_1 \cdot R(D_2) \cdot \ldots \cdot R(D_k)$. By considering each descendant in turn it follows that $A \Rightarrow^* w$.

Only-if-part. Assume $A \Rightarrow^* w$ in k steps, for some $k \geq 1$. If $k = 1$ then $A \to w$ and there is certainly a partial derivation tree for w and A.

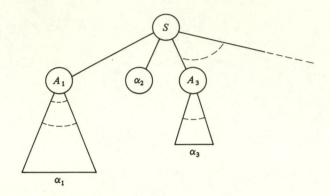

Figure 2.1.5. Derivation Tree for Theorem 2.1.

Assume the result holds for all $j \leq k-1$ and that $A \Rightarrow X_1 X_2 \ldots X_m \Rightarrow^*$ w. Then there is a partial derivation tree for w and each X_i for $1 \leq i \leq m$ that is a nonterminal, and clearly $A \rightarrow X_1 X_2 \ldots X_m$. Thus T_w is a derivation tree for w and A.

(2) follows directly from (1), putting $S = A$. □

Note also that the if-part argument shows that there is a 1–1 correspondence between derivation trees and leftmost derivations. It is equally possible to consider the descendants in right to left order, hence there is also a 1–1 correspondence between derivation trees and rightmost derivations. A parser might thus produce a rightmost derivation instead of a derivation tree as its output and still fulfil its task. This is most useful in theoretical models of parsers, whereas the tree building is of more practical use.

The question arises: does every sentential form have a *unique* corresponding derivation tree? The answer is: in general, no. Consider the grammar $G_2 = (\{L, M\}, \{,, ;, \mathbf{a}, (,)\}, P_2, L)$ where P_2 is

$$
\begin{array}{ll}
L \rightarrow L;L & L \rightarrow (M) \\
L \rightarrow L,L & M \rightarrow L \\
L \rightarrow \mathbf{a} & M \rightarrow \Lambda
\end{array}
$$

which generates the same language as G_1 in a superficially more attractive way. Consider the sentence **a,a;a**. G_2 permits the construction of two separate derivation trees for this sentence as shown in Figure 2.1.6.

This is an undesirable situation, since the grammar is intended to impose a structure on sentences. Grammars such as G_2 which permit

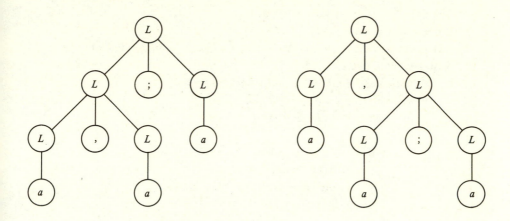

Figure 2.1.6. Derivation Trees for **a,a;a** *in* G_2.

more than one structure are said to be ambiguous. That is, a grammar G is *ambiguous* if, for some $w \in L(G)$ there is more than one derivation tree. (Equivalently, if there is more than one rightmost derivation.) A CFL is ambiguous if it is generated by an ambiguous grammar (thus $L(G_1) = L(G_2)$ is ambiguous). It is *inherently ambiguous* if it is generated *only* by ambiguous grammars. Inherently ambiguous languages do exist (see [HoUl79]).

Since an ambiguous grammar is of little direct use for syntax analysis it would be helpful to have an algorithm for determining whether an arbitrary CFG is ambiguous. Unfortunately, it can be shown (although it is outside the scope of this book to do so) that this problem is formally undecidable, i.e., no such algorithm can be devised. However, it is possible to determine that certain grammars are unambiguous; in particular, the LR parser generating techniques, which form the subject of subsequent chapters, are guaranteed to reject any ambiguous grammar.

Before leaving the subject of derivations it is convenient to introduce a few more definitions related to it.

Given a context free grammar $G = (N, T, P, S)$, a nonterminal $A \in N$ is said to be *left recursive* if and only if $A \Rightarrow_G^+ A\psi$ for some $\psi \in (N \cup T)^*$, *right recursive* if and only if $A \Rightarrow_G^+ \psi A$ for some $\psi \in (N \cup T)^*$ and *self embedding* if and only if $A \Rightarrow_G^+ \psi_1 A \psi_2$ for some $\psi_1, \psi_2 \in (N \cup T)^+$. The significance of these properties will appear later. For the moment it is worth remarking that if any symbol in the nonterminal alphabet of a

Algorithm 2.1. Identification of Nullable Nonterminals

let $G = (N, T, P, S)$ be a CFG
let *nullables, newnullables* $= \emptyset, \emptyset$
for each $A \rightarrow \alpha \in P : \alpha = \Lambda$ **do** *newnullables* := *newnullables* $\cup \{A\}$
until *newnullables* $= \emptyset$ **do**
{   *nullables* := *nullables* $\cup$ *newnullables*
       newnullables := $\emptyset$
       for each $A \rightarrow \alpha \in P$ **do**
       {   **let** $i = 1$
           while $i \leq |\alpha|$ **do**
                  if $\alpha(i) \in$ *nullables*
                  then $\alpha := \alpha(1 \ldots i - 1) \cdot \alpha(i + 1 \ldots)$
                  else $i := i + 1$
           if $\alpha = \Lambda$ **then** *newnullables* := *newnullables* $\cup \{A\}$
       }
}

grammar is both left and right recursive, then that grammar is definitely ambiguous.

A production $A \rightarrow \beta$ of G is said to be *useful* if $S \Rightarrow^* uAw \Rightarrow u\beta w \Rightarrow^* uvw$ for some $u, v, w \in T^*$, i.e., if the production can be used at one step in the derivation of some terminal string in $L(G)$. Otherwise, the production is said to be *useless*. A nonterminal is useless unless it is the subject of some useful production. Finally, a nonterminal A is said to *nullable* if $A \Rightarrow^* \Lambda$.

It is helpful to be able to detect both useless productions and nullable nonterminals, the former because the parser generating algorithms to be described generally assume that all productions are useful and may go seriously awry if this is not so, the latter because, it will be seen, the presence of nullable nonterminals has a profound effect on some of the computations required for LR parser generation. The tasks of identifying useless and nullable symbols are similar so an algorithm (Algorithm 2.1) will only be given for the latter. (Backhouse [Back79] gives a detailed algorithm, with a proof, for eliminating useless productions.)

A suitable data structure for the sets *nullables* and *newnullables* is a bit vector of length $|N|$. A further optimization of this algorithm is possible by taking a first pass over the grammar and eliminating from consideration any nonterminal which is the subject only of productions with a terminal symbol somewhere in the right hand side, since clearly these cannot be nullable.

2.2   Bottom Up Parsing

The main concern of this book is parsing or, as it has now been expressed, attempting to construct a derivation tree for a sentence $w = t_1 t_2 \ldots t_m$ of the language generated by a context free grammar. The properties of the derivation tree indicate that its frontier will match the given sentence and that its root will be labelled with the start symbol of the grammar; the parser's task is to identify the internal structure of the tree which corresponds to the syntactical structure of the sentence according to the rules embodied in the productions of the grammar. The situation facing the parser can be illustrated as in Figure 2.2.1.

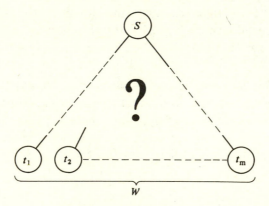

Figure 2.2.1. The Parsing Problem

These two fixed parts of the tree provide alternative starting points for the tree construction and suggest two immediately obvious ways in which to proceed with the task. Either start with the sentence symbol and attempt to construct the tree from the root to the leaves in imitation of the way in which sentences are generated by the grammar, or work in the opposite direction from the leaves to the root. These two strategies are usually referred to as *top down* and *bottom up*, respectively, for fairly obvious reasons. LR parsers are one particular variety of bottom up parser and it is instructive, before going into the details of LR parsing to consider a general description of the bottom up approach.

Notice first that choosing to proceed from the bottom upwards still leaves a choice, in principle at least, about which direction to proceed across the tree. In theory either direction is possible but it is more practical to consider symbols in the order in which they are intended to be read, conventionally left to right (although it should be understood that this convention has nothing to do with the way the symbols are written on paper in their usual form which could quite well be top to bottom or right to left). This makes input much simpler and also simplifies the interface between the syntax analyser and any subsequent processing which may be required.

A bottom up parser, by working from the symbols of a sentence back towards the sentence symbol of the grammar, is constructing a derivation in reverse. That is, it performs steps in which a string of the form $\alpha\beta\gamma$ is replaced by $\alpha A\gamma$ where $A \to \beta$ is a production, so that the relation $\alpha A\gamma \Rightarrow \alpha\beta\gamma$ holds, but the replacement goes in the opposite direction to that implied by the arrow. Such a replacement is called a *reduction*. If $\gamma \in T^*$, i.e., A is the rightmost nonterminal in $\alpha A\gamma$, the reductions will form a rightmost derivation in reverse. Most importantly, this reduction sequence is the one naturally produced by scanning sentential forms from left to right.

Consider then the operation of a parser which works by repeatedly scanning a sentential form from left to right to find substrings which match the right hand side of a production, replacing them by the subject of that production to produce a new sentential form. Such a parser for G_1 given the string **a;a,a** could proceed as follows:

string	reduce by	
a;a,a	$P \to \mathbf{a}$	(1)
P**;a,a**	$E \to P$	(2)
E**;a,a**	$L \to E$	(3)
L**;a,a**	$P \to \mathbf{a}$	(4)
L**;**P**,a**	$E \to P$	(5)
L**;**E**,a**	$L \to L;E$	(6)
L**,a**	$P \to \mathbf{a}$	(7)
L**,**P	$E \to P$	(8)
L**,**E	$L \to E$	(9)
L**,**L		

The parser cannot perform another reduction since no substring of L,L matches the right hand side of any production; indeed, L,L is not a sentential form in G_1. It is obvious that what has gone wrong is that the wrong reduction was performed in step (6). One way to cope with such problems is to allow the parser to *backtrack*: when it gets stuck, it

Algorithm 2.2. Bottom Up Parsing

let $G = (N, T, P, S)$ be a CFG
let $parse(stack, rest) = $ **valof**
{   **if** $stack = S \wedge rest = \Lambda$
     then resultis true
     else {   **for each** $A \rightarrow \beta : \exists \alpha \in (N \cup T)^* : stack = \alpha\beta$
           do if $parse(stack(1 \ldots |stack| - |\beta| \cdot A, rest)$ ‖ reduce
             then resultis true
             if $rest \neq \Lambda$
             then resultis $parse(stack \cdot rest(1), rest(2 \ldots))$ ‖ shift
             else resultis false
       }
}

$parse(\Lambda, input)$

should undo reductions until it reaches a place where an alternative was possible and then try that. This gives rise to Algorithm 2.2, the general bottom up parsing algorithm with backtracking.

Backtracking requires some bookkeeping to keep track of which productions have already been tried as possible reductions for a particular sentential form. This can be handled most conveniently using a recursive procedure *parse* that takes two parameters. The first is the prefix of the sentential form that has been considered by the algorithm so far; the parser treats the string like a stack, with its top at the right, replacing symbols on top of it during reductions. Since rightmost sentential forms are being produced, the substring being replaced must be on top of the stack. The second parameter to *parse* is the remaining unscanned input. If this is empty and the stack has been reduced to the start symbol, the parse is successful, and the result true is returned. Otherwise, each possible reduction is made in turn, and the resulting sentential form is passed recursively as a new stack; if any of these recursive calls leads to a successful parse, the result true is passed back as the recursion unwinds. Otherwise, after all possibilities have been exhausted, if there is remaining input its first symbol is pushed on to the stack. This is referred to as *shifting*, and the shifted input is considered for possible reductions by a recursive call. If there is no input left to shift, the attempted parse has failed, and the result false is returned so that the calling procedure can try any further alternatives. If false percolates right back up to the first level call of *parse* the input is not a sentence.

Any parser that manipulates a stack of partially parsed input in this way is called a *shift-reduce* parser. The recursive mechanism is being used to create multiple copies of the stack and input, and to remember previous states, to permit backtracking. As well as the overhead implied, this means that a backtracking parser must be able to buffer its entire input; this may present a nontrivial problem in realistic applications, such as compilers.

Backtracking presents other problems. The first of these is its inefficiency: the space required by the algorithm to parse a string of length n is linearly proportional to n but the time in the worst case is exponential in n. Because of the rate at which exponential functions grow, such behaviour is not acceptable. Practically useful algorithms must have time requirements which only increase with the input length in a polynomial manner; all else being equal, the preferred algorithm will be a linear one.

A second problem with backtracking concerns the undoing of the effects of reductions as failed recursive calls return. It is important to remember that a syntax analyser is never going to be used in isolation; there will be associated 'semantic' actions such as code generation, interpretation or evaluation. At the very least, the syntax analyser will be producing a tree as its output to be handed on to later stages for processing. If reductions are to be undone then partially built trees must be discarded, implying the need for some form of garbage collection in the system, or perhaps code must somehow be un-generated (which may invalidate the resolution of jump destinations and so on) or the actions of an interpreter must be reversed, which may simply be impossible. All these complications can be avoided if backtracking can be avoided.

Finally, the use of a backtracking algorithm seriously interferes with the parser's ability to provide accurate diagnosis of syntax errors in its input. Indeed, the best that is possible is for such a parser to announce 'this input contains a syntax error of some sort, somewhere', which is hardly satisfactory. It is generally agreed that a primary requirement for compilers and interactive systems is that they produce good, clear and accurate error messages. For this reason alone, most compiler writers would rule out backtracking methods of syntax analysis.

A bottom up parser avoids backtracking if it is able to identify those substrings of a sentential form whose reduction will eventually lead to a successful parse. Such a string is colloquially referred to as a handle. More precisely, if $\gamma \in (N \cup T)^*$ is a sentential form of the CFG $G = (N, T, P, S)$ then a *handle* of γ is a triple (A, β, i) where $A \in N$, $\beta \in$

$(N \cup T)^*$ and $i \geq 0$ such that

$$\exists \alpha \in (N \cup T)^*, w \in T^*: S \Rightarrow_R^* \alpha A w \Rightarrow_R \alpha \beta w = \gamma \wedge i = |\alpha \beta|$$

This full definition identifies the position of the substring within γ and the particular production it is appropriate to reduce by, as well as imposing the required condition that the reduction be a step in a successful parse. All these are necessary to unambiguously identify the handle, but often it is enough to identify the substring β, and this practice will usually be followed.

A bottom up parser should, therefore, only perform a reduction if it has a handle on the top of its stack. The backtracking parser achieves this by trial and error; to eliminate the backtracking, an algorithm is needed to identify handles from the information available when the reduction is to be performed. LR parsers work in this manner making use of all the contextual information provided by the progress of the parse up to that point and also using the next few unshifted characters of the string being parsed.

2.3   Recognizers

In order to understand how an LR parser works and how it can be generated from a context free grammar, it is necessary to have a mathematical description of the operation of a parser and to understand the relationship between it and a grammar. Appropriate models are found in automata theory and two in particular are of interest: finite state machines and pushdown automata.

Finite state machines are useful in modelling a wide range of phenomena which can be characterized as systems capable of being in one of a finite number of different states and of changing state in response to discrete inputs. A finite state machine is fully described by specifying the alphabet from which these inputs are taken, the set of states the machine can be in, the transitions between states in response to the inputs and, additionally, an initial state from which the machine starts its operation and some final states where it stops.

Accordingly, a *finite state machine (FSM)* is defined as a 5-tuple $(Q, \Sigma, \delta, q_0, F)$ where Q is a finite, non-empty set of states, Σ is an alphabet, $\delta: Q \times \Sigma \rightarrow Q$ is the transition function, $q_0 \in Q$ is the initial state and $F \subseteq Q$ are the final states.

An FSM can be depicted as a black box whose only contact with the outside world is via a reading head which scans a tape made up of discrete squares on each of which is a character from Σ (see Figure 2.3.1).

At each step in its operation the machine is in some state q, reads a character, X say, changes state to $\delta(q, X)$ and moves the reading head one square on to the next character. If it is in a state $q \in F$ then it halts.

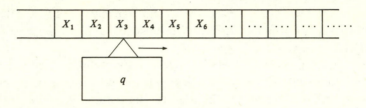

Figure 2.3.1. A Finite State Machine

If the sequence of symbols on the tape is considered as a string then it is apparent that some strings will lead the machine into a final state starting from the initial state q_0. Such strings are said to be *accepted* by the FSM and thus an FSM can be said to define a language by the set of strings over Σ which it accepts, since this is obviously a subset of Σ^* and so a language by definition. This can be expressed neatly by defining a function $\delta^* : Q \times \Sigma^* \to Q$ related to δ thus

$$\delta^*(q, \Lambda) = q$$
$$\delta^*(q, sa) = \delta(\delta^*(q, s), a) \text{ for } s \in \Sigma^*, a \in \Sigma$$

The language accepted by an FSM $M = (Q, \Sigma, \delta, q_0, F)$ is $L(M) = \{\, s \mid \delta^*(q_0, s) \in F \,\}$.

It is convenient to represent FSMs by pictures called transition diagrams. In these diagrams states are shown as circles containing the name of the state and transitions are indicated by labelled arrows: if $p = \delta(q, X)$ then an arrow labelled X will lead from the circle labelled q to that labelled p. Since δ is a function there will only be one arrow labelled with each $X \in \Sigma$ leading from each circle. Final states are indicated by using double circles; the initial state is marked by an unlabelled arrow with no state at its tail. An example is shown in Figure 2.3.2.

It is conventional to allow δ to be a partial function, i.e., $\delta(q, X)$ is not defined for every combination of $q \in Q$ and $X \in \Sigma$, so not every state has a transition for every symbol. If M is in a state q, the next symbol is X and $\delta(q, X)$ is undefined, then M can announce an error – the input is not in $L(M)$. If this seems an unwarranted modification then consider adding a new state Ω such that $\delta(q, X) = \Omega$ for all q and X for which the transitions were previously undefined, and $\delta(\Omega, X) = \Omega$ for all X.

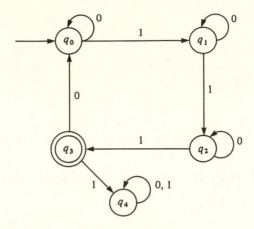

Figure 2.3.2. A Transition Diagram.

Then, reading X from q will never lead to acceptance. Nevertheless, presentation is neater if δ is partial and so it will be taken to be so from now on.

It is easier to demonstrate things about the languages accepted by the class of FSMs by considering similar machines called nondeterministic finite state machines, or NFSMs for short. As will be shown, these accept the same class of languages as the FSMs just defined (which are, in fact, deterministic FSMs) but provide more direct proofs.

An NFSM is just like an FSM except that it relaxes the restriction that at most one of the arrows leaving a state may be labelled with a particular symbol X. Formally, an NFSM is a 5-tuple $(Q, \Sigma, \delta, q_0, F)$ where Q, Σ, q_0 and F are as for an FSM but $\delta: Q \times \Sigma \to 2^Q$ is the transition function. For each combination of state and symbol it specifies a subset of Q as the possible successor states. It may be helpful to imagine the NFSM as being in several states at once, making state transitions in parallel. Alternatively, the machine can be imagined trying each possible transition in turn to see whether any one eventually leads to a final state. In the latter case, the analogy with the backtracking algorithm of the previous section should not be missed.

It is somewhat less straightforward to extend δ to δ^* in this case. The requirement is that, for a set of states P, $\delta^*(P, s)$ should be the set of states in which the NFSM will be after having read the string s, starting in some state $q \in P$. The machine still cannot change state without reading an input symbol, so

$$\delta^*(P, \Lambda) = P$$

The set of states the machine is in after reading a string sa will comprise all those states it can be in after reading the a from any of the states it was in after reading the prefix s, so, for any $s \in \Sigma^*, a \in \Sigma$

$$\delta^*(P, sa) = \bigcup_{p \in \delta^*(P,s)} \delta(p, a)$$

The following lemma shows that this δ^* behaves in a similar way to that defined for deterministic FSMs.

Lemma 2.2. $\forall P \subseteq Q, s \in \Sigma^*, a \in \Sigma : \delta^*(\delta^*(P, s), a) = \delta^*(P, sa)$

Proof Let $D = \delta^*(P, s)$.

$$\begin{aligned}
\delta^*(\delta^*(P, s), a) &= \delta^*(D, a) \\
&= \bigcup_{p \in \delta^*(D, \Lambda)} \delta(p, a) \\
&= \bigcup_{p \in D} \delta(p, a) \\
&= \delta^*(P, sa)
\end{aligned}$$

$\square$

The language accepted by an NFSM $M = (Q, \Sigma, \delta, q_0, F)$ is

$$L(M) = \{\, s \mid \delta^*(\{q_0\}, s) \cap F \neq \emptyset \,\}$$

The following important theorem shows the equivalence between NFSMs and FSMs.

Theorem 2.3. *If a language L is accepted by an NFSM M, then there exists an FSM M' accepting L.*

Proof: The method of proof is to show how to construct an M' and then to show that $L(M') = L(M)$.

Let $M = (Q, \Sigma, \delta, q_0, F)$. Construct $M' = (Q', \Sigma, \delta', q_0', F')$ where $Q' = 2^Q$, $F' = \{\, q' \in Q' \mid q' \cap F \neq \emptyset \,\}$, $q_0' = \{q_0\}$ and $\delta'(q', a) = \bigcup_{q \in q'} \delta(q, a)$. Note that since the states $q' \in Q'$ are subsets of Q, M' is deterministic. Clearly, $\delta'^*(q_0', \Lambda) = \delta^*(\{q_0\}, \Lambda) = \{q_0\}$.

Let $s = ta$ and suppose as inductive hypothesis that $\delta'^*(q_0', t) = \delta^*(\{q_0\}, t) = P$, say. Then $\delta'^*(q_0', ta) = \delta'^*(P, a) = \bigcup_{p \in P} \delta(p, a)$, by construction. But $\delta^*(\{q_0\}, ta) = \bigcup_{p \in P} \delta(p, a)$. Hence $\delta'^*(q_0', ta) = \delta^*(\{q_0\}, ta)$.

Thus $\delta'^*(q_0', s) = \delta^*(\{q_0\}, s)$ for all $s \in \Sigma^*$. Further, $\delta'^*(q_0', s) \in F'$ iff $\delta^*(\{q_0\}, s) \cap F \neq \emptyset$ by construction. Therefore $L(M') = L(M)$. $\square$

The construction used in this proof provides the basis for an algorithm for building FSMs from NFSMs. In practice, the size of the set 2^Q is prohibitively large, so it is necessary to generate only those subsets which are actually accessible from the start state; this is quite easily done and provides a reasonably efficient algorithm. Further transformations are then possible to produce an equivalent FSM with the minimum number of states. See [HoUl79,RayS83] for details.

Theorem 2.3 shows that allowing nondeterminism does not extend the class of languages accepted by FSMs. Therefore, it is legitimate to determine limits on this class by investigating NFSMs even though, in practice, it is more useful to construct FSMs. In fact, as will be proved shortly, FSMs can only be constructed to recognize a subset of the CFLs known as the regular languages. This class of languages can be defined in a number of equivalent ways; the most useful for present purposes is by imposing restrictions on the form of productions permitted in a CFG.

A *right linear (RL) grammar* is a CFG in which all productions are of the form:

$$\left. \begin{array}{l} A \to aB \\ \text{or } A \to a \end{array} \right\} \qquad A, B \in N, a \in T \cup \{\Lambda\}$$

A language generated by a right linear grammar is a *regular language*.

Sentential forms generated by RL grammars contain at most one nonterminal and that will be at the right hand end. This rather obvious fact may be proved formally as follows.

Lemma 2.4. *If $G = (N, T, P, S)$ is a RL grammar and $S \Rightarrow^*_G \gamma$ then either $\gamma \in T^*$ or $\exists \alpha \in T^*, A \in N : \gamma = \alpha A$.*

Proof By induction on the length of derivation.
Base: clearly if $\gamma = S$, $\alpha = \Lambda$ and $A = S$.
Induction: Assume $S \Rightarrow^* \beta = \alpha A \Rightarrow \gamma$ for some $\alpha \in T^*$, $A \in N$. Then either $\exists a \in T \cup \{\Lambda\} : A \to a \wedge \gamma = \alpha a$ which is in T^* or $\exists B \in N, a \in T \cup \{\Lambda\} : A \to aB \wedge \gamma = \alpha aB$, which is in $T^* N$. □

Clearly right linear grammars are a proper subset of context free grammars; it is also the case, although it will not be proved here, that the regular languages are a proper subset of the context free languages. The class of languages recognized by FSMs is precisely the regular languages. This is proved by showing how to construct an NFSM M from a RL grammar G such that $L(M) = L(G)$. This construction thus provides a solution to the parsing problem for the special case of RL grammars.

Theorem 2.5. *If a language is generated by a right linear grammar G then there exists an FSM M_G such that $L(M_G) = L(G)$.*

Proof Let $G = (N, T, P, S)$. Construct an NFSM $M = (Q, T, \delta, q_0, F)$ as follows.

$$Q = \{ [A] \mid A \in N \} \cup \{ [A \to a] \mid A \to a \in P \wedge a \in T \}$$

$$q_0 = [S]$$

$$F = \{ [A \to a] \mid A \to a \in P \wedge a \in T \} \cup \{ [A] \mid A \to \Lambda \in P \}$$

and for symbols $A, B \in N, a \in T$

$$\delta([A], a) = \{ [A \to a] \mid A \to a \in P \}$$

$$\delta([A], a) = \{ [B] \mid \exists C \in N : A \to aC \in P \wedge C \Rightarrow^* B \}$$

The last clause deals with productions of the form $A \to B$ without introducing transitions under Λ, an extension which causes considerable extra complications.

This construction ensures that non-final states bear the names of the nonterminal symbols in sentential forms whose terminal prefix leads to them from the initial state, and final ones the last production used in a derivation of a sentence accepted in them.

Lemma 2.5a. $[A] \in \delta^*([S], \alpha)$ iff $\exists A \in N, \alpha \in (N \cup T)^* : S \Rightarrow^*_G \alpha A$.

Proof The if-part is shown by induction on the length of derivation in G.

Base: If $A = S$ then $\alpha = \Lambda$ and $[S] \in \delta^*([S], \Lambda)$ certainly.

Induction: Suppose $S \Rightarrow^* \gamma B \Rightarrow \gamma b A = \alpha A$, for some $\gamma \in T^*$, $b \in T \cup \{\Lambda\}$ and $B \in N$. Assume, as hypothesis, that $[B] \in \delta^*([S], \gamma)$. Since $B \to bA$, by construction, if $b \in T$ then $[A] \in \delta^*([B], b)$ so, by Lemma 2.2 $[A] \in \delta^*([S], \gamma b) = \delta^*([S], \alpha)$. If $b = \Lambda$, $B \Rightarrow A$ so $[A] \in \delta^*([S], \gamma) = \delta^*([S], \alpha)$.

Only-if is shown by a similar induction on $|\alpha|$.   □

Now, if $S \Rightarrow^* w$ then the last step in the derivation has one of two forms. a) $S \Rightarrow^* \alpha A \Rightarrow \alpha a = w$. In this case, $[A] \in \delta^*([S], \alpha)$ and $[A \to a] \in \delta([A], a)$ by construction, so $[A \to a] \in \delta^*([S], w)$. But $[A \to a] \in F$ so $w \in L(M)$, b) $S \Rightarrow^* \alpha A \Rightarrow \alpha = w$. Thus $A \to \Lambda \in P$ so $[A] \in F$. But $[A] \in \delta^*([S], \alpha)$ and $\alpha = w$ so $w \in L(M)$.

The reverse implication is similar. Thus, $w \in L(M)$ iff $w \in L(G)$. M_G can be constructed from M by the method of Theorem 2.3.   □

The converse of Theorem 2.5 is also true, but will not be needed, so a proof is omitted.

Example. Let $G_3 = (\{N, X\}, \{0, 1\}, P, N)$ where P consists of:

$$N \to 0$$
$$N \to 1X$$

$$X \to 0X$$
$$X \to 1X$$
$$X \to \Lambda$$

G_3 is a RL grammar generating binary numbers with no leading zeros. Applying the construction of Theorem 2.5 gives an NFSM with the transition diagram shown in Figure 2.3.3.

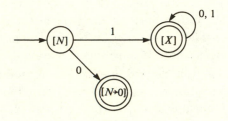

Figure 2.3.3. FSM Constructed for G_3

It is easy to see that a grammar $G = (N, T, P, S)$ which includes only productions of the form $A \to wB$ or $A \to w$ with $A, B \in N$ and $w \in T^*$ also generates a regular language, since an equivalent RL grammar can be constructed by successively stripping single terminals off the front of w, i.e. if there is a production $A \to a_1 a_2 \ldots a_k B$ replace it by

$$A \to a_1 A_1$$
$$A_1 \to a_2 A_2$$
$$\vdots$$
$$A_{k-1} \to a_k B$$

Henceforth this extended form of production will be allowed in RL grammars.

Finite state machines and their properties play an important role in the theory of LR parsing but they do not, in themselves, provide an adequate model of a parser such as that described in section 2.2. The FSM lacks any memory corresponding to the stack used in Algorithm 2.2; it is for this reason that its recognition abilities are confined to regular languages. Consider, for example, the language $L = \{a^k b^k \mid k \geq 1\}$, which is not regular. Intuitively, it is easy to see that the reason no FSM can recognize L (i.e., accept all and only those input strings which belong to L) is that it is necessary somehow to keep a count of the number of as in order to make sure that the number of bs matches. The only way an FSM can 'remember' anything is by being in a particular state after reading it. In this case, to distinguish a^i from a^j when $j \neq i$, it is necessary that $\delta^*(q_0, a^i) \neq \delta^*(q_0, a^j)$ for all $j \neq i$. But the FSM has only a finite number of states, so there is always a string containing too many as to be remembered in this way. If there is some $j \neq i$ for which $\delta^*(q_0, a^i) = \delta^*(q_0, a^j)$ then the machine is bound to accept the string $a^j b^i$ which is not in L. [†] Adding memory in the form of a stack extends the power of an FSM sufficiently to enable it to recognize context free languages. The last-in first-out property of the stack enables the machine to remember left contexts in the required manner while avoiding the unappealing extension to infinite sets of states.

A parser as it has been defined is expected to produce some output in the form of a derivation or derivation tree. Therefore, the model will also be extended to include an output tape onto which the machine may write symbols.

The machine produced by augmenting an FSM with a stack is known as a *pushdown automaton (PDA)*. The stack is a string over some stack alphabet, with its top at the right hand end. The manipulations permitted on the stack are restricted to the replacement of a sequence of symbols from its top end by another, possibly empty, sequence. The information in the stack may also be used to select the moves the machine makes; this is done by selecting the next state, the stack replacement and the symbol to be written to the output on the basis of the current state, the string on the top of the stack and, optionally, the next input symbol, although this may be ignored, allowing the machine to manipulate its stack without reading any input. (Most authors prefer to restrict the machine to examining and replacing the single topmost stack symbol, instead of an arbitrary string on top of the stack. It is easy to simulate a PDA as defined here by one in the more restricted form by adding extra states, but this seems to complicate the notation

---

[†] The foregoing argument can be tightened up into a proof of the 'Pumping Lemma' for FSMs: Let $L \subseteq \Sigma^*$ be a regular language. There is a constant n such that $\forall z \in L : |z| \geq n$ implies $\exists u, v, w \in \Sigma^* : z = uvw \wedge |uv| \leq n \wedge |v| \geq 1 \wedge \forall i \geq 0 : uv^i w \in L$. (See [HoU79].) Context free languages that are not regular do not automatically admit families of strings in this way, so that typically, as in the example, an FSM will accept too many strings to be a recognizer.

unnecessarily.)

Thus, a pushdown automaton is a 7-tuple $M = (Q, \Sigma, \Gamma, \Omega, \delta, q_0, F)$ where Q is the set of states, Σ, Γ and Ω are three, not necessarily disjoint, alphabets: the input, stack and output alphabets, respectively. $\delta: Q \times (\Sigma \cup \{\Lambda\}) \times \Gamma^+ \to 2^K$ where $K = Q \times \Gamma^* \times \Omega$ is the transition function, q_0 is the initial state, and $F \subseteq Q$ are the final states. The possibility $|\delta(q, a, \gamma)| = \infty$ for some q, a and γ must be forbidden. Note that the machine is nondeterministic.

The machine's operation can be described in terms of *configurations*. A configuration is a member of $Q \times \Gamma^* \times \Sigma^* \times \Omega^*$, consisting of the current state, the stack contents, the unread input and the output produced. Each move of the PDA transforms its configuration in accordance with the relation $\vdash$ ('moves to') defined on configurations as follows: For $p, q \in Q, \alpha, \gamma \in \Gamma^*, \beta \in \Gamma^+, a \in \Sigma \cup \{\Lambda\}, z \in \Sigma^*, \omega \in \Omega \cup \{\Lambda\}, \varphi \in \Omega^*$:

$$(q, \alpha\beta, az, \varphi) \vdash (p, \alpha\gamma, z, \omega\varphi) \text{ if and only if } (p, \gamma, \omega) \in \delta(q, a, \beta)$$

The case $a = \Lambda$ corresponds to the stack manipulations made without reading any input. The machine starts in the configuration $(q_0, \Lambda, z, \Lambda)$, i.e., in the initial state, with an empty stack and some input string z and an empty output tape, and halts when it enters a final state.

In LR parsing there is always a simple relationship between the current state and stack contents, and the halting condition may be expressed without reference to final states, so it is only necessary to consider configurations in $\Gamma^* \times \Sigma^* \times \Omega^*$.

The shift-reduce parsing algorithm of section 2.2 for a grammar $G = (N, T, P, S)$ can be modelled by a PDA with $\Gamma = N \cup T$, $\Sigma = T$ and $\Omega = P$ and a moves relation for $\alpha, \beta, \gamma \in (N \cup T)^*, A \in N, z \in T^*, \Pi \in P^*$ satisfying

$$(\alpha\beta, z, \Pi) \vdash (\alpha A, z, (A \to \beta) \cdot \Pi) \text{ iff } A \to \beta \in P \qquad (2.3.1)$$

i.e., a reduce move, and

$$(\gamma, az, \Pi) \vdash (\gamma a, z, \Pi) \text{ for all } a \in T \qquad (2.3.2)$$

i.e., a shift move. The nondeterministic PDA models an algorithm with backtracking.

The machine halts when its stack contains only the symbol S and the input is exhausted, i.e., in the configuration (S, Λ, Π) and Π will be the sequence of productions used in a rightmost derivation of the input. Notice that this makes final states unnecessary, but it does require that $S \Rightarrow^+ S$ is impossible.

Theorem 2.6. *If $G = (N, T, P, S)$ is an arbitrary CFG such that $S \not\Rightarrow^+$*

S and ⊢ is the moves relation of a PDA satisfying (2.3.1) and (2.3.2) then $\forall z \in T^*: S \Rightarrow^*_R z$, using the sequence of productions $\Pi \in P^*$ if and only if $(\Lambda, z, \Lambda) \vdash^* (S, \Lambda, \Pi)$.

The proof is quite simple, since the moves relation ensures that, in any configuration (γ, z, Π), γz is a right sentential form. This begs the question of whether it is possible to construct such a PDA; the proof of that is similar to that of Theorem 2.5 but depends on a normal form theorem for CFGs. For details see [HoUl79, RayS83, AhUl72].

It is possible to define a deterministic PDA by imposing restrictions on δ. Firstly, insist that each state $q \in Q$ has at most one successor and stack top replacement for each input symbol, top stack string combination. This requires $\forall a \in \Sigma \cup \{\Lambda\}, \alpha, \beta \in \Gamma^*: |\delta(q, a, \beta)| \leq 1$ and if $\delta(q, a, \alpha\beta) \neq \emptyset$ then $\delta(q, a, \beta) = \emptyset$. Secondly, there must never be a choice whether to read the next symbol or not, so, if $\delta(q, \Lambda, \beta) \neq \emptyset$ then $\forall a \in \Sigma: \delta(q, a, \beta) = \emptyset$. Unfortunately, whereas NFSMs turned out to be no more powerful than FSMs the corresponding statement is not true for PDAs: the class of languages recognized by deterministic PDAs is a proper subset of the CFLs, often known as the *deterministic languages*. Fortunately, most programming languages are deterministic, so the methods of parsing deterministic languages are of considerable practical interest. The class of languages that can be recognized by LR parsers is, in fact, the class of deterministic languages.

3

Simple LR Parsing

3.1   LR(0) Parsers

LR(k) parsers are so called because they operate in the manner of bottom up parsers described in section 2.2., scanning the input from *L*eft to right, producing the reverse of a *R*ightmost derivation, and use k characters of unscanned input to produce deterministic behaviour. The family of parsing techniques related to LR(k) parsers is distinguished by the fact that, in deciding whether to perform a reduction, they make use of all the contextual information that is available in the prefix of the input string that has already been parsed. In the most basic of the LR techniques, LR(0), this is all the information that is used; the more powerful variants supplement this left context information by considering the first few characters of so far unread input. This chapter describes informally the simplest such variant, SLR(1) parsers, in order to introduce important ideas behind the whole family of techniques.

First it is necessary to consider LR(0) parsers. If $G = (N, T, P, S)$ is a CFG and there is a derivation of the form $S \Rightarrow^*_R \alpha A w \Rightarrow_R \alpha \beta w$ with $\alpha, \beta \in (N \cup T)^*, A \in N$ and $w \in T^*$ then, if a shift-reduce parser has $\alpha\beta$ on its stack it may be correct to reduce by $A \rightarrow \beta$. The set of all such stack strings for which the reduction could be a step in a successful parse is known as the *LR(0) context* of the production $A \rightarrow \beta$, written $LR0C(A \rightarrow \beta)$; i.e.,

$LR0C(A \rightarrow \beta)$

$$= \{\, \alpha\beta \in (N \cup T)^* \mid \exists w \in T^*\colon S \Rightarrow^*_R \alpha A w \Rightarrow_R \alpha\beta w \,\}$$

A parser should perform a reduction by $A \rightarrow \beta$ only if its stack contents is a member of $LR0C(A \rightarrow \beta)$. However, it may be the case that some string $\alpha\beta$ is a member of the LR(0) context set of two or more different productions. Alternatively, a situation may arise where there is a string $\alpha\beta \in LR0C(A \rightarrow \beta)$, but there is also a non-empty terminal string t, such that $\alpha\beta t \in LR0C(B \rightarrow \delta)$ for some production $B \rightarrow \delta$. In the first case, the parser cannot choose one reduction in preference to the other when it has $\alpha\beta$ on its stack. In the second case, since there is a sequence of shift moves which reads the symbols of t, transforming the stack contents into a member of $LR0C(B \rightarrow \delta)$, the parser cannot decide whether to reduce immediately by $A \rightarrow \beta$ or perform a shift move, so as to eventually be able to reduce by $B \rightarrow \delta$. Thus, using the LR(0) contexts to decide when to reduce only provides a deterministic parser if neither of these situations can arise, so that the stack contents is all that is needed to determine whether a particular reduction should take place. In that case, G is said to be an LR(0) grammar. For an LR(0) grammar the problem of whether to perform a reduction thus becomes the problem of identifying LR(0) contexts on the stack. Fortunately, this is a relatively simple task, because of the following result.

Theorem 3.1. *Let $G = (N, T, P, S)$ be a CFG. Then $LR0C(G) = \bigcup_{A \rightarrow \beta \in P} LR0C(A \rightarrow \beta)$ is a regular language.*

Proof Construct the grammar $F = (\{\, [A] \mid A \in N \,\}, N \cup T, P_F, [S])$ where for each production $A \rightarrow X_1 X_2 \ldots X_n$ in P, P_F includes the productions

$$[A] \rightarrow X_1 X_2 \ldots X_{j-1}[X_j] \qquad 1 \leq j \leq n, X_j \in N$$
$$\text{and } [A] \rightarrow X_1 X_2 \ldots X_n$$

F is right linear, so $L(F)$ is regular. Furthermore, it is easy to see that, for $\psi \in (N \cup T)^*$, $[S] \Rightarrow_F^* \psi$ if and only if

$$\exists \alpha, \beta \in (N \cup T)^*, A \in N, w \in T^*: S \Rightarrow_{GR}^* \alpha A w \Rightarrow_{GR} \alpha \beta w \wedge \psi = \alpha\beta$$

since derivations in F 'shadow' those in G, with the rightmost nonterminal in the sentential forms of G corresponding to a nonterminal $[A]$ in the sentential forms of F. Thus, $\psi \in L(F)$ iff $\exists A \rightarrow \beta \in P : \psi \in LR0C(A \rightarrow \beta)$, so that $LR0C(G)$ is a regular language. $\square$

It is therefore possible, given an LR(0) grammar G, to construct from it an RL grammar F, and then, using algorithms based on Theorems 2.5 and 2.3 to build a deterministic FSM to recognize strings in $LR0C(G)$. Because of the LR(0) condition, no final state will have any outgoing transitions. Such states are therefore *reduce states*; since a string in $LR0C(G)$ has just been recognized the handle on top of the stack can be replaced as one step in the parse. The production to be used can be obtained by mapping final states to productions of G by a function Reduce, such that Reduce($[[A] \rightarrow X_1 X_2 \ldots X_n]$) = $A \rightarrow X_1 X_2 \ldots X_n$.

The construction of such a FSM, known as the *characteristic FSM of G*, provides the basis of a parser, whose operation is described by

Algorithm 3.1. LR(0) Parsing

let $G = (N, T, P, S)$ be an LR(0) CFG
let $M = (Q, N \cup T, \delta, q_0, F)$ be G's characteristic FSM
let Reduce: $F \to P$ map reduce states to corresponding productions
let $\gamma = input$
let $stack = \Lambda$
let $q = q_0$
until $stack = S \wedge \gamma = \Lambda$ **do**
{   **if** $q \notin F$
        then   {   ‖   shift
                        let $X = \gamma(1)$
                        $\gamma := \gamma(2 \ldots)$
                        if $\delta(q, X)$ is undefined
                        then *error*
                        else { $stack := stack \cdot X$; $q := \delta(q, X)$ }
                    }
        else   {   ‖   reduce
                        let $A \to \beta = \text{Reduce}(q)$
                        $stack := stack(1 \ldots |stack| - |\beta|) \cdot A$
                        if $stack = S \wedge \gamma \neq \Lambda \wedge \delta(q_0, S)$ is undefined
                        then *error*
                        else { $q := q_0$
                                    for $i = 1$ **to** $|stack| - 1$ **do** $q := \delta(q, stack(i))$
                                    unless $stack = S \wedge \gamma = \Lambda$ **do** $q := \delta(q, A)$
                                }
                    }
        }
}

Algorithm 3.1. This is a shift-reduce algorithm. Since there is no back-tracking, and thus no need to remember stacks, the recursion of Algorithm 2.2 can be unwrapped into an iterative form. The characteristic FSM is used to control when a reduction takes place; since the sentential form produced by a reduction consists of the remaining input appended to the stack, the FSM must scan the stack after the reduction before considering any more input symbols, unless the stack contains only the start symbol. In that case, if there is no remaining input, the parse is successful; otherwise it is possible that the remaining symbols are super-fluous. This can be detected, since $\delta(q_0, S)$ will be undefined if $S \Rightarrow^* Sz$ is impossible for all $z \in T^+$.

There may be strings $\gamma \notin L(G)$ which will cause this algorithm to attempt to shift symbols from beyond the end of γ. To prevent this, an *endmarker symbol* $\dashv$ should be appended to γ; it corresponds to an end of file indication in a real input. $\delta(q, \dashv)$ is undefined for all q, so strings not in $L(G)$ will always cause an error (even if they are a prefix of some string which is in $L(G)$). It is convenient to assume that $\dashv \in T$, but never appears on the right hand side of any production (i.e., $P \subseteq N \times (N \cup T \setminus \{\dashv\})^*$).

The algorithm as just presented has another weakness: if the string γ has the form $\alpha\beta w$ before reduction, after reduction it will be $\alpha A w$. The characteristic FSM will now return to state q_0 and scan the updated stack containing αA. Since it is a deterministic FSM, having re-read α it will be in the same state it was in after reading it the first time; the second scanning is wasted if it is possible to remember the state the machine entered after reading α initially. This is easily done by providing the parser with a stack on which it pushes each state as it enters it. When the machine reduces by a production $A \to \beta$, in the context $\alpha\beta$, $|\beta|$ states are popped off the stack and the current state is set to the new stack top. This state is $\delta^*(q_0, \alpha)$, the state it would have been in after re-scanning α. Only the following transition under A need be made as part of the reduction, so that only the terminals of the input need be read, in a single scan, left to right, as in Algorithm 3.2.

The A-successor required by the reduction is guaranteed to be defined, except in the special case mentioned above in connection with Algorithm 3.1: if the start symbol S is not left recursive $\delta(q_0, S)$ will be undefined. This transition will only be required if the input is some string wz such that $S \Rightarrow^* Sz \Rightarrow^* wz$, with $|z| > 0$. In that case, $wz \notin L(G)$, so an error should be reported, but a special test is needed to prevent the parser from trying to change to a nonexistent state. (S might be left recursive, so it is not correct to report an error whenever $A = S \wedge \sigma = q_0 \wedge \gamma \neq \dashv$; see the following example.)

Example.

Let $G_4 = (\{L, E\}, \{(,), ,, \mathbf{a}\}, P_4, L)$ where P_4 consists of

$$L \to L,E \qquad E \to \mathbf{a}$$
$$L \to E \qquad E \to (L)$$

Algorithm 3.2. Improved LR(0) Parsing

let $G = (N, T, P, S)$ be an LR(0) CFG
let $M = (Q, N \cup T, \delta, F)$ be G's characteristic FSM
let Reduce: $F \to P$ map reduce states to corresponding productions
let $\gamma = input \cdot \dashv$
let $\sigma = q_0$ ‖   state stack
let $q, X = q_0, \gamma(1)$
let $accepted = $ **false**
while $\neg accepted$ **do**
{   **if** $q \notin F$
     then { $\gamma := \gamma(2 \dots)$
           if $\delta(q, X)$ is undefined **then** *error*
                         else { $q := \delta(q, X)$; $X := \gamma(1)$ }
           $\sigma := \sigma \cdot q$
         }
     else {   **let** $A \to \beta = $ Reduce(q)
           $\sigma := \sigma(1 \dots |\sigma| - |\beta|)$
           if $A = S \wedge \sigma = q_0$
           then if $\gamma = \dashv$ **then** *accepted* := **true**
                      else if $\delta(q_0, S)$ is undefined **then** *error*
           unless *accepted* **do** { $q := \delta(\sigma(|\sigma|), A)$; $\sigma := \sigma \cdot q$ }
         }
}

The corresponding grammar F_4 has productions
$$[L] \to [L]$$
$$[L] \to L, [E] \qquad [E] \to \mathbf{a}$$
$$[L] \to L, E \qquad [E] \to ([L]$$
$$[L] \to [E] \qquad [E] \to (L)$$
$$[L] \to E$$

In G_4 there is a rightmost derivation $L \Rightarrow L, E \Rightarrow L, \mathbf{a}$. Corresponding to this in F_4 is the derivation $[L] \Rightarrow L, [E] \Rightarrow L, \mathbf{a}$, and $L, \mathbf{a} \in LR0C(E \to \mathbf{a})$.

The characteristic FSM's transition diagram is shown in Figure 3.1.1, where reduce states have been indicated by double circles annotated with the corresponding production.

Note that no reduce states have outgoing transitions, hence it can be deduced that G_4 is LR(0). Given the input $\mathbf{a}, (\mathbf{a}, \mathbf{a})$ to parse, Algorithm

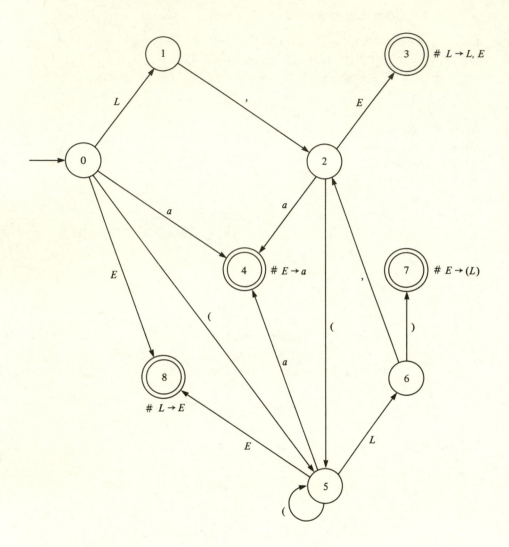

Figure 3.1.1 CFSM Transition Diagram for G_4

3.2 behaves as shown in Figure 3.1.2.

The LR(0) parsing algorithm can be described abstractly in a succinct fashion by defining an LR(0) *automaton* (LRA). An LR(0) automaton for a CFG $G = (N, T, P, S)$ is a 6-tuple $(Q, V, P, q_0, \delta, \text{Reduce})$ where Q is the set of LR(0) states, $V = N \cup T$, P is the production set of G, $q_0 \in Q$ is the initial state, $\delta : Q \times V \rightarrow Q$ is the transition function and

unscanned input	state stack	reduction
a,(a,a)⊣	0	
,(a,a)⊣	04	$E \rightarrow$ **a**
,(a,a)⊣	08	$L \rightarrow E$
,(a,a)⊣	01	
(a,a)⊣	012	
a,a)⊣	0125	
,a)⊣	01254	$E \rightarrow$ **a**
,a)⊣	01258	$L \rightarrow E$
,a)⊣	01256	
a)⊣	012562	
)⊣	0125624	$E \rightarrow$ **a**
)⊣	0125623	$L \rightarrow L,E$
)⊣	01256	
⊣	012567	$E \rightarrow (L)$
⊣	0123	$L \rightarrow L,E$
		accept

Figure 3.1.2. Example Parse by Algorithm 3.2.

Reduce: $Q \rightarrow 2^P$ is the reduce function.

The operation of Algorithm 3.2 can be described by moves between configurations as in a PDA. For an LR(0) automaton, the stack component of the configuration is a string in Q^* and the input is in $T^* \cdot \{\dashv\}$. The output should be a representation of the parse; as mentioned in section 2.1, a convenient representation is the sequence of productions used to reduce the input. Thus, a configuration is a member of $Q^* \times T^* \cdot \{\dashv\} \times P^*$, and the current state of the parser will always be the top stack element. The moves of the parser are as follows: shift moves, where

$$(\rho q, az, \Pi) \vdash (\rho qp, z, \Pi) \text{ if } p = \delta(q, a) \text{ is defined}$$

and reduce moves, where

$$(\rho p \sigma q, z, \Pi) \vdash (\rho pr, z, (A \rightarrow \beta) \cdot \Pi) \text{ if}$$

$$\text{Reduce}(q) = A \rightarrow \beta \text{ and } |\sigma q| = |\beta| \text{ and } \delta(p, A) = r$$

The initial configuration is $(\Lambda, z\dashv, \Lambda)$ where z is the string to be parsed. The machine halts in a configuration $(\rho q, \dashv, \Pi)$ if $\text{Reduce}(q) = S \rightarrow \alpha$ for some $\alpha \in (N \cup T)^*$ and $|\alpha| = |\rho q|$. It should be noted that $S \Rightarrow^+ S$ must again be impossible.

3.2   The Item Set Construction

The construction of the previous section is rarely used in practice in the form presented; instead, a method of producing the characteristic FSM directly from the grammar is preferred as the basis of most LR parser constructors. This method will be described informally in this section; a more formal description and proof are deferred until the next chapter.

The method is based on the use of *items*. An item is a production with a distinguished position in its right hand side, i.e., it is a triple (A, α, β) such that $A \rightarrow \alpha\beta \in P$. Usually, an item is written as a production with a dot in its right hand side: $A \rightarrow \alpha \cdot \beta$ represents the item (A, α, β). Either α or β or both may be Λ in which case they are omitted. The intention of this notation is to indicate how much of a production has been seen at a particular point in the parsing process. Thus, if $A \rightarrow XYZ$ were a production, the item $A \rightarrow X \cdot YZ$ would correspond to a situation where a string derivable from X had been seen as a suffix of the scanned input and a string derivable from YZ was expected, leading to a reduction of XYZ to A. In the construction process, items are grouped together into *item sets* which comprise all items which might correspond to a particular 'state of the parse'. The way this is done is best introduced by an example.

Consider again the grammar G_4 whose productions are reproduced here for convenience.

$$L \rightarrow L,E \qquad E \rightarrow \mathbf{a}$$
$$L \rightarrow E \qquad E \rightarrow (L)$$

A parser for G_4 will start having seen no input and hoping to see a string derivable from L. This situation can be represented by the items $L \rightarrow \cdot L,E$ and $L \rightarrow \cdot E$. Since the latter implies that the next thing to be expected in the input is a string derivable from E, and since $E \rightarrow \mathbf{a}$, it follows that in this same initial situation a string derivable from $\mathbf{a}$ ($\mathbf{a}$ itself) is expected. Thus the item $E \rightarrow \cdot \mathbf{a}$ also corresponds, as does the item $E \rightarrow \cdot(L)$ taken from the other production with E as its subject. This gives the initial item set

$$\Im_0 = \{ L \rightarrow \cdot L,E$$
$$L \rightarrow \cdot E$$
$$E \rightarrow \cdot \mathbf{a}$$
$$E \rightarrow \cdot(L) \}$$

The construction of the parser using items works by identifying item sets with states of the characteristic FSM. $\Im_0$ is clearly the initial state;

the other states can be found by considering its possible successors. Consider, for example, what should happen if the first character of the input is a left bracket. In that situation, since $E \to (L)$ and the opening bracket has been seen the parser must expect a string derivable from $L)$ to reduce the whole to E. This corresponds to the item $E \to (\cdot L)$. Similar reasoning to that used in adding items to $\Im_0$ leads to an item set for this situation

$$\Im_(= \{ E \to (\cdot L)$$
$$L \to \cdot L,E$$
$$L \to \cdot E$$
$$E \to \cdot \mathbf{a}$$
$$E \to \cdot (L) \}$$

Furthermore, if the parser was initially in the state $\Im_0$, having seen the left bracket it would change state to $\Im_($, so that $\delta(\Im_0, () = \Im_($. $\Im_0$ will have successor states for each of the symbols following the dot in items of $\Im_0$, and each of these successors will have two parts: a *nucleus* consisting of items in which the dot has been moved over to follow the symbol, and a *closure* formed by adding items with the dot at the start of the right hand side of productions whose subject is a symbol following the dot in an item already in the item set. The symbol, if any, following the dot in an item is called its *successor symbol*; the item set whose nucleus comprises the items formed by moving the dot across successor symbol X for items in an item set $\Im$ is called $\Im$'s X-successor. An item in which the dot appears at the end of the production's right hand side has no successor and no successor symbol.

Each successor to $\Im_0$ will have its own successors computed in the same way as $\Im_($. This computation of successors will eventually halt to give the LR(0) *collection of item sets*. For G_4 this collection is shown in Figure 3.2.1 where nucleus items are separated from closure items by a broken line. Several points should be observed: the LR(0) collection is a set and thus contains no duplicate item sets. Thus the **a**-successors to states 0, 2 and 5 are all the same item set 4. It is this fact that ensures that the computation will terminate (since a grammar is finite the number of items produced from it is finite, so the number of possible item sets is finite, although large). Whereas this fact is fairly obvious in a description of the construction, it must be remembered if the construction is to be programmed: after computing a successor item set, a program must check that it is not already present before adding it to the LR(0) collection. The FSM to be produced by the construction process

Item Set	Items	Successors
0	$L \rightarrow \cdot L,E$ $L \rightarrow \cdot E$ $---------$ $E \rightarrow \cdot \mathbf{a}$ $E \rightarrow \cdot (L)$	$L \Rightarrow 1$ $E \Rightarrow 8$ $\mathbf{a} \Rightarrow 4$ $(\Rightarrow 5$
1	$L \rightarrow L \cdot ,E$	$, \Rightarrow 2$
2	$L \rightarrow L, \cdot E$ $-------$ $E \rightarrow \cdot \mathbf{a}$ $E \rightarrow \cdot (L)$	$E \Rightarrow 3$ $\mathbf{a} \Rightarrow 4$ $(\Rightarrow 5$
3	$L \rightarrow L,E \cdot$	$\#L \rightarrow L,E$
4	$E \rightarrow \mathbf{a} \cdot$	$\#E \rightarrow \mathbf{a}$
5	$E \rightarrow (\cdot L)$ $--------$ $L \rightarrow \cdot L,E$ $L \rightarrow \cdot E$ $E \rightarrow \cdot \mathbf{a}$ $E \rightarrow \cdot (L)$	$L \Rightarrow 6$ $E \Rightarrow 8$ $\mathbf{a} \Rightarrow 4$ $(\Rightarrow 5$
6	$E \rightarrow (L \cdot)$ $L \rightarrow L \cdot ,E$	$) \Rightarrow 7$ $, \Rightarrow 2$
7	$E \rightarrow (L) \cdot$	$\#E \rightarrow (L)$
8	$L \rightarrow E \cdot$	$\#L \rightarrow E$

Figure 3.2.1. Item Set Construction for G_4

is to be deterministic, so each item set can have only one successor for any symbol. Thus the set 5 has one L-successor (set 6) whose nucleus comprises both the items obtained by moving the dot over L in items in set 5.

An item with a dot at the right hand end obviously corresponds to the situation where a handle has been found and should trigger a reduce action; in Figure 3.2.1 a reduction by $A \rightarrow \beta$ is indicated by the annotation $\#A \rightarrow \beta$. If the transitions and reductions are abstracted away from the actual sets of items the result is an FSM identical to that obtained in section 3.1 by the construction of Theorem 3.1. In fact, as will be shown in Chapter 4, the item set construction will always produce the LR(0) characteristic FSM.

The item set construction can be neatly summarized by defining a relation $\downarrow$ on items. For all $A, B \in N$, $\alpha, \beta, \gamma \in (N \cup T)^*$

$$A \rightarrow \alpha \cdot B\beta \downarrow B \rightarrow \cdot \gamma \text{ iff } A \rightarrow \alpha B\beta \in P \wedge B \rightarrow \gamma \in P \qquad (3.2.1)$$

and for a set of items $\Im$

$$\text{closure}(\Im) = \{\, I \mid \exists I' \in \Im \colon I' \downarrow^* I \,\} \tag{3.2.2}$$

where $\downarrow^*$ is the reflexive transitive closure of $\downarrow$. Thus $\text{closure}(\Im)$ gives all the items added to $\Im$ by successive $\downarrow$ steps. The X-successor nucleus of an item set $\Im$ is given by

$$\text{succ}(\Im, X) = \{\, A \to \alpha X \cdot \beta \mid A \to \alpha \cdot X\beta \in \Im \,\} \tag{3.2.3}$$

(Thus $\text{succ}(\Im, X) = \emptyset$ if $\Im$ has no X-successor.) The initial item set is

$$\Im_0 = \text{closure}(\{\, S \to \cdot\alpha \mid S \to \alpha \in P \,\}) \tag{3.2.4}$$

If $G = (N, T, P, S)$ is a CFG, then its LR(0) automaton $LRA = (Q, N \cup T, P, q_0, \delta, \text{Reduce})$ can be constructed with

$$q_0 = \Im_0$$

$$\delta(q, X) = \text{closure} \cdot \text{succ}(q, X) \text{ for } q \in Q, X \in N \cup T$$

$$\text{Reduce}(q) = \{\, A \to \beta \mid A \to \beta \cdot \in q \,\} \text{ for } q \in Q$$

where Q is identified with the subset of the set of all item sets for G for which $\delta^*(q_0, w) \neq \emptyset$ for some w. It is thus the smallest Q satisfying

$$Q = \{q_0\} \cup \{\, q \mid \exists X \in (N \cup T), p \in Q \colon q = \delta(p, X) \,\} \cup \{\emptyset\}$$

It is customary to omit the transitions to $\emptyset$ and use a partial δ, as in section 2.3; the expressions '$\delta(q, X) = \emptyset$' and '$\delta(q, X)$ is undefined' are to be understood as equivalent.

A recursive algorithm (Algorithm 3.3.) for constructing the LR(0) automaton follows almost immediately from these definitions.

It is worth looking at the data structures that would be used in implementing this algorithm as part of a parser generator and at the coding-level improvements that could be made.

The algorithm requires some internal representation of the grammar and of the nonterminal and terminal symbols. It is worthwhile using a symbol table for these and performing simple lexical analysis when the grammar is read by the program so that symbols can be represented by codes or symbol table addresses internally. The symbol table will have to distinguish between terminals and nonterminals in such a way that the predicate *isnonterminal* may be implemented. The productions can most conveniently be represented by a pair of vectors, *subject* and *rhs*. For the ith production (in some ordering), the entry in *subject* is the code for its subject, the entry in *rhs* points to a vector containing the codes for the symbols of the right hand side. A count in word 0 of this vector could be used for the length of the right part. An item $A \to \alpha \cdot \beta$ can then be represented as a pair (p, j) where $A \to \beta$ is the pth production

Algorithm 3.3. Item Set Construction

let $G = (N, T, P, S)$
let $C = \emptyset$ ‖ LR(0) collection
let $\delta = \emptyset$

proc *successors*(I)
    for $X \in (N \cup T)$ **do**
    {   **let** $XsuccI = closure(succ(I, X))$
      $\delta(I, X) := XsuccI$
      if $XsuccI \neq \emptyset \wedge XsuccI \notin C$ **do**
      { $C := C \cup \{XsuccI\}$
        successors$(XsuccI)$
      }
    }

where *closure*(I) =**valof**
{   **let** $C = I$
    repeat
      for $i \in C$ **do**
      {   **let** $X = succ.sym(i)$
        if *isnonterminal*(X) **do**
          for all $X \rightarrow \beta \in P$ **do** $C := C \cup \{X \rightarrow \cdot\beta\}$
      }
    until no more items are added to C
    resultis C
}

and *succ*(I, X) =**valof**
{   **let** $s = \emptyset$
    for $i \in I \mid succ.sym(i) = X$ **do**
      $s := s \cup \{A \rightarrow \alpha X \cdot \beta \mid i = A \rightarrow \alpha \cdot X\beta\}$
    resultis s
}

let *initial.set*$= closure(\{S \rightarrow \cdot\alpha \mid S \rightarrow \alpha \in P\})$
$C := initial.set$
successors$(initial.set)$

and $|\alpha| = j$. The successor symbol of this item would then be (in BCPL)
`rhs!p!(i+1)`.

    Item sets are lists of items. If space is not a serious consideration, it is
worthwhile keeping items' successor symbols in the list and maintaining

Algorithm 3.4. Improved Closure Computation

```
proc closure(I) = valof
{      let c = I
       for i ∈ I do
       {    let X = succ.sym(i)
            if isnonterminal(X) do
            { for X → α ∈prods(X) ‖ list of productions with subject X
                 do c := c ∪ { B → ·β | X → α ↓*_p B → β }
            }
       }
       resultis c
}
```

the list in order of successor symbols. This ensures that all items with the same successor symbol can be dealt with at once; keeping lists in some order also speeds up the search for item sets already present in C (the innocuous-looking test $X succ I \notin C$ in the procedure *successors*). A real program would not iterate through all vocabulary symbols, but only process the actual items present using their successor symbols.

The procedure given for computing closure sets, while effective, is not particularly efficient, and the computation will be duplicated for many items. The approach suggested by the abstract version of the algorithm of precomputing $\downarrow^*$ using fast RTC techniques is also rather impractical because the relation is defined on items and the set of all items is a large one. However, since all items added by the closure operation are of the form $A \rightarrow \cdot\beta$ with the dot at the beginning of the right hand side this relation actually has a more constrained shape. Items are contributed to the closure set either because an item in the nucleus has a dot before a nonterminal or because an item already added by closure is for a production whose right hand side begins with a nonterminal. This suggests a better way to compute the closure by keeping a list for each nonterminal of those productions of which it is the subject and a relation $\downarrow_p$ defined on *productions* such that $A \rightarrow B\alpha \downarrow_p B \rightarrow \beta$, so $A \rightarrow \cdot\alpha \downarrow B \rightarrow \cdot\beta$ iff $A \rightarrow \alpha \downarrow_p B \rightarrow \beta$. This is a much smaller relation whose RTC can comfortably be computed. The closure can then be computed using Algorithm 3.4.

Apart from possible diagnostic use, the item sets themselves are of no use once the LR(0) automaton has been produced, so it is best to map item sets to integers representing states and to record the transitions of the characteristic FSM in a data structure completely separate from the item sets; these can be garbage collected once the item set construction is complete.

3.3   Inadequate States and the Use of Lookahead

Figure 3.3.1 shows the result of applying the item set construction to the grammar G_1 of section 2.1. The corresponding FSM is shown in Figure 3.3.2, and it will be seen that, unlike the FSM produced for G_4, it includes states (3, 6, 7, and 8) for which a reduce action is indicated but which also have outgoing transitions under grammar symbols. It can be deduced that G_1 is not an LR(0) grammar: for example, for any string $\psi \in LR0C(L \rightarrow L;E)$, there is a string $\psi,a \in LR0C(P \rightarrow a)$, following a path from state 3 to state 12. This violates the LR(0) condition. Any state q in an LR(0) automaton for which $|\text{Reduce}(q)| = 1$ but for which $\delta(q, X)$ is defined for some symbol X is said to have a *shift-reduce conflict*. The LR(0) condition can also be violated if a string ψ is in the LR(0) contexts of two or more different productions. This would manifest itself in the LR(0) automaton by a state q with $|\text{Reduce}(q)| > 1$; such a state is said to have a *reduce-reduce conflict*. Any state of an LR(0) automaton with either a shift-reduce or a reduce-reduce conflict is called an *inadequate state* and it is clear that the parsing algorithm given previously will not work correctly for LR(0) automata with inadequate states.

Although it is not immediately apparent from the definition given previously whether or not the LR(0) condition is a severe restriction on the forms of grammars, experience has shown that most grammars for programming languages are not LR(0). Indeed, the fact that G_1 is not LR(0) illustrates the fact that the syntax of expressions with more than one level of operator priority destroys the LR(0)-ness of a grammar. How can LR techniques be adapted to parse non-LR(0) grammars?

The LR(0) algorithm already makes use of as much information as is available from the left context of the reduction; to improve on it requires making use of additional information from its right context, i.e., from the characters of the so-far unparsed input. The theory to be developed in chapter 4 considers the use of the next k characters of input, for arbitrary integer k. However, for practical purposes, k should be small, and in most cases $k = 1$ is used. The LR(1) context of a production $A \rightarrow \beta$

$$L \to L;E \qquad E \to P$$
$$L \to E \qquad P \to \mathbf{a} \qquad M \to \Lambda$$
$$E \to E,P \qquad P \to (M) \qquad M \to L$$

Item Set	Items	Successors
0	$L \to \cdot L;E$ $L \to \cdot E$ $E \to \cdot E,P$ $E \to \cdot P$ $P \to \cdot(M)$ $P \to \cdot \mathbf{a}$	$L \Rightarrow 1$ $E \Rightarrow 8$ $P \Rightarrow 9$ $(\Rightarrow 6$ $\mathbf{a} \Rightarrow 12$
1	$L \to L \cdot ;E$	$; \Rightarrow 2$
2	$L \to L; \cdot E$ $E \to \cdot E,P$ $E \to \cdot P$ $P \to \cdot(M)$ $P \to \cdot \mathbf{a}$	$E \Rightarrow 3$ $P \Rightarrow 9$ $(\Rightarrow 6$ $\mathbf{a} \Rightarrow 12$
3	$L \to L;E\cdot$ $E \to E \cdot ,P$	$\#L \to L;E$ $, \Rightarrow 4$
4	$E \to E, \cdot P$ $P \to \cdot(M)$ $P \to \cdot \mathbf{a}$	$P \Rightarrow 5$ $(\Rightarrow 6$ $\mathbf{a} \Rightarrow 12$
5	$E \to E,P\cdot$	$\#E \to E,P$
6	$P \to (\cdot M)$ $M \to \cdot$ $M \to \cdot L$ $L \to \cdot L;E$ $L \to \cdot E$ $E \to \cdot E,P$ $E \to \cdot P$ $P \to \cdot(M)$ $P \to \cdot \mathbf{a}$	$M \Rightarrow 10$ $\#M \to \Lambda$ $L \Rightarrow 7$ $E \Rightarrow 8$ $P \Rightarrow 9$ $(\Rightarrow 6$ $\mathbf{a} \Rightarrow 12$

Figure 3.3.1. Item Set Construction for G_1

Item Set	Items	Successors
7	$M \rightarrow L \cdot$ $L \rightarrow L \cdot ; E$	$\#M \rightarrow L$ $; \Rightarrow 2$
8	$L \rightarrow E \cdot$ $E \rightarrow E \cdot , P$	$\#L \rightarrow E$ $, \Rightarrow 4$
9	$E \rightarrow P \cdot$	$\#E \rightarrow P$
10	$P \rightarrow (M \cdot)$	$) \Rightarrow 11$
11	$P \rightarrow (M) \cdot$	$\#P \rightarrow (M)$
12	$P \rightarrow \mathbf{a} \cdot$	$\#P \rightarrow \mathbf{a}$

Figure 3.3.1. Item Set Construction for G_1 (continued)

can be defined in a similar way to the LR(0) context (see section 3.1) as

$LR1C(A \rightarrow \beta)$

$$= \{ \alpha\beta a \in (N \cup T)^*T \mid \exists w \in T^*: S \dashv \Rightarrow_R^* \alpha A a w \Rightarrow_R \alpha\beta a w \}$$

i.e., the LR(1) context is that portion of a sentential form extending one symbol beyond the handle. Notice that, in order to deal properly with the end of the string, it is necessary to consider strings derivable from $S \dashv$, where $\dashv$ is the endmarker symbol introduced in section 3.1.

Using the additional context means extending the domain of the function Reduce of the LR automaton to take account of this *lookahead symbol*, as it is called, so that Reduce is defined with functionality $Q \times T \rightarrow 2^P$ and a reduce move is as follows:

$(\rho p \sigma q, az, \Pi) \vdash (\rho p r, az, (A \rightarrow \beta) \cdot \Pi)$ iff

$$\text{Reduce}(q, a) = A \rightarrow \beta \wedge |\sigma q| = |\beta| \wedge \delta(p, A) = r$$

The definition of a shift move is unaffected.

The problem, of course, is to compute Reduce so that the LR(1) automaton makes its reductions in the correct LR(1) context. In the general case this is quite tricky, but a useful insight into the operation of LR parsers which do take some right context into account may be gained by looking at a simplified approximation to LR(1) parsers: the simple LR(1), or SLR(1), parsers of DeRemer [DeRe71].

The reasoning behind SLR(1) parsing is as follows: if the parser is about to reduce by $A \rightarrow \beta$ then it should only do so if the next input symbol could follow the nonterminal A in *some* right sentential form

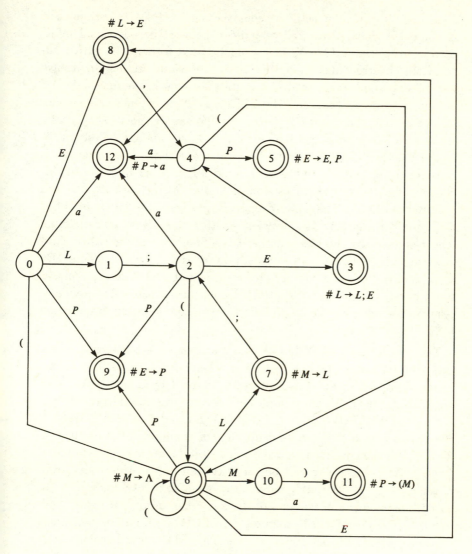

Figure 3.3.2. LR(0) CFSM for G_1

(not necessarily the one resulting from the reduction). This can be summarized by defining a function FOLLOW: $N \to 2^T$ as

$$\text{FOLLOW}(A) = \{\, a \in T \mid \exists \alpha \in (N \cup T)^*, w \in T^*: S\dashv \Rightarrow_R^* \alpha A a w \,\}$$

Then the simple LR(1) context of a production $A \to \beta$ is

$$SLR1C(A \to \beta) = LR0C(A \to \beta) \cdot \text{FOLLOW}(A)$$

This, too, is a regular set, but constructing an FSM to recognize it is not quite what is required to build a parser; the additional information from the FOLLOW set should be used to help the LR(0) automaton, constructed as described in the previous section, to resolve the parsing conflicts in inadequate states. This is because only the handle is to be reduced and the SLR(1) context extends one symbol beyond it. If $\gamma\beta a \in SLR1C(A \to \beta)$ the parser must not actually shift the a before making its reduction, it should merely investigate it to see whether to reduce or to perform more shifts. A reduction is considered appropriate whenever a could follow A so Reduce(q, a) includes $A \to \beta$ if the LR(0) version of Reduce(q) includes $A \to \beta$ and $a \in$ FOLLOW(A). The parsing algorithm (Algorithm 3.2) is modified to give Algorithm 3.5. The decision whether to shift or reduce can no longer be made by checking whether q is a final state of the LR(0) characteristic FSM because of the possibility of shift-reduce conflicts. By using Reduce, the final states can be dispensed with, leaving a parser based purely on the LR automaton. The use of a lookahead symbol also removes the necessity for a special test for errors following a reduction to S.

The computation of FOLLOW sets must now be considered. As a first step, it should be apparent that where a nonterminal A occurs in the right hand side of a production followed by a terminal a then $a \in$ FOLLOW(A). So, for example considering yet again the productions of G_1, ; $\in$ FOLLOW(L), , $\in$ FOLLOW(E) and) $\in$ FOLLOW(M). But this is not all that can be deduced. For example, if the production $E \to E,P$ is used during a derivation in G_1 producing, say, the sentential form $\gamma E,Pw$ then there will be sentential forms $\gamma P,v$ derivable from it using $E \to P$, so that , must be a member of FOLLOW(P). In general, if there is a production of the form $A \to \alpha Ba\gamma$ with $A, B \in N$, $\alpha, \gamma \in (N \cup T)^*$ and $a \in T$, then $a \in$ FOLLOW(C) for all nonterminals C such that $B \Rightarrow^* \beta C$ for some $\beta \in (N \cup T)^*$. Furthermore, it is necessary to consider the case where two nonterminals occur next to each other on the right hand side of a production. By a similar reasoning, if $A \to \alpha BC\gamma$ is a production then FOLLOW(B) includes all terminals a such that $C \Rightarrow^* a\beta$. These possibilities are illustrated in Figure 3.3.3.

Clearly, the possibilities may be combined as in Figure 3.3.4.

To summarize, define, for all $X \in N \cup T$

$$\text{START}(X) = \{a \mid X \Rightarrow^* a\beta, \text{ for some } \beta \in (N \cup T)^*\}$$
$$\text{and FINISH}(X) = \{a \mid X \Rightarrow^* \beta a, \text{ for some } \beta \in (N \cup T)^*\}$$

Algorithm 3.5. LR Parsing with One Symbol Lookahead

let $G = (N, T, P, S)$ be an SLR(1) CFG
let $LRA = (Q, N \cup T, P, q_0, \delta, \text{Reduce})$ be G's SLR(1) automaton
let $\gamma = input \cdot \dashv$
let $\sigma = q_0$ ‖ state stack
let $q, X = q_0, \gamma(1)$
let $accepted = \textbf{false}$

while $\neg accepted$ **do**
{   **if** $\text{Reduce}(q, X)$ is undefined
       then { $\gamma := \gamma(2\ldots)$
              if $\delta(q, X)$ is undefined
              then *error*
              else { $q := \delta(q, X)$; $X := \gamma(1)$ }
              $\sigma := \sigma \cdot q$
        }
     else {   **let** $A \to \beta = \text{Reduce}(q, X)$
            $\sigma := \sigma(1 \ldots |\sigma| - |\beta|)$
            $accepted := A = S \wedge \gamma = \dashv \wedge \sigma = q_0$
            unless $accepted$ **do** { $q := \delta(\sigma(|\sigma|), A)$; $\sigma := \sigma \cdot q$ }
        }
}

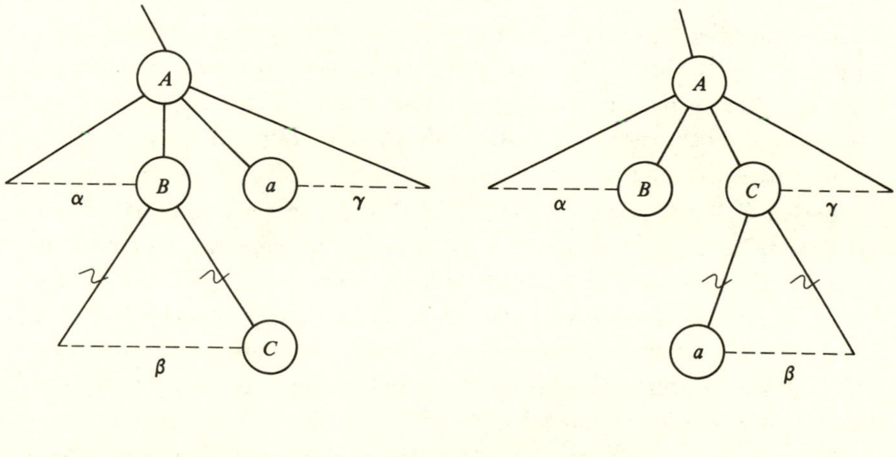

Figure 3.3.3. Contributions to FOLLOW

(hence, if $X \in T$, $\text{START}(X) = \text{FINISH}(X) = X$). If $A \to X_1 X_2 \ldots X_k$

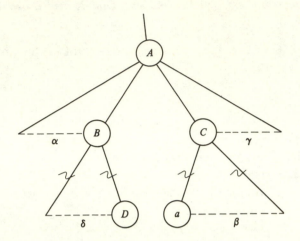

Figure 3.3.4. Combining the possibilities

is a production, then $\text{START}(X_{i+1}) \subseteq \text{FOLLOW}(\text{FINISH}(X_i))$ for $1 \leq i \leq k - 1$. A first attempt to compute START and FINISH efficiently might be to define relations $\ll$ ('can immediately start with') and $\gg$ ('can immediately finish with') as follows

$$X \ll Y \quad \text{iff } X \rightarrow Y\beta \text{ is a production for some } \beta \in (N \cup T)^*$$

$$X \gg Y \quad \text{iff } X \rightarrow \beta Y \text{ is a production for some } \beta \in (N \cup T)^*$$

and computing $\text{START}(X) = \{ a \in T \mid X \ll^* a \}$ and $\text{FINISH}(X) = \{ a \in T \mid X \gg^* a \}$, using fast RTC techniques. However, this would not be quite correct, for it is possible for the situations in Figure 3.3.5 to arise. In both cases, $a \in \text{FOLLOW}(E)$, since $D \Rightarrow^* \Lambda$.

By observing that $X \Rightarrow^* a\beta$ iff $\exists \gamma \colon X \Rightarrow^* \gamma a\beta \wedge \gamma \Rightarrow^* \Lambda$, it becomes apparent that the correct START and FINISH sets are computed from the reflexive transitive closure of $\ll$ and $\gg$ if these are redefined as $X \ll Y$ iff $X \rightarrow \gamma Y\beta$ is a production, for some $\beta, \gamma \in (N \cup T)^*$ where $\gamma \Rightarrow^* \Lambda$ and $X \gg Y$ iff $X \rightarrow \beta Y\gamma$ is a production. A string $\gamma \Rightarrow^+ \Lambda$ if and only if γ consists of nonterminals $A_1 A_2 \ldots A_n$, such that $A_i \Rightarrow^* \Lambda$, for $1 \leq i \leq n$. Such nullable nonterminals can be identified using the algorithm given in section 2.1.

This is still not quite enough, since it is possible to have the situation shown in Figure 3.3.6. and similar situations corresponding to the more elaborate cases just discussed. Here $\text{FOLLOW}(B) \supseteq \text{START}(C)$. Thus, the amalgamation of START sets to give FOLLOW sets must consider not just adjacent pairs of symbols, but pairs of symbols separated by

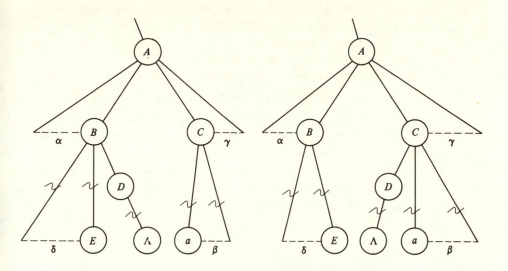

Figure 3.3.5. Effect of nullable nonterminals

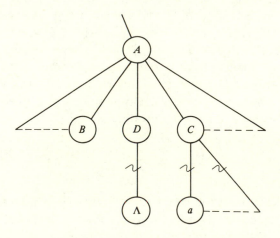

Figure 3.3.6. Intervening nullable nonterminals

nullable nonterminals. Thus, if $A \rightarrow X_1 X_2 \ldots X_k$, then for $1 \leq i \leq k-1$, START$(X_{i+1}) \supseteq$ FOLLOW(FINISH(X_j)) for $1 \leq j \leq i$ such that, for $1 \leq m \leq j$, $X_m \Rightarrow^* \Lambda$.

Finally, since all strings to be parsed have $\dashv$ appended to serve as an endmarker, it is necessary to add $\dashv$ to FOLLOW(A) for all $A \in$ FINISH(S) where S is the start symbol.

These rules can be applied to G_1 more or less by inspection since there are no pairs of adjacent nonterminals. This gives

$$\text{FOLLOW}(L) = \{;,), \dashv\}$$
$$\text{FOLLOW}(E) = \{;, ,,), \dashv\}$$
$$\text{FOLLOW}(M) = \{)\}$$
$$\text{FOLLOW}(P) = \{;, ,,), \dashv\}$$

In fact, only FOLLOW(L) and FOLLOW(M) are required to resolve the parsing conflicts in the inadequate states. In states 3 and 8 the reduction to L is performed only if the next symbol is ;,) or $\dashv$; if it is a comma, then that is shifted. Similarly, in states 6 and 7, a reduction to M occurs only if the lookahead symbol is), otherwise, either a shift is performed or an error is announced.

3.4   Augmented Grammars

A device often employed to deal with the complications caused by the end of string is to incorporate the $\dashv$ symbol directly in the language, by allowing it to appear on the right hand side of a production. Given a CFG $G = (N, T, P, S)$, construct an *augmented grammar* $G' = (N \cup \{S'\}, T, P \cup \{S' \to S\dashv\}, S')$, where $S' \notin N$ is a new sentence symbol. Clearly $L(G') = L(G) \cdot \{\dashv\}$; this makes it explicit that strings end in $\dashv$ and simplifies some of the lookahead computations involved in parser generation. However, it is important to be clear about what is going on. As a concrete example, consider G'_1, the augmented grammar for G_1, which has the following productions.

$$
\begin{array}{lll}
L' \to L\dashv & E \to E,T & P \to (M) \\
L \to L;E & E \to P & M \to \Lambda \\
L \to E & P \to \mathbf{a} & M \to L
\end{array}
$$

Applying the item set construction to G'_1 gives the FSM, part of which is shown in Figure 3.4.1. Consider state 13 which is entered after shifting $\dashv$. The appropriate action to take is obviously to reduce to L' and then halt; however, this is not what happens if Algorithm 3.5 is applied. Instead, the parser must attempt to look beyond the $\dashv$ to evaluate Reduce(13, a), which, of course, it cannot – this is precisely the problem that addition of $\dashv$ to the input was supposed to solve. What has really been produced by this construction is a parser for $L(G_1)$ (not $L(G'_1)$) with extra transitions added so the machine will go from state 0 to 13, under $L\dashv$ corresponding to the right hand side of the augmenting production $L' \to L\dashv$. State 13 must, therefore, be specially treated as an *accept state*, and the action

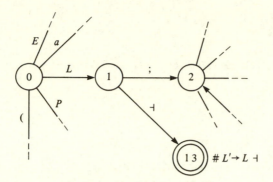

Figure 3.4.1. Part of the CFSM for G'_1

in this state is to halt successfully, irrespective of lookahead symbol.

In fact, any grammar which includes a production $S \rightarrow \alpha\dashv$ where S is the start symbol, $\alpha \in (N \cup T)^+$, $\dashv$ is the endmarker symbol and S and $\dashv$ do not appear in any other production will have an LR automaton with a state such as 13 which is entered only under a $\dashv$-transition and for which acceptance is the correct parsing action. This is a convenient way of implementing a parser and makes for clean termination as well as simplifying lookahead compuations. For purposes of expounding the theory of LR parsers, however, use of augmented grammars is confusing and it will be avoided except in some of the practical discussion.

4

Introduction to LR Theory

4.1 LR(k) Parsers and Grammars

In this section, the behaviour of an LR(k) parser, for arbitrary $k \geq 0$, will be formalized. This will permit the formulation of a condition which must be satisfied by derivations if a grammar is to be parsable by the LR(k) method. It will also provide a basis for the deduction of some important properties of such grammars.

Some additional notation is required, and it will be convenient to observe some notational conventions in order to prevent repetitions and a plethora of quantifiers. Throughout this chapter, then, let $G = (N, T, P, S)$ be an arbitrary CFG with no useless symbols in which $S \not\Rightarrow^+ S$. Unless otherwise stated, free variables are to be understood to be universally quantified, with letters denoting members of particular sets as shown in Figure 4.1.1. Thus, for example, $A \Rightarrow^* z \ldots$ is shorthand for $\forall A \in N, z \in T^*: A \Rightarrow^* z \ldots$. Similarly, $\exists A: \ldots A \ldots$ is short for $\exists A \in N: \ldots A \ldots$. (In turn, of course, $\forall x \in S: px$ is a shorthand for $\forall x: x \in S$ implies px whereas $\exists x \in S: px$ is short for $\exists x: x \in S \wedge px$.)

Figure 4.1.1. Notational Conventions

$$G = (N, T, P, S)$$

early, upper case Roman letters	$A, B, C, \ldots$	$\in N$
early, lower case Roman letters	$a, b, c, \ldots$	$\in T$
	u, v	$\in T^k$
	X	$\in N \cup T$
late, lower case Roman letters	$\ldots, x, y, z$	$\in T^*$
lower case Greek letters	$\alpha, \beta, \ldots, \omega$	$\in (N \cup T)^*$
except	π	$\in P$
	Π	$\in P^*$

Most of these are standard conventions, but note carefully that $|u| = |v| = k$; this is an important part of some formulas involving these letters. Subscripted and primed versions of letters naturally obey the same conventions as their undecorated counterparts.

For any integer $k \geq 0$, $k : z$ denotes the prefix of z of length k, i.e., $k : z = u$ where $z = uv$ and $|u| = k$. The possibility that $|z| < k$ will not arise: all input strings are assumed to be terminated by k endmarkers. $\perp$ will be used to denote $\dashv^k$.

All derivations will be rightmost. The notation $\alpha_0 \overset{\Pi}{\Rightarrow} \alpha_m$ is used to mean that $\alpha_0 \Rightarrow^*_R \alpha_m$ and Π is the sequence of productions used in the derivation.

Just as the LR(0) and SLR(1) algorithms were refinements of the shift-reduce algorithm, so the formal model of the LR(k) parser is a refinement of the PDA introduced at the end of section 2.3. Its desired behaviour can be described by imposing restrictions on the 'moves to' relation on configurations. The idea that a parser can make its moves on the basis of left context and the next k characters of unread input is captured by insisting that, for a given stack contents (i.e., left context), the machine makes the same move for all remaining inputs that appear to be the same on the basis of their first k symbols. Let $\vdash$ denote the moves relation of such a machine. $\vdash$ will describe a subset of the moves given by (2.3.1) and (2.3.2), so these become

$$(\alpha\beta, z, \Pi) \vdash (\alpha A, z, (A \to \beta) \cdot \Pi) \text{ implies } A \to \beta \in P \qquad (4.1.1)$$

and

$$(\gamma, az, \Pi) \vdash (\gamma a, z, \Pi) \text{ implies } a \in T \qquad (4.1.2)$$

The additional restrictions just described can be expressed as

$$(\alpha\beta, z, \Pi) \vdash (\alpha A, z, (A \to \beta) \cdot \Pi) \wedge k : z = k : y$$
$$\text{implies } (\alpha\beta, y, \Pi') \vdash (\alpha A, y, (A \to \beta) \cdot \Pi') \quad (4.1.3)$$

$$(\gamma, az, \Pi) \vdash (\gamma a, z, \Pi) \wedge k : az = k : by$$
$$\text{implies } (\gamma, by, \Pi') \vdash (\gamma b, y, \Pi') \quad (4.1.4)$$

The parser is also required to accept exactly the strings in $L(G)$, and produce a rightmost derivation, so

$$(\Lambda, z \perp, \Lambda) \vdash^* (S, \perp, \Pi) \text{ iff } S \perp \overset{\Pi}{\underset{R}{\Rightarrow}}^* z \perp \qquad (4.1.5)$$

Remember that $S \Rightarrow^+ S$ is forbidden. $\vdash$ is referred to as a *parsing relation* and whenever the symbol is used it is assumed to have the properties just given. The important fact about the LR algorithms of Chapter 3 was that they eliminated backtracking. To be a model of such an algorithm, an automaton must be deterministic, i.e., $\vdash$ must be a partial function.

Since these conditions capture precisely the intuitive notion of an LR parser as a device which makes its parsing decisions using left context and restricted lookahead and does not perform backtracking, they will be taken as the basis of the definition of an LR(k) grammar.

A grammar G is an *LR(k) grammar* if and only if it permits an automaton with a deterministic moves relation $\vdash$ to satisfy (4.1.3), (4.1.4) and (4.1.5).

One important property of LR(k) grammars can be deduced immediately.

Theorem 4.1. *If G is an LR(k) grammar, G is unambiguous.*

Proof. Since, for an LR(k) grammar, $\vdash$ is a partial function, the parser's output is uniquely determined for any input z. ($S \not\Rightarrow^+ S$ rules out the possibility that $(\Lambda, z, \Lambda) \vdash^+ (S, \perp, \Pi) \vdash^+ (S, \perp, \Pi' \cdot \Pi)$ for any z.) But this output comprises the sequence of productions in a rightmost derivation of z because of (4.1.1). Hence, this rightmost derivation is unique, so, by definition, G is unambiguous. ☐

Recall that, in section 3.1, an informal argument was given to the effect that an LR parser must perform a reduction whenever it has a handle on top of its stack; that is, its reductions must correspond to the application of a production as part of a rightmost derivation. It can be shown that this is the case for a parser satisfying (4.1.5).

First, an intermediate result is required.

Lemma 4.2.

$$S \perp \Rightarrow^* \alpha A w \overset{\Pi}{\Rightarrow} zw \text{ implies } (\Lambda, zw, \Lambda) \vdash^* (\alpha A, w, \Pi)$$

Proof. By induction on the length of $S \perp \Rightarrow^* \alpha A w$. If the derivation is of length 0 then $\alpha = \Lambda$, $A = S$ and $w = \perp$. Certainly $(\Lambda, zw, \Lambda) \vdash^* (S, \perp, \Pi)$ by (4.1.5).

Suppose that $S \perp \overset{\Pi'}{\Rightarrow} \gamma B x \overset{\Pi''}{\Rightarrow} zw$ implies $(\Lambda, zw, \Lambda) \vdash^* (\gamma B, x, \Pi'')$. Since $(\Lambda, zw, \Lambda) \vdash^* (S, \perp, \Pi' \cdot \Pi'')$ by (4.1.5), and Π' defines a unique sequence of reductions $(\gamma B, x, \Pi'') \vdash^* (S, \perp, \Pi' \cdot \Pi'')$. If $S \perp \overset{\Pi'}{\Rightarrow} \gamma B x \Rightarrow \alpha A w \overset{\Pi}{\Rightarrow} zw$ then $\Pi'' = (B \to \beta A y) \cdot \Pi$ with $\alpha = \gamma \beta$ and $w = yx$. Then, by the definition of shift and reduce moves $(\alpha A, w, \Pi) \vdash^* (\gamma B, x, \Pi'')$. But $(\Lambda, zw, \Lambda) \vdash^* (S, \perp, \Pi' \cdot \pi \cdot \Pi)$, giving the situation shown in Figure 4.1.2, so the correct output $\Pi' \cdot \pi \cdot \Pi$ will only be produced if $(\Lambda, zw, \Lambda) \vdash^* (\alpha A, w, \Pi)$. ☐

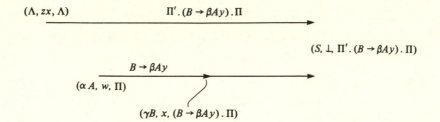

Figure 4.1.2. Parser Moves for Proof of Lemma 4.2

Lemma 4.3.

$S \perp \Rightarrow^* \alpha Aw \Rightarrow \alpha\beta w$ implies $(\alpha\beta, w, \Pi) \vdash (\alpha A, w, (A \to \beta) \cdot \Pi))$

and $S \perp \Rightarrow^* \rho Bw \Rightarrow \rho\gamma w \wedge \psi ay = \rho\gamma$ implies

$$(\psi, ayw, \Pi) \vdash (\psi a, yw, \Pi)$$

Proof. Since G has no useless nonterminals $\exists z, \Pi: S \perp \Rightarrow^* \alpha Aw \overset{\Pi}{\Rightarrow} zw$. Applying Lemma 4.2 gives $(\Lambda, zw, \Lambda) \vdash^* (\alpha A, w, (A \to \beta) \cdot \Pi))$. But this reduction must have been performed from the configuration $(\alpha\beta, w, \Pi)$, so $(\alpha\beta, w, \Pi) \vdash (\alpha A, w, (A \to \beta) \cdot \Pi))$.

If $S \perp \Rightarrow^* \rho Bw \Rightarrow^* \psi ayw \Rightarrow^* zayw$ then $\exists \Pi: (\Lambda, zayw, \Lambda) \vdash^*$ $(\rho B, w, (B \to \gamma) \cdot \Pi)$. As before, this must mean that $(\Lambda, zayw, \Lambda) \vdash^*$ $(\rho\gamma, w, \Pi)$ or, rewriting $\rho\gamma$, $(\Lambda, zayw, \Lambda) \vdash^* (\psi ay, w, \Pi)$. Since $ay \in TT^*$ and derivations are rightmost, ay can only get onto the stack via a series of shifts, so $(\psi, ayw, \Pi) \vdash (\psi a, yw, \Pi)$. $\qquad \square$

Since $\vdash$ satisfies (4.1.3), Lemma 4.3 implies that

$$S \perp \Rightarrow^* \alpha Auy \Rightarrow \alpha\beta uy \text{ implies } (\alpha\beta, uz, \Pi) \vdash (\alpha A, uz, (A \to \beta) \cdot \Pi))$$
$$(4.1.6)$$

Thus configurations $(\alpha\beta, uz, \Pi)$ with α, β and u satisfying the above condition precede reductions in the parser; the string $\alpha\beta u$ contains all the information which determines this move. Recalling section 3.1 therefore the set of all such strings is defined to be the LR(k) context of $A \to \beta$.

$$LRC(A \to \beta) = \{ \alpha\beta u \mid \exists y: S \perp \Rightarrow^* \alpha Auy \Rightarrow \alpha\beta uy \}.$$

(Remember that $u \in T^k$.) The LR(k) contexts of G are the set $LRC(G) = \bigcup_{A \to \beta \in P} LRC(A \to \beta)$. These contexts are related to the moves of a parser as follows.

Lemma 4.4. *Any relation $\vdash$ satisfying (4.1.1)–(4.1.4) is a parsing relation iff*

$$\alpha\beta u \in LRC(A \to \beta) \text{ implies } (\alpha\beta, uw, \Pi) \vdash (\alpha A, uw, (A \to \beta) \cdot \Pi)) \quad (a)$$

$$\exists x\colon x \neq \Lambda \wedge \psi ux \in LRC(G) \wedge k : aw = u \text{ implies } (\psi, aw, \Pi) \vdash (\psi a, w, \Pi)$$

$$(b)$$

Proof. It is necessary to show that (4.1.5) is true iff (a) and (b) are true. First, suppose (a) and (b) are true. The 'only if' part of (4.1.5) is a consequence of (4.1.1) and (4.1.2). To show that $S \perp \overset{\Pi}{\underset{R}{\Rightarrow}} z \perp$ implies $(\Lambda, z \perp, \Lambda) \vdash^* (S, \perp, \Pi)$, let the derivation have an intermediate step $S \perp \Rightarrow^* \gamma Bvz \Rightarrow \gamma\delta yvz = \psi uxz$ where $x \neq \Lambda$. Figure 4.1.3 shows the relationship between $\psi ux = \gamma\delta yv$ and any string aw for which (b) holds.

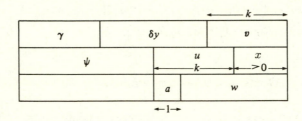

Figure 4.1.3. Strings in Proof of Lemma 4.4.

This should help make clear that condition (b) implies $(\gamma\delta, yvz, \Pi) \vdash^*$ $(\gamma\delta, vz, \Pi)$. (a) is then applicable, showing $(\gamma\delta, yvz, \Pi) \vdash^* (\gamma B, vz, (B \to \delta y) \cdot \Pi)$. Induction shows that this in turn implies $S \perp \overset{\Pi}{\Rightarrow} z$ iff $(\Lambda, z, \Lambda) \vdash^* (S, \perp, \Pi)$, so $\vdash$ is a parsing relation.

If, on the other hand, $\vdash$ is a parsing relation, (a) follows straight away by expanding the definition of $LRC(A \to \beta)$ and applying (4.1.3). For (b), assume now $B \to \delta \in P$, so $S \perp \Rightarrow^* \rho Bz \Rightarrow \rho\delta z = \psi uxz$, if $\psi ux \in LRC(B \to \delta)$, where $|u| = k$ and $|x| > 0$. Let $by = ux$; by Lemma 4.3 $(\psi, byz, \Pi) \vdash (\psi b, yz, \Pi)$. Now, $k : by = u$ and $u = k : aw$ (given) so 4.1.2 (which is true for any parsing relation $\vdash$) implies $(\psi, aw, \Pi) \vdash (\psi a, w, \Pi)$. $\qquad\square$

Notice that the implications in (a) and (b) only hold from left to right: the moves defined thereby are necessary for a parsing relation, but a parser may be able to make other, additional moves and still parse correctly all the strings in $L(G)$. This is undesirable behaviour (although, as will be seen in chapter 5, it is necessary if a practical parser is to be achieved), so a particular parser, the *canonical LR(k) parser* is defined to make only the moves it needs to, i.e., for the canonical parser the implications hold in both directions. This parser is minimal, since any other correct parser makes at least those moves made by the canonical parser. Let $\vdash_c$ denote the moves relation of the canonical LR(k) parser. Then, by definition,

$\alpha\beta u \in LRC(A \to \beta)$ if and only if

$$(\alpha\beta, uw, \Pi) \vdash_c (\alpha A, uw, (A \to \beta) \cdot \Pi)) \quad (4.1.7)$$

$\exists x : x \neq \Lambda \wedge \psi ux \in LRC(G) \wedge k : aw = u$ if and only if

$$(\psi, aw, \Pi) \vdash_c (\psi a, w, \Pi) \quad (4.1.8)$$

(4.1.7) and (4.1.8) differ from the conditions (a) and (b) of Lemma 4.4 only in that 'if and only if' replaces 'implies'. Hence $\vdash_c$ is a parsing relation. According to the definition of an LR(k) grammar, G is LR(k) if and only if its canonical LR(k) parser is deterministic, meaning that $\vdash_c$ associates at most one successor with any configuration. This means $\psi u \in LRC(A \to \beta) \wedge \psi u \in LRC(B \to \delta) \wedge |u| = k$ implies $A \to \beta = B \to \delta$ to make (4.1.7) deterministic, and $\psi u \in LRC(G) \wedge \psi ux \in LRC(G) \wedge |u| = k$ implies $x = \Lambda$ to make moves defined by (4.1.7) and (4.1.8) disjoint. (Compare these with reduce-reduce and shift-reduce conflicts.) Combining the two conditions provides a succinct characterization of LR(k) grammars.

Theorem 4.5. *G is LR(k) if and only if*

$$\psi ux \in LRC(B \to \delta) \wedge \psi u \in LRC(A \to \beta) \text{ implies}$$

$$x = \Lambda \wedge A \to \beta = B \to \delta.$$

This theorem permits an alternative characterization of LR(k) grammars in terms of derivations, which needs to make no reference to the moves of an automaton.

Consider two derivations $S \perp \Rightarrow^* \alpha Auw \Rightarrow \alpha\beta uw$ and $S \perp \Rightarrow^* \gamma Bvx \Rightarrow \gamma\delta vx$. Suppose that $\exists x' : \gamma\delta v = \alpha\beta ux'$, so $\gamma Bvx \Rightarrow \alpha\beta uy$ where $y = x'x$. Since $\gamma\delta v \in LRC(B \to \delta)$ and $\alpha\beta u \in LRC(A \to \beta)$ Theorem 4.5 implies that $x' = \Lambda$ whence $x = y$. Since the theorem also states that $B \to \delta = A \to \beta$ it follows that, in fact, $\alpha = \gamma$ and $u = v$ by adding up the length of substrings of $\gamma\delta v$ and $\alpha\beta u$. These conclusions prove the 'only if' part of the following theorem. The 'if' part is left to the reader; the details of both parts may be found in [Heil77].

Theorem 4.6. *G is LR(k) if and only if*

$$S \perp \Rightarrow^* \alpha Auw \Rightarrow \alpha\beta uw$$

$$\text{and } S \perp \Rightarrow^* \gamma Bvx \Rightarrow \alpha\beta uy$$

where $|u| = |v| = k$ *implies* $\alpha = \gamma$, $A = B$, $v = u$ *and* $x = y$.

Or, to paraphrase this result rather crudely, for an LR(k) grammar, if two sentential forms appear to be the same on the basis of left context and k characters of lookahead, then they must be reduced in the same way. The condition of Theorem 4.6 is often taken as the definition of LR(k). The proofs in this section show that it is equivalent to the notion of a grammar that can be parsed deterministically bottom up, using k characters of lookahead.

Unfortunately, as Knuth showed in [Knu65], for an arbitrary grammar, it is not possible to determine whether there is any value of k for which it is LR(k).

Theorem 4.7. *For a given CFG G it is undecidable whether there is any value of* $k \geq 0$ *such that G is an LR(k) grammar.* [†]

If, however, some particular value of k is given, it is always possible to determine whether G is LR(k) by attempting to construct an LR(k) parser for G. The construction of LR(k) parsers will therefore now be considered and analysed in detail.

4.2   Parser Construction

The item set construction given in section 3.2 for LR(0) parsers can be extended to produce LR(k) parsers by using items which include a k character lookahead string as an extra component. Thus, an LR(k) item for $G = (N, T, P, S)$ is of the form (A, α, β, u) where $A \to \alpha\beta \in P$ and $u \in T^k$ is a lookahead string of length k. The item (A, α, β, u) is written $[A \to \alpha \cdot \beta, u]$. The intuitive meaning of the part $A \to \alpha \cdot \beta$ is the same as in the LR(0) case. The string u is intended to be k characters which can follow $\alpha\beta$ in some sentential forms of which it is the handle. The following function is required in order to compute these lookahead strings.

$$\text{first}_k(\alpha) = \{ v \mid |v| = k \wedge \exists x : \alpha \Rightarrow^* vx \}$$

[†] A proof of a general undecidability result from which this theorem follows as a simple consequence may be found in [Heil83].

The construction of a parser is based on the same functions as were used in the LR(0) item set construction, and the following details should be read in conjunction with its description in section 3.2.

As before, items are grouped into item sets and successor item sets are computed. For any $X \in N \cup T$ the X-successor of an item set is given by

$$\text{succ}(\Im, X) = \{ [A \rightarrow \alpha X \cdot \beta, u] \mid [A \rightarrow \alpha \cdot X\beta, u] \in \Im \} \qquad (4.2.1)$$

(c.f. 3.2.3), i.e., the lookahead string remains the same. The computation of closure items introduces new lookahead strings.

$$[A \rightarrow \alpha \cdot B\beta, u] \downarrow [B \rightarrow \cdot\delta, v] \text{ , for all } v \in \text{first}_k(\beta u). \qquad (4.2.2)$$

(c.f. 3.2.1). Again as before, the closure of a set of items is

$$\text{closure}(\Im) = \{ I \mid \exists I' \in \Im : I' \downarrow^* I \} \qquad (4.2.3)$$

The initial item set is

$$\Im_0 = \text{closure}(\{ [S \rightarrow \cdot\alpha, \perp] \mid S \rightarrow \alpha \in P \}) \qquad (4.2.4)$$

A grammar will be LR(k) iff, for all item sets $\Im$, if $[A \rightarrow \alpha\cdot, u] \in \Im$ then, for all items $[B \rightarrow \delta\cdot, u'] \in \Im$, $u' \neq u$, and, for items $[B \rightarrow \gamma \cdot a\beta, v] \in \Im$, $u \notin \text{first}_k(a\beta v)$. This will be proved later, but it should be clear that if this condition is satisfied a parser based on item sets may make unique parsing decisions using a k character lookahead string. Abstracting away from the item sets gives the LR(k) automaton for $G = (N, T, P, S)$, $LRA = (Q, N \cup T, P, q_0, \delta, \text{Reduce})$ where Q is the set of item sets, $q_0 = \Im_0$, $\delta(q, X) = \text{closure} \cdot \text{succ}(q, X)$ for all $q \in Q$ and $X \in N \cup T$ and $\text{Reduce}(q, u) = \{ A \rightarrow \alpha \mid [A \rightarrow \alpha\cdot, u] \in q \}$ for all $q \in Q$, $u \in T^k$.

Example.

Let $G_5 = (\{S, A, B, C\}, \{a, b, c\}, P_5, S)$ where P_5 consists of

$$
\begin{array}{ll}
S \rightarrow AB & B \rightarrow aCb \\
A \rightarrow a & C \rightarrow \Lambda \\
A \rightarrow aa & C \rightarrow c
\end{array}
$$

G_5 appears to be LR(2), since two characters of lookahead are required to determine whether an initial a is to be reduced to A or is part of an aa to be reduced after the second a is shifted. One character of lookahead is insufficient because an A is followed by a B which begins with an a.

The nucleus of the initial LR(2) item set is $[S \rightarrow \cdot AB, \dashv\dashv]$. Closure gives $[A \rightarrow \cdot a, v]$ and $[A \rightarrow \cdot aa, v]$ where $v \in \text{first}_2(B\dashv\dashv)$. By inspection, $\text{first}_2(B\dashv\dashv) = \{ab, ac\}$, so the initial item set is $\{[S \rightarrow \cdot AB, \dashv\dashv], [A \rightarrow$

Item Set	Items	Successors
0	$[S \to \cdot AB, \dashv\dashv]$ $[A \to \cdot a, ab]$ $[A \to \cdot aa, ab]$ $[A \to \cdot a, ac]$ $[A \to \cdot aa, ac]$	$A \Rightarrow 1$ $a \Rightarrow 7$
1	$[S \to A \cdot B, \dashv\dashv]$ $[B \to \cdot aCb, \dashv\dashv]$	$B \Rightarrow 2$ $a \Rightarrow 3$
2	$[S \to AB\cdot, \dashv\dashv]$	$\#S \to AB$
3	$[B \to a \cdot Cb, \dashv\dashv]$ $[C \to \cdot, b\dashv]$ $[C \to \cdot c, b\dashv]$	$C \Rightarrow 4$ $\#C \to \Lambda$ $c \Rightarrow 6$
4	$[B \to aC \cdot b, \dashv\dashv]$	$b \Rightarrow 5$
5	$[B \to aCb\cdot, \dashv\dashv]$	$\#B \to aCb$
6	$[C \to c\cdot, b\dashv]$	$\#C \to c$
7	$[A \to a\cdot, ab]$ $[A \to a \cdot a, ab]$ $[A \to a\cdot, ac]$ $[A \to a \cdot a, ac]$	$\#A \to a$ $a \Rightarrow 8$ $\#A \to a$ $a \Rightarrow 8$
8	$[A \to aa\cdot, ab]$ $[A \to aa\cdot, ac]$	$\#A \to aa$ $\#A \to aa$

Figure 4.2.1. LR(2) Item Sets for G_5.

$\cdot a, ab], [A \to \cdot aa, ab], [A \to \cdot a, ac], [A \to \cdot aa, ac]\}$. The successor computation is straightforward; the complete collection of LR(2) item sets for G_5 is shown in Figure 4.2.1, which shows that G_5 is indeed an LR(2) grammar. For example, if the input is $aab\dashv$ and the parser has read a and gone to state 7, it will perform a reduction since the 2 character lookahead string is ab and not aa as it would need to be for a shift.

An algorithm is needed to compute first_k. Reasonably efficient algorithms are known for generating $\text{first}_k(A)$ for all $A \in N$, whence $\text{first}_k(\beta)$ can be computed for any β as required (see, for example [Back79]). In general, however, only the case $k = 1$ is used and the function START used in computing SLR(1) lookahead sets is sufficient, since $\text{START}(A) = \text{first}_1(A)$; the algorithm given in section 3.3 is thus suitable for computing one character lookahead strings.

The main question of interest is whether the construction just outlined produces a parser that is correct. To establish this, it is necessary to formalize the construction in order to describe the parser produced in the same terms as the model of section 4.1. The way to approach this is by considering how items can be related to LR(k) contexts. This is done by introducing special right linear grammars whose nonterminals are LR(k) items and whose productions model steps in the construction. (The technique is similar to the one used in section 3.1 to show that LR(0) contexts are regular.)

The LR(k) *item grammar* of $G = (N, T, P, S)$ is $I(G) = (I_k \cup \{[S]\}, N \cup T, P_I, [S])$ where I_k is the set of LR(k) items of G and P_I consists of productions of the form

$$[A \to \alpha \cdot X\beta, u] \to X[A \to \alpha X \cdot \beta, u]$$
$$[A \to \alpha \cdot B\beta, u] \to [B \to \cdot\delta, v] \text{ for all } v \in \text{first}_k(\beta u)$$

together with

$$[S] \to [S \to \cdot\alpha, \perp] \text{ for all } S \to \alpha \in P.$$

Observe in passing that $L(I(G)) = \emptyset$.

Derivations in $I(G)$ are related to derivations in G by the following important lemma.

Lemma 4.8.

$$\text{For } I_1, I_2 \in I_k, \exists \Pi: I_1 \overset{\Pi}{\Rightarrow} \gamma I_2 \wedge |\Pi| = |\gamma|$$
$$\text{iff } \exists A, \alpha, \beta, \gamma, u: I_1 = [A \to \alpha \cdot \gamma\beta, u] \wedge \qquad (a)$$
$$I_2 = [A \to \alpha\gamma \cdot \beta, u]$$

$$[A \to \alpha \cdot \beta, u] \overset{\Pi}{\Rightarrow}_{I(G)} \gamma [C \to \rho \cdot \sigma, v] \wedge |\Pi| > |\gamma|$$
$$\text{iff } \exists \omega, w: \beta u \Rightarrow_G^* \omega C v w \Rightarrow_G \omega\rho v w = \gamma \sigma v w \qquad (b)$$

Proof. (a) If I_1 and I_2 are of the required form and $\gamma = X_1 X_2 \ldots X_m$, then the item grammar has productions $[A \to \alpha X_1 \ldots \cdot X_i \ldots X_m\beta, u] \to X_i[A \to \alpha X_1 \ldots X_i \cdot \ldots X_m\beta, u]$ for $1 \le i \le m$ so there is a derivation $[A \to \alpha \cdot X_1 X_2 \ldots X_m\beta, u] \Rightarrow X_1[A \to \alpha X_1 \cdot X_2 \ldots X_m\beta, u] \Rightarrow^* X_1 X_2 \ldots X_m[A \to \alpha X_1 X_2 \ldots X_m \cdot \beta, u]$. i.e., $[A \to \alpha \cdot \gamma\beta, u] \overset{\Pi}{\Rightarrow} \gamma[A \to \alpha\gamma \cdot \beta, u]$ where $|\Pi| = |\gamma|$. Similarly, the only derivation of length $|\gamma|$ must have productions of the same form, so that I_1 and I_2 can only be as required.

(b) 'If' is proved by induction on $\beta u \Rightarrow_G^* \omega C v w$. If this derivation is of length 0, $\beta u = \omega C v w$ so $[A \to \alpha \cdot \beta, u] = [A \to \alpha \cdot \omega C x, u]$ for some $x \in T^*$. By (a), $[A \to \alpha \cdot \beta, u] \Rightarrow^* \omega[A \to \alpha\omega \cdot C x, u]$ and this derives $\omega[C \to \cdot\rho\sigma, v] \Rightarrow^* \omega\rho[C \to \rho \cdot \sigma, v] = \gamma[C \to \rho \cdot \sigma, v]$ and the length of this derivation is $|\gamma| + 1$.

If the length of the initial derivation is greater than 0, then C must have been introduced somewhere within it so

$$\beta u \Rightarrow^* \psi B y \Rightarrow \psi \delta_1 C \delta_2 y \Rightarrow^* \psi \delta_1 C v w \Rightarrow \psi \delta_1 \rho \sigma v w.$$

Assume as inductive hypothesis that $\beta u \Rightarrow^* \psi B y \Rightarrow \psi \delta_1 C \delta_2 y$ implies $[A \to \alpha \cdot \beta, u] \overset{\Pi}{\Rightarrow} \psi \delta_1 [B \to \delta_1 \cdot C \delta y, k : y] \wedge |\Pi| > |\psi \delta_1|$. The derivation then proceeds as in the previous case, giving $\psi \delta_1 [B \to \delta_1 \cdot C \delta y, k : y] \Rightarrow^*$ $\psi \delta_1 \rho [C \to \rho \cdot \sigma, v]$, so $[A \to \alpha \cdot \beta, u] \overset{\Pi'}{\Rightarrow} \gamma [C \to \rho \cdot \sigma, v] \wedge |\Pi'| > |\gamma|$.

The proof of 'only if' proceeds similarly by induction on $|\gamma|$. If $|\gamma| = 0$ then $[A \to \alpha \cdot \beta, u] \Rightarrow [C \to \rho \cdot \sigma, v]$ which is impossible unless $\rho = \Lambda$ and $C \to \cdot \sigma$ in which case $\beta u \Rightarrow \sigma \beta' u$ where $\beta = C \beta'$. Furthermore, $v \in \text{first}_k(\beta' u)$ so $\beta u \Rightarrow \sigma v \psi \Rightarrow^* \sigma v w = \gamma \sigma v w$, since $|\gamma| = 0$.

For the induction, assume that $[A \to \alpha \cdot \beta, , u] \Rightarrow^* \gamma' [B \to \theta \cdot \psi, v']$ implies $\beta u \Rightarrow^* \omega B v' w' \Rightarrow \omega \theta \psi v' w' = \gamma' \psi v' w'$. This holds for all $\psi \in (N \cup T)^*$ and thus for $\psi = C \psi'$. Now $[B \to \theta \cdot C \psi', v'] \Rightarrow [C \to \cdot \rho \sigma, v] \Rightarrow^* \rho [C \to \rho \cdot \sigma, v]$ implies $C \to \rho \sigma$ and $v \in \text{first}_k(\psi' v')$ so $\gamma' \psi v' w' \Rightarrow \gamma' \rho \sigma \psi' v' w' = \gamma \rho v w$. $\qquad \square$

Lemma 4.8 immediately permits item grammars to be related to $\text{LR}(k)$ contexts.

Theorem 4.9. $\psi u \in LRC(A \to \beta)$ *if and only if* $[S] \Rightarrow^*_{I(G)} \psi [A \to \beta \cdot, u]$.

Proof. Suppose $S \to \alpha \in P$, then $[S] \Rightarrow_{I(G)} [S \to \cdot \alpha, \perp]$. Substituting in Lemma 4.8 shows that $[S \to \cdot \alpha, \perp] \Rightarrow^* \psi [A \to \beta \cdot, u]$ if and only if $\alpha \perp \Rightarrow^* \omega A u w \Rightarrow \omega \beta u w = \psi u w$. But, since $S \perp \Rightarrow \alpha \perp$ this says precisely that $\psi u \in LRC(A \to \beta)$. $\qquad \square$

Derivations in the item grammar are thus based on LR contexts; transitions in an FSM built from the item grammar will therefore trace out LR contexts. Theorems 2.3 and 2.5 show how to construct such a machine.

If $I(G) = (I_k \cup \{[S]\}, N \cup T, P_I, [S])$ is the item grammar for G, then construct an NFSM $M_1 = (I_k \cup \{[S]\}, N \cup T, \delta_1, [S], \emptyset)$ with

$$\delta_1([A \to \alpha \cdot X \beta, u], X) = \{ I \in I_k \mid [A \to \alpha X \cdot \beta, u] \Rightarrow^*_{I(G)} I \} \quad (4.2.5)$$

$$\delta_1([S], X) =$$

$$\{ I \in I_k \mid [S \to \cdot \alpha, \perp] \Rightarrow^*_{I(G)} X I \wedge S \to \alpha \in P \} \quad (4.2.6)$$

Because $I(G)$ has no productions of the form $[A \to \alpha \cdot \beta, u] \to X$ for $X \in N \cup T \cup \{\Lambda\}$, there are no final states.

The nondeterminism can be removed from M_1 by the construction of Theorem 2.3 to give $M_2 = (Q_2, N \cup T, \delta_2, q_{20}, \emptyset)$ where $Q_2 = 2^{I_k \cup \{[S]\}}$,

$q_{20} = \{[S]\}$ and for $q \in Q_2$, $X \in N \cup T$, $\delta_2(q, X) = \bigcup_{p \in q} \delta_1(p, X)$. It should be clear, $\delta_2(q, X) = \{I \in I_k \mid \exists I_1 \in q: I_1 \Rightarrow^* XI\}$ by this construction. But, from (4.2.2), $I_1 \downarrow I_2$ iff $I_1 \Rightarrow_{I(G)} I_2$, and, from (4.2.1), $\text{succ}(\Im, X) = \{I \mid \exists I_1 \in \Im: I_1 \Rightarrow XI\}$, whence $\delta_2(q, X) = \text{closure} \cdot \text{succ}(q, X) = \delta(q, X)$, the transition function of G's LR(k) automaton built by the item set construction. Also $q_{20} = q_0$, its initial state. Thus, the states and transitions of the LR(k) automaton are the same as those of the machine built from the item grammar. The transition function δ can thereby be shown to be related to the LR(k) contexts as required.

Lemma 4.10. *If* $LRA = (Q, N \cup T, P, q_0, \delta, \text{Reduce})$ *is the LR(k) automaton built by the item set construction for G then*

$$\psi u \in LRC(A \to \beta) \text{ iff } [A \to \beta\cdot, u] \in \delta^*(q_0, \psi) \qquad (a)$$

$$\exists x: x \neq \Lambda \wedge \psi ux \in LRC(G) \text{ iff}$$

$$\exists [A \to \alpha \cdot a\beta, v] \in \delta^*(q_0, \psi): u \in \text{first}_k(a\beta v) \qquad (b)$$

Proof. From the above discussion, $\delta = \delta_2$, constructed from $I(G)$, whence $\delta^*(q_0, \psi) = \{I \mid [S] \Rightarrow^*_{I(G)} \psi I\}$. (a) then follows immediately from Theorem 4.9.

For (b), suppose $\exists a, y, v': \psi ux = \psi ayv'$ where $|v'| = k$. Certainly $x \neq \Lambda$. If $\psi ayv' \in LRC(B \to \delta)$ Theorem 4.9 states $[S] \Rightarrow^* \psi ay[B \to \delta\cdot, v]$. The symbol a must have been introduced as part of the right hand side of some production $A \to \alpha a\beta$, say, so for some v

$$[S] \Rightarrow^* \psi[A \to \alpha \cdot a\beta, v] \Rightarrow \psi a[A \to \alpha a \cdot \beta, v] \Rightarrow^* \psi ay[B \to \delta\cdot, v']$$

If $\beta \in T^*$, $[A \to \alpha a\beta\cdot, v] = [B \to \delta\cdot, v']$ so $y = \beta$ and $v = v'$; $\psi ux = \psi a\beta v$ and $u \in \text{first}_k(a\beta v)$. Otherwise, applying Lemma 4.8 to $[A \to \alpha \cdot a\beta, v] \Rightarrow^* ay[B \to \delta\cdot, v']$ gives $a\beta v \Rightarrow^* ayv'w = uxw$ so $u \in \text{first}_k(a\beta v)$.

The reverse implication follows a similar pattern. If $[A \to \alpha \cdot a\beta, v] \in \delta^*(q, \psi)$ then if $\beta \in T^*$, $[S] \Rightarrow^* \psi[A \to \alpha \cdot a\beta, v]$ so by (a), $\psi a\beta v \in LRC(A \to \alpha a\beta)$. But $u \in \text{first}_k(a\beta v)$ here means that $u = k : a\beta v$. Since $|u| = |v| = k$ and $|a| = 1$, $\exists x: x \neq \Lambda \wedge \psi ux \in LRC(A \to \alpha a\beta) \subseteq LRC(G)$.

Otherwise, since $u \in \text{first}_k(a\beta v)$ there is a derivation $a\beta v \Rightarrow^* yBv'w \Rightarrow yzv'w$ with $|v'| = k$ and $u = k : yzv'$. Lemma 4.8 here gives $[A \to \alpha \cdot a\beta, v] \Rightarrow^* yz[B \to z\cdot, v']$. The computation of δ makes $[B \to z\cdot, v'] \in \delta^*([A \to \alpha\cdot a\beta, v], yz)$, but since $[A \to \alpha\cdot a\beta, v] \in \delta^*(q_0, \psi)$, $[B \to z\cdot, v'] \in \delta^*(q_0, \psi yz)$, whence, using (a), $\psi yzv' \in LRC(B \to z)$. Since $a\beta v \Rightarrow^* yBv'w$, $|y| \geq 1$ so $\exists x: x \neq \Lambda \wedge \psi ux \in LRC(G)$. $\square$

Combining this result with the definition of the canonical LR(k)

parser's moves relation shows that

$$(\psi, aw, \Pi) \vdash_c (\psi a, w, \Pi) \text{ iff}$$

$$\exists [A \to \alpha \cdot a\beta] \in \delta^*(q_0, \psi): k : aw \in \text{first}_k(a\beta v) \quad (4.2.7)$$

$$(\alpha\beta, uw, \Pi) \vdash_c (\alpha A, uw, (A \to \beta) \cdot \Pi)) \text{ iff}$$

$$[A \to \beta \cdot, u] \in \delta^*(q_0.\alpha\beta) \quad (4.2.8).$$

Alternatively

$$(\alpha\beta, uw, \Pi) \vdash_c (\alpha A, uw, (A \to \beta) \cdot \Pi)) \text{ iff}$$

$$A \to \beta \in \text{Reduce}(\delta^*(q_0, \alpha\beta), u).$$

By definition, G is LR(k) if and only if $\vdash_c$ is deterministic. The condition required for this to be the case is defined as follows: a set of items q is *consistent* if

$$[A \to \beta \cdot, u] \in q \wedge [B \to \delta \cdot, u] \in q \text{ implies } A \to \beta = B \to \delta$$

and $[A \to \alpha \cdot a\beta, v] \in q \wedge [B \to \delta \cdot, u] \in q$ implies $u \notin \text{first}_k(a\beta v)$.

An automaton is consistent iff all its states are consistent, which immediately gives the following.

Theorem 4.11. *G is an LR(k) grammar iff its LR(k) automaton is consistent.*

The moves defined by (4.2.7) and (4.2.8) require the computation of $\delta^*(q_0, \psi)$ for stack contents ψ which is naturally done after a reduction, by scanning the stack as in Algorithm 3.1. The optimization obtained by stacking states must be incorporated into the model.

If $[A \to \alpha \cdot \beta, u] \in \delta^*(q_0, \psi)$ then, in $I(G)$, $\exists \sigma: [S] \Rightarrow [S \to \cdot\sigma, \perp]$ $\Rightarrow^* \psi[A \to \alpha \cdot \beta, u]$ by construction of δ. Lemma 4.8 then shows that $S \perp \Rightarrow \sigma \perp \Rightarrow^* wAuw \Rightarrow w\alpha\beta uw = \psi\beta uw$. i.e., $\exists \gamma: \psi = \gamma\alpha$. This means, among other things, that if the parser is in a state q, u is the lookahead string and $[A \to \alpha \cdot, u] \in q$ then α will be on top of the stack and the machine need not check before making a reduction. The symbols on the stack are not needed at all and the machine does not need to re-scan its input to compute $\delta^*(q_0, \psi)$, so the optimization may be made by replacing the stack of symbols by a stack of states $q_1 q_2 \ldots q_n$ where $\forall i, 1 < i \le n: \exists X_i: \delta(q_{i-1}, X_i) = q_i$. Such a sequence is called a *path*, and if $X_1 X_2 \ldots X_n = \alpha$, then $q_1 q_2 \ldots q_n$ may be written $[q_1 : \alpha]$. $\text{Top}(q_1 q_2 \ldots q_n) = q_n$. The moves of this automaton are given by the relation $\vdash'$ where

$$([q_0 : \psi], aw, \Pi) \vdash' ([q_0, \psi a], w, \Pi) \text{ iff}$$

$$[A \to \alpha \cdot a\beta, v] \in \text{Top}([q_0 : \psi]) \wedge k : aw \in \text{first}_k(a\beta v) \quad (4.2.9)$$

$([q_0 : \alpha\beta], uw, \Pi) \vdash' ([q_0, \alpha A], uw, (A \to \beta) \cdot \Pi))$ iff

$$A \to \beta \in \text{Reduce}(\text{Top}([q_0 : \alpha\beta]), u) \quad (4.2.10)$$

The initial configuration is $([q_0 : \Lambda], z \perp, \Lambda) = (q_0, z \perp, \Lambda)$. The accepting configuration would appear to be $([q_0 : S], \perp, \Pi)$, but if S does not appear on the right hand side of any production, $\delta(q_0, S)$ will be undefined. Instead, acceptance must be by configurations $([q_0 : \alpha], \perp, \Pi)$ for some α such that $S \to \alpha \in P$. In practice, this is implemented by checking whether the stack, after popping the handle, holds only q_0, whenever a reduction by such a production is made (cf. Algorithm 3.5).

Theorem 4.12. $S \Rightarrow \alpha \overset{\Pi}{\Rightarrow} w$ *if and only if* $[S \to \alpha \cdot, \perp] \in \delta^*(q_0, \alpha)$ *and* $(q_0, w \perp, \Lambda) \vdash'^* ([q_0 : \alpha], \perp, \Pi)$.

Proof. By a simple induction on Π; the details will be omitted. □

To summarize the results of this section, the item set construction produces an automaton from G whose transition function δ computes LR(k) contexts and which is deterministic if and only if G is an LR(k) grammar. Because of the results of section 4.1, the moves made by this automaton are those defined by the canonical LR(k) parsing relation, but this is inefficient because it requires the continual re-scanning of the stack; by stacking states instead of symbols and redefining the moves relation suitably, a correct and efficient LR(k) parser is obtained.

4.3   Relationships among Grammars and Languages

The LR(k) property is a property of *grammars*, not, as so far defined, of languages. This is illustrated trivially by the two following sets of productions.

$$1 : \quad S \to Sab \qquad 2 : \quad S \to SaS$$
$$S \to b \qquad\qquad\quad S \to b$$

In both cases the language generated is $\{ b(ab)^n \mid n \geq 0 \}$ but whereas 1 is LR(0), 2, being ambiguous, is not LR(k) for any k. It is nevertheless useful to be able to talk about the languages which can be generated by some LR(k) grammar, hence the following definitions.

A CFL L is an *LR(k) language*, $k \geq 0$, iff it is $L(G)$ for some LR(k) grammar G. L is an *LR language* iff it is an LR(k) language for some k.

The set of LR(k) languages turns out to be the same as another theoretically interesting class of languages. A CFL L is an *(empty stack) deterministic context free language (DCFL)* iff it is recognized by some deterministic pushdown automaton. The PDA used to model a shift-reduce parser in section 2.3 can be modified to recognize in this way, by adding the move $(S, \Lambda, \Pi) \vdash (\Lambda, \Lambda, \Pi)$. A string $z \in \Sigma^*$ is recognized by M iff $(\Lambda, z, \Lambda) \vdash^* (\Lambda, \Lambda, \omega)$ for some ω, hence the qualification 'empty stack'. The original treatments of PDAs included final states in their definition and recognition was defined analogously to the way it is defined for FSMs, so that, informally, a string is recognized if it causes the machine to enter a final state when its input is exhausted. In the case of nondeterministic PDAs these notions define the same languages but in the deterministic case recognition by final states defines a slightly larger class. The difference is technical but the effect is that the languages recognized by empty stack are that subset of the languages recognized by final state possessing the *prefix property*: there are no two strings x_1 and x_2 in the language such that $\exists x \neq \Lambda : x_1 = x_2 x$. The implication is that if L is recognized by final state, then $L \cdot \{\dashv\}$ is recognized by empty stack. Usually, it is the languages recognized by final state that are referred to as DCFLs elsewhere in the literature. Where the distinction is important languages recognized by empty stack will be called es-DCFLs and those by final state fs-DCFLs.

Theorem 4.13. *If L is an LR language, then L is an fs-DCFL.*

Proof. (Outline) Since L is $L(G)$ for some LR(k) grammar G, its LR(k) automaton is deterministic. It is not, however, a PDA, because of its lookahead capability. It can be turned into one by adding additional states to remember lookahead strings (for the full details of the construction, see [Harr78] or [Knu65]). The canonical LR automaton accepted in a configuration $(\Lambda, \dashv^k, \Pi)$, so the PDA built from it will be in a configuration (Λ, Λ, Π) having read the k-lookahead string and changed state into one of its additional states. There is no guarantee that this is the only time the stack becomes empty, so it is necessary that this state be final. The PDA so constructed therefore accepts the language $L \cdot \{\dashv^k\}$ by final state. Ginsburg and Greibach have shown [GiGr66] that if a language L_0 is an fs-DCFL and R is regular, then the language L' such that $L_0 = L' \cdot R$ is also an fs-DCFL. $\{\dashv^k\}$ is regular, so L is an fs-DCFL. $\qquad\qquad\square$

Perhaps surprisingly, a stronger result than the simple converse of Theorem 4.13 is true.

Theorem 4.14. *If L is an es-DCFL then L is $L(G)$ for some LR(0) grammar G.*

The proof of this theorem consists in the familiar procedure of defining a grammar which models the transitions of a PDA accepting L and then showing that this grammar is LR(0). The detailed proof is lengthy and tedious; since it is readily available elsewhere, it will be omitted. The form of the construction permits the deduction of the following.

Corollary. *If L is an fs-DCFL then L is $L(G)$ for some LR(1) grammar G.*

This seems intuitively reasonable, since $L \cdot \{\dashv\}$ is an es-DCFL and hence LR(0). Since the endmarker only introduces one extra symbol into the language one might expect that a single symbol of lookahead would be sufficient to eliminate any parsing conflicts introduced by removing it, given that the parsing decision to shift it when encountered at the end of a string could be made without lookahead.

Combining these results demonstrates that the LR languages do not form a proper hierarchy.

Theorem 4.15. *If L is an LR(k) language, for some $k \geq 0$, then L is an LR(1) language and $L \cdot \{\dashv\}$ is an LR(0) language.*

In contrast, the LR(k) *grammars* do form a hierarchy: trivially, if G is LR(k) then G is LR(m), for all $m \geq k$. On the other hand, for all $k \geq 0$ there are grammars which are LR(k) but not LR($k - 1$). In particular, consider the family of grammars G_k defined as follows, for all $k \geq 0$.

$$G_k = (\{S, A_0, \ldots, A_k\}, \{a\}, P_k, S) \text{ where } P_k \text{ consists of:}$$

$$S \rightarrow A_0$$

$$\left. \begin{array}{l} A_i \rightarrow a \\ A_i \rightarrow A_{i+1}a \end{array} \right\} \text{ for } 0 \leq i < k.$$

$$A_k \rightarrow a$$

Each G_k is an LR(k) grammar. This can be seen most easily by considering the LR(m) item set construction applied to G_k for some $m \geq 0$. The initial item set will consist of $[S \rightarrow \cdot A_0, \dashv^m]$ and pairs of items of the form $[A_i \rightarrow \cdot A_{i+1}a, a^i\dashv^{m-i}]$ and $[A_i \rightarrow \cdot a, a^i\dashv^{m-i}]$ for $0 \leq i \leq m$, and, in the case that $k > m$, $[A_i \rightarrow \cdot A_{i+1}, a^m]$ and $[A_i \rightarrow \cdot a, a^m]$ for $m < i < k$, and finally $[A_k \rightarrow \cdot a, a^m]$ or $[A_k \rightarrow \cdot a, a^k\dashv^{m-k}]$, if $k < m$ (see Figure 4.3.1). This item set has an a-successor consisting of $[A_i \rightarrow a\cdot, a^i\dashv^{m-i}]$ for $0 \leq i \leq m$ and, if $m \leq k$, $[A_i \rightarrow a\cdot, a^m]$ for $m < i \leq k$. Clearly, this state is inadequate unless $m \geq k$, hence G is LR(k), but not LR($k - 1$).

Theorem 4.15 seems to imply that, providing the endmarker symbol is incorporated into the language via its grammar, it is only necessary

$$\begin{bmatrix} S \to \cdot A_0 & , & \dashv^m \\ A_0 \to \cdot A_1 & , & \dashv^m \\ A_1 \to \cdot A_2 & , & m : a\dashv^m \\ \vdots & & \\ A_i \to \cdot A_{i+1} & , & m : a^i\dashv^m \\ \vdots & & \\ A_{k-1} \to \cdot A_k a & , & m : a^k\dashv^m \\ A_0 \to \cdot a & , & \dashv^m \\ A_1 \to \cdot a & , & m : a\dashv^m \\ \vdots & & \\ A_k \to \cdot a & , & m : a^m\dashv^m \end{bmatrix}$$

has

a-successor

$$\begin{bmatrix} A_0 \to a\cdot & , & m : \dashv^m \\ A_1 \to a\cdot & , & m : a\dashv^m \\ \vdots & & \\ A_k \to a\cdot & , & m : a^k\dashv^m \end{bmatrix}$$

Figure 4.3.1. LR(m) Item Set Construction for G_k.

to consider LR(0) grammars and parsers. Theoretically, this is so, but the practical difficulties associated with this approach are apparent in the grammar $G_6 = (\{S, L, L_0, L_1, E, P\}, \{(,), \mathbf{a}, ,, ;, \dashv\}, P_6, S)$ with P_6 comprising

$$S \to L$$
$$L \to L_0 E\dashv$$
$$L \to E\dashv$$
$$E \to E,P$$
$$E \to P$$

$$P \to \mathbf{a}$$
$$P \to (L_1$$
$$L_0 \to E;$$
$$L_1 \to L_0 E)$$
$$L_1 \to E)$$
$$L_1 \to)$$

$L(G_6) = L(G_1)\cdot\{\dashv\}$, where G_1 is the grammar for lists used in Chapters 2 and 3. Whereas G_1 was LR(1) (with the endmarker being required to follow all lists, but not explicitly in the language), G_6 is LR(0). It is far from apparent that $L(G_6)$ is what it is supposed to be, and it does a certain amount of violence to the phrase structure of the language, where ; and , are naturally to be considered binary operators with two sublists as their operands. It is unlikely that a user of a parser generating system, with this structure in mind, would come up with G_6 as a description of it. This should be sufficient reason for the writer of a parser generator to make the additional effort required to deal with LR(1) grammars, or at least a substantial subset of them, such as the LALR(1) grammars to be described in Chapter 5. As a further incentive, it will be noticed that G_6 is somewhat larger than G_1 and it leads to an LR(0) parser with more states, many of which correspond to large item sets.

A further class of grammars of interest consists of the grammars which can be parsed deterministically top-down. Although it is not the concern of this book to compare the merits of the two approaches, an examination of the relationships between the grammars each can handle is instructive.

A top-down parsing method which successively expands nonterminals until a terminal string is obtained which matches the input is naturally associated with leftmost derivations, assuming it reads its input from left to right. The grammars which permit the construction of a leftmost derivation in a single scan using only k characters of lookahead to assist in making parsing decisions are known as LL(k) grammars (left to right scan of the input producing a leftmost derivation with k characters of lookahead) and are the top-down analogue of LR(k) grammars. Formally, they are defined thus:

G is an *LL(k) grammar* iff $S \perp \Rightarrow^*_L wCw \wedge C \rightarrow \gamma \in P \wedge C \rightarrow \delta \in P \wedge \text{first}_k(\gamma w) \cap \text{first}_k(\delta w) \neq \emptyset$ implies $\gamma = \delta$. Note that the derivation is leftmost and that whereas it made sense to define an LR(k) grammar in terms of the moves of an automaton, since LR(k) grammars are asociated with bottom-up parsing, LL(k) grammars are best defined directly in terms of derivations. The definition says that where C appears as the leftmost nonterminal in a left sentential form, the decision as to which production to use to expand it may be made uniquely on the basis of the next k characters of input.

Assuming that G contains no useless symbols, the LL(k) condition is immediately violated if G is left recursive. Suppose some nonterminal A is immediately left recursive in G (the case of indirect left recursion is almost as simple, but the argument is slightly obscured, so it will be left as an exercise). Then, since G is reduced, there must be productions $A \rightarrow A\alpha$ and $A \rightarrow \beta$, for some $\alpha \in (N \cup T)^+$ and $\beta \in (N \cup T)^*$ (to avoid circularities), and a derivation $S \perp \Rightarrow_L wAw \Rightarrow^*_L wA\alpha^k w$. Now, the A in the final sentential form of this derivation may be expanded using either of the productions with A as subject, so the LL(k) condition requires $\text{first}_k(A\alpha^{k+1}w) \cap \text{first}_k(\beta\alpha^k w) = \emptyset$. But $A \rightarrow \beta$, so $A\alpha^{k+1}w \Rightarrow \beta\alpha^{k+1}w$, whence $\text{first}_k(\beta\alpha^{k+1}w) \subseteq \text{first}_k(A\alpha^{k+1}w)$, and, whatever the length of β, $\text{first}_k(\beta\alpha^{k+1}w) = \text{first}_k(\beta\alpha^k w)$, so the LL($k$) condition cannot be satisfied. However, left recursive grammars have been seen which are LR(k) (e.g. G_1). Thus, there are grammars which are LR(k) but not LL(k). Are there, on the other hand, grammars which are LL(k) but not LR(k)?

The answer is negative, and although top-down parsers are usually implemented by recursive descent, making no use of items or anything like them, item grammars can be used to provide a proof of this. Two rather technical lemmas, both due to Heilbrunnerare required, and will be quoted without proof (see [Heil81] for these). The first relates leftmost and rightmost derivations, the second deduces a condition on the item grammar of an LL(k) grammar.

Lemma 4.16.

$$B \Rightarrow_L^* wA\psi \text{ implies } \exists\omega\colon(\omega \Rightarrow^* w \land \forall z \in L(\psi)\colon B \Rightarrow_R^* \omega Az)$$

$$B \Rightarrow_R^* \omega Az \text{ implies } \exists\psi\colon(\psi \Rightarrow^* z \land \forall w \in L(\omega)\colon B \Rightarrow_L^* wA\psi)$$

where

$$L(\psi) = \{\, x \in T^* \mid \psi \Rightarrow^* x \,\}.$$

Lemma 4.17. *For LL(k) grammars, if*

$$[S] \Rightarrow^* \psi[A \to \alpha \cdot \beta, u] \land [S] \Rightarrow^* \psi[B \to \rho \cdot \sigma, v]$$

$$\land \text{ first}_k(\beta u) \cap \text{first}_k(\sigma v) \neq \emptyset$$

then $[A \to \alpha \cdot \beta] \Rightarrow^* [B \to \rho \cdot \sigma]$ *or* $[B \to \rho \cdot \sigma] \Rightarrow^* [A \to \alpha \cdot \beta]$.

Note all derivations are in the item grammar; $[B \to \rho \cdot \sigma]$ is shorthand for $[B \to \rho \cdot \sigma, \Lambda]$.

Theorem 4.18. *Every LL(k) grammar is LR(k).*

Proof. A grammar is LR(k) iff its LR(k) automaton is consistent (Theorem 4.11), so it is sufficient to show that the consistency conditions are necessarily satisfied by LL(k) grammars. Suppose, in contradiction, that for some state q there are items $[A \to \alpha\cdot, u] \in q$ and $[B \to \rho\cdot, u] \in q$, where $A \to \alpha \neq B \to \delta$. Then there is a string ψ such that $[S] \Rightarrow^* \psi[A \to \alpha\cdot, u]$ and $[S] \Rightarrow^* \psi[B \to \delta\cdot, u]$, so, according to Lemma 4.17 $[A \to \alpha\cdot] \Rightarrow^* [B \to \delta\cdot]$ or $[B \to \delta\cdot] \Rightarrow^* [A \to \alpha\cdot]$, which is impossible unless $A \to \alpha = B \to \delta$.

Suppose instead that there are items $[A \to \alpha\cdot, u] \in q$ and $[B \to \rho\cdot a\sigma, v] \in q$ with $u \in \text{first}_k(a\sigma v)$. Then, it follows by the same argument that

$$[A \to \alpha\cdot] \Rightarrow^* [B \to \rho \cdot a\sigma] \text{ or } [B \to \rho \cdot a\sigma] \Rightarrow^* [A \to \alpha]$$

which is impossible, given the way in which the item grammar is constructed. □

Thus, the LL(k) grammars are properly contained in the LR(k) grammars, for any k.

4.4   Complexity Results

It is important to know how much time a parser will take to analyse an input string and how much space (i.e., memory) it will need. The precise answer in any implementation depends on the chosen data representation and the precise code used to perform parsing actions. General conclusions can be drawn by considering the behaviour of the abstract model of the parser which has been developed in this chapter. In this context, the questions to be answered are: how many moves will the canonical LR(k) automaton for G make in parsing a string $w \in L(G)$? How many states are there in the automaton?

The first of these questions can be given an eminently satisfactory answer.

Theorem 4.19. *There exist constants a, b such that the number of moves made by the canonical LR(k) automaton in parsing a string w is $\leq a|w| + b$.*

Proof. The proof of this theorem requires two results concerning the length of derivations. Although these are not entirely obvious, they will be stated without proof, since these are lengthy and technical.

Lemma 4.19a. *For every unambiguous context free grammar, there are constants c and d such that*

$$A \Rightarrow^j w \text{ implies } j \leq c|w| + d.$$

Lemma 4.19b. *For every LR(k) grammar, there is a constant p such that*

$$S \Rightarrow^*_R \alpha\gamma\beta y \text{ and } \gamma \Rightarrow^* \Lambda \text{ implies } |\gamma| < p.$$

Assume that $(\Lambda, wz, \Lambda) \vdash^j (\psi, z, \Pi)$. Similar reasoning to that used to justify stacking parser states shows that, for some σ and u, $\psi\sigma u \in LRC(G)$ and $S \overset{\Pi}{\Rightarrow} \psi\sigma uy$ for some y. It is not hard to see that $\psi \overset{\Pi}{\Rightarrow} w$. ψ may be written as $\psi = \psi_0 X_1 \psi_1 X_2 \ldots X_n \psi_n$ where, for each i, $X_i \Rightarrow^{j_i} x_i$ for some $x_i \neq \Lambda$ and $\psi_i \Rightarrow^{m_i} \Lambda$, such that $x_1 x_2 \ldots x_n = w$ and $\Sigma j_i + \Sigma m_i = |\Pi|$. For all i, Lemma 4.19b states that $|\psi_i| < p$, so, by Lemma 4.19a, $m_i \leq d \cdot p$. Lemma 4.19a also shows that each $j_i \leq c|x_i| + d$, so that $\Sigma j_i \leq nd + c\Sigma|x_i| = nd + c|w| \leq (c+d)|w|$ (because n must be $\leq |w|$). Now, $j = |w| + |\Pi| = |w| + \Sigma j_i + \Sigma m_i$, so $j \leq |w| + dp + (c+d)|w|$ whence $j \leq a|w| + b$, with $a = (c+d+1)$, $b = d$. In particular, if $(\Lambda, z, \Lambda) \vdash^j (S, \perp, \Pi)$ the inequality holds, as required. □

Since the stack can only grow as a result of a shift or a reduction of the empty string, its maximum length is bounded by the number of such moves, and thus by a linear function of $|w|$.

It would be surprising indeed if a parser could analyse its input without examining every character of it, so a linear algorithm is an optimum one (if no use is made of parallelism). Furthermore, it turns out in practice that the constants of proportionality are small and the primitive moves of the LR(k) automaton can be efficiently programmed on present-day computers. It is therefore justifiable to refer to LR parsers as efficient.

Matters are less clear and less satisfactory when the number of states of the LR(k) automatonis considered. The usual approach adopted is to try and find bounds on the number of states as functions of the size of the grammar. If $G = (N, T, P, S)$ then the size of G, written $|G|$ is $\sum_{A \rightarrow \alpha \in P} |A\alpha|$.

Each production $A \rightarrow \alpha$ produces $|A\alpha|$ different LR(0) items, each of which is followed by a terminal string of length k to form an LR(k) item. $|T|$ is certainly less than $|G|$ so the number of different k-lookahead strings that may appear in each item is less than $|G|^k$. Thus, the number of different items is less than $|G|^{k+1}$. Each state in the LR(k) automaton corresponds to a subset of the set of all items, so the maximum possible number of states is $2^{|G|^{k+1}}$. Since this estimate takes no account of the way the item set construction actually computes lookahead strings, which depends on the structure of the grammar, it seems highly likely that for $k > 0$ this doubly exponential upper bound is too high, and, indeed, no grammars have been exhibited which actually display this behaviour. Nevertheless, it has proved difficult to establish tighter upper bounds.

It is known that for $k = 0$ there are grammars whose LR(k) automata have state sets whose size is exponential in the size of the grammar. Consider the family of grammars, defined for $n > 0$ as $G_n = (\{A_0, \ldots A_n\}, \{1, 0, a, a_0, \ldots a_n\}, P_n, A_0)$ with productions

$$A_0 \rightarrow a$$
$$\left.\begin{array}{l} A_{i-1} \rightarrow 1A_ia_{i-1} \\ A_i \rightarrow 0A_ia_i \\ A_i \rightarrow 0A_0a_i \end{array}\right\} \quad 1 \leq i \leq n$$
$$A_n \rightarrow 1A_0a_n$$

The LR(0) parser for G_n has a number of states proportional to $2^{c|G_n|}$, for a constant $c < 1$ [Ukko85]. Energetic readers may convince themselves of this by starting the item set construction for a general G_n and observing how 0-successors spawn new states after each A_i is added by closure.

This result is rather disappointing, since there are other, less powerful, bottom-up parsing methods (e.g., precedence techniques) which always work with polynomial size parsers, and it is well known that the growth rate of any polynomial is tractable compared with that of any exponential function. However, Purdom [Pur74] has produced statistics to show that for many grammars the number of states of the LR(0) parser (and hence of the LALR(1) parser, see Chapter 5) is linear in the size of the grammars. These purely statistical results seem to demonstrate that the sort of grammars which people actually write do not have the kind of convoluted structure required to spawn LR(0) states in an exponential way, even though it is possible to devise grammars which do do this.

For the case $k > 0$ it is not known whether grammars exist for which the canonical LR(k) automaton has as many states as predicted by the upper bound of $2^{|G|^{k+1}}$. It is conjectured that none does, although this has not been proved. Ukkonen [Ukko85] has shown that much smaller bounds exist for certain restricted forms of grammar. For grammars without right recursion the number of LR(k) states is $\leq |G|^{k|G|} \cdot 2^{|G|}$. For regular grammars the bounds are independent of k: if G is left linear the number of states is $\leq |G| + 1$, if right linear, it is $\leq 2^{|G|}$.

The final complexity issue to be discussed is the computational complexity of the parser construction process itself. The space requirements are essentially determined by the size of the automaton being built, so the results just cited are applicable and the space requirement of an LR(k) parser generator is at least exponential in the size of the grammar being processed. Provided closure and first$_k$ computations are done once and for all at the start of processing (as noted in sections 3.2 and 4.2) using the techniques described in the appendix, which have polynomial time complexity, the computation of the item sets will be dominated by the successor computations which have the same upper bound, since every state has to be processed. This processing is in turn dominated by the search required to check whether an item set has already been added; the actual complexity thus depends on the data structure used to hold item sets at this point. At worst, the search is linear in the number of item sets, giving a worst case of $2^{2|G|^{k+1}}$. Even when $k = 0$ this is potentially a substantial overhead.

It has been shown, nevertheless, that for fixed k it is possible to *test* for the LR(k) property in time bounded by $|G|^{k+2}$ [HuSU75]. The algorithm employed is based on nondeterministic FSMs equivalent to those built from the item grammar for G, but parameterized in the lookahead string that is to be part of the item corresponding to a reduction.

5

Practical LR Parser Construction

5.1   LALR(k) Grammars and Parsers

Practical experience appears to bear out the theoretical prediction that, for $k \geq 1$, the number of states in an LR(k) automaton built using the algorithm of section 4.2 is prohibitively large (see e.g., [AnEH73]). LR(0) parsers have a relatively modest number of states but are nondeterministic for most grammars of interest. This nondeterminism can often be resolved by augmenting the LR(0) automaton with lookahead information, either taken from the LR(k) automaton or deduced from the structure of the LR(0) automaton itself. At the time of writing, this is the most practically important of the LR parser generating techniques. Its essence is captured by the following definition.

A grammar G is a *lookahead LR(k) grammar (LALR(k) grammar)* if and only if parsing conflicts in its LR(0) automaton can be resolved correctly by computing *lookahead sets*, $LA(q, A \rightarrow \beta) \subseteq T^k$ for each reduction by a production $A \rightarrow \beta$ in a state q, such that, for all $u \in LA(q, A \rightarrow \beta)$, $A \rightarrow \beta \in \text{Reduce}(q, u)$. Conflicts are resolved correctly if, for all q, u, $|\text{Reduce}(q, u)| \leq 1$ and if $|\text{Reduce}(q, u)| = 1$, $\forall [B \rightarrow \gamma \cdot a\delta, v] \in q : u \notin \text{first}_k(a\delta v)$ and the parser still accepts exactly the strings in $L(G)$.

This definition does not specify any algorithm for computing the lookahead sets, it merely says that G is LALR(k) if *any* such set can be computed. One example of lookahead computation has already been seen in section 3.3, where $LA(q, A \rightarrow \beta)$ was taken as the easily computed set FOLLOW(A). This is not always successful, even in situations where k symbols of lookahead should be sufficient to resolve conflicts, because the computation does not take into account the context in which the reduction is to take place. This is evident because the SLR lookahead set is independent of q. Making use of this contextual information leads to smaller lookahead sets (which are more likely to resolve conflicts). The problem in producing parsers for LALR(k) grammars is that of finding efficient algorithms to compute the smallest lookahead sets.

The full LR(k) method of section 4.2 uses all the available contextual information in its computation. One method of computing lookahead sets (which is *not* efficient but conveys most clearly the nature of the technique) is to take the lookahead strings associated with reductions in the LR(k) automaton and use them as the lookahead sets for reductions in the LR(0) automaton which correspond to them, in a particular sense. This sense can be understood by considering the relationship between the LR(k) and LR(0) automata for the same grammar.

Suppose $G = (N, T, P, S)$ is a CFG. Let $LRA0 = (Q^0, N \cup T, P, q_0^0, \delta^0, \text{Reduce}^0)$ be its LR(0) automaton, and let $LRA = (Q, N \cup T, P, q_0, \delta, \text{Reduce})$ its LR(k) automaton. Define a function core: $Q \rightarrow Q^0$ by

$$\text{core}(q) = \{ A \rightarrow \alpha \cdot \beta \mid [A \rightarrow \alpha \cdot \beta, u] \in q \}.$$

It follows from the way in which the LR(k) automaton was constructed that $\text{core}(\delta(q, X)) = \delta^0(\text{core}(q), X)$. Hence, by induction, for any $\psi \in (N \cup T)^*$, $\text{core}(\delta^*(q_0, \psi)) = \delta^{0*}(\text{core}(q_0), \psi) = \delta^{0*}(q_0^0, \psi)$.

This suggests that to shrink the LR(k) parser to the size of the LR(0) parser the latter should be used to compute δ but all items of the LR(k) parser which differ only in their lookahead components from the LR(0) items of a state should be included in that state. Hence, when computing Reduce the lookahead information in items of the form $[A \rightarrow \alpha \cdot, u]$ is available. More precisely, define the *lookahead completion* of $q^0 \in Q^0$ as

$$\text{LAC}(q^0) = \{ [A \rightarrow \alpha \cdot \beta, u] \mid$$
$$\exists q \in Q : [A \rightarrow \alpha \cdot \beta, u] \in q \wedge \text{core}(q) = q^0 \}$$
$$= \bigcup_{q \in Q \mid \text{core}(q) = q^0} q.$$

The LALR(k) automaton for G is $LALRA(G) = (Q^l, N \cup T, P, q_0^l, \delta^l, \text{Reduce}^l)$ where $Q^l = \{ \text{LAC}(q^0) \mid q^0 \in Q^0 \}$, $q_0^l = \text{LAC}(q_0^0)$ and for $q^l \in Q^l$, $\delta^l(q^l, X) = q^{l'}$ iff $\exists q^0 \in Q^0 : q^l = \text{LAC}(q^0) \wedge q^{l'} = \text{LAC}(\delta^0(q^0, X))$. As usual, $\text{Reduce}^l(q^l, u) = \{ A \rightarrow \alpha \mid [A \rightarrow \alpha \cdot, u] \in q^l \}$, whence $LA(q^l, A \rightarrow \alpha) = \{ u \mid [A \rightarrow \alpha \cdot, u] \in q^l \}$. The automaton still makes its moves as if it were the canonical LR(k) parser, i.e.,

$$(\alpha\beta, uw, \Pi) \vdash_{LALRA} (\alpha A, uw, (A \rightarrow \beta) \cdot \Pi) \text{ iff } [A \rightarrow \beta \cdot, u] \in \delta^{l*}(q_0^l, \alpha\beta)$$

and

$$(\psi, aw, \Pi) \vdash_{LALRA} (\psi a, w, \Pi) \text{ iff}$$

$$\exists [A \rightarrow \alpha \cdot a\beta, v] \in \delta^{l*}(q_0^l, \psi) : k : aw \in \text{first}_k(a\beta v)$$

In practice, the usual optimizations of stacking states and shifting on the basis of the next symbol only will be made, giving a moves relation $\vdash'_{LALRA}$ analogous to the relation defined by (4.2.9) and (4.2.10).

G is an LALR(k) grammar iff $LALRA(G)$ is consistent (cf. Theorem 4.11). An LALR(k) grammar is thus defined in terms of the item sets in its LALR(k) automaton. This is somewhat unsatisfactory, since it is not clear how this can be related to any other properties of the grammar. However, it seems to be the best one can do (cf. [DePe82]), suggesting that the LALR property is intimately bound up with the parser construction method.

The construction is illustrated in Figures 5.1.1 and 5.1.2 for G_1, whose LR(0) item sets are in Figure 3.3.1. To save space, the shorthand $A \to \alpha \cdot \beta \,/\, u_1 \ldots u_n$ is being used for the set of items $[A \to \alpha \cdot \beta, u_1] \ldots [A \to \alpha \cdot \beta, u_n]$ in an obvious way. G_1 is LALR(1), the parsing conflicts of its LR(0) automaton having been resolved by this construction. In fact, G_1 is SLR(1), but there are LALR(k) grammars which are not SLR(k) (for the same k). This is illustrated by the grammar with productions

$$
\begin{array}{lll}
S \to AbB & A \to aB & \\
 & & B \to A \\
S \to B & A \to c &
\end{array}
$$

which is easily verified to be LALR(1) but not SLR(1).

Figures 5.1.1 and 5.1.2 also show how the additional states of the full LR(1) automaton come about. Consider states 3 and 9 of the LR(1) parser, which get merged into state 3 of the LALR(1) parser. In the original state 3 the item $[L \to L;E\cdot, \dashv]$ corresponds informally to a state of the parse in which a list at the outermost level has been scanned; it can only, therefore, be followed by an endmarker. In state 9, on the other hand, the items $[L \to L;E\cdot,)]$ and $[L \to L;E\cdot, ;]$ correspond to lists which are part of a bracketed sublist of a larger list; they must be followed by either a semicolon or a closing bracket. This case can be distinguished from state 3 because state 9 is a successor, via 7 and 8, of state 6 which can only be entered after shifting an opening bracket. Merging the two loses this information, which in this case doesn't matter, since the decision of whether to shift or reduce is not affected by bracketing level, only by the relative binding power of the , and ; operators. State 8 is distinct from state 2, even though it involves no reduction, because it enables the parser to distinguish shifts which will *eventually* lead to a reduction in which) is a legitimate following symbol from those in which it is not, but $\dashv$ is. Similar remarks apply to all pairs of states which have been merged in this LALR(1) parser.

$$L \to L;E$$
$$L \to E \qquad P \to \mathbf{a} \qquad M \to \Lambda$$
$$E \to E,P \quad P \to (M) \quad M \to L$$
$$E \to P$$

Item Set	Items	Successors
0	$L \to \cdot L;E \mathbin{/} \dashv, ;$ $L \to \cdot E \mathbin{/} \dashv, ;$ $E \to \cdot E,P \mathbin{/} \dashv, ;, ,$ $E \to \cdot P \mathbin{/} \dashv, ;, ,$ $P \to \cdot (M) \mathbin{/} \dashv, ;, ,$ $P \to \cdot \mathbf{a} \mathbin{/} \dashv, ;, ,$	$L \Rightarrow 1$ $E \Rightarrow 22$ $P \Rightarrow 21$ $(\Rightarrow 6$ $\mathbf{a} \Rightarrow 20$
1	$L \to L \cdot ;E \mathbin{/} \dashv, ;$	$; \Rightarrow 2$
2	$L \to L; \cdot E \mathbin{/} \dashv, ;$ $E \to \cdot E,P \mathbin{/} \dashv, ;, ,$ $E \to \cdot P \mathbin{/} \dashv, ;, ,$ $P \to \cdot (M) \mathbin{/} \dashv, ;, ,$ $P \to \cdot \mathbf{a} \mathbin{/} \dashv, ;, ,$	$E \Rightarrow 3$ $P \Rightarrow 21$ $(\Rightarrow 6$ $\mathbf{a} \Rightarrow 20$
3	$L \to L;E \cdot \mathbin{/} \dashv, ;$ $E \to E \cdot ,P \mathbin{/} \dashv, ;, ,$	$\#L \to L;E$ $, \Rightarrow 4$
4	$E \to E, \cdot P \mathbin{/} \dashv, ;, ,$ $P \to \cdot (M) \mathbin{/} \dashv, ;, ,$ $P \to \cdot \mathbf{a} \mathbin{/} \dashv, ;, ,$	$P \Rightarrow 5$ $(\Rightarrow 6$ $\mathbf{a} \Rightarrow 20$
5	$E \to E,P \cdot \mathbin{/} \dashv, ;, ,$	$\#E \to E,P$
6	$P \to (\cdot M) \mathbin{/} \dashv, ;, ,$ $M \to \cdot \mathbin{/})$ $M \to \cdot L \mathbin{/})$ $L \to \cdot L;E \mathbin{/} ;,)$ $L \to \cdot E \mathbin{/} ;,)$ $E \to \cdot E,P \mathbin{/} ;, ,,)$ $E \to \cdot P \mathbin{/} ;, ,,)$ $P \to \cdot (M) \mathbin{/} ;, ,,)$ $P \to \cdot \mathbf{a} \mathbin{/} ;, ,,)$	$M \Rightarrow 18$ $\#M \to \Lambda$ $L \Rightarrow 7$ $E \Rightarrow 13$ $P \Rightarrow 14$ $(\Rightarrow 12$ $\mathbf{a} \Rightarrow 17$
7	$L \to L \cdot ;E \mathbin{/} ;,)$ $M \to L \cdot \mathbin{/})$	$; \Rightarrow 8$ $\#M \to L$

Figure 5.1.1. LR(1) Item Sets for G_1

Item Set	Items	Successors
8	$L \to L; \cdot E \,/\, ;,)$ $E \to \cdot E,P \,/\, ;,,,)$ $E \to \cdot P \,/\, ;,,,)$ $P \to \cdot (M) \,/\, ;,,,)$ $P \to \cdot \mathbf{a} \,/\, ;,,,)$	$E \Rightarrow 9$ $P \Rightarrow 14$ $(\Rightarrow 12$ $\mathbf{a} \Rightarrow 17$
9	$L \to L;E \cdot \,/\, ;,)$ $E \to E \cdot ,P \,/\, ;,,,)$	$\#L \to L;E$ $, \Rightarrow 10$
10	$E \to E, \cdot P \,/\, ;,,,)$ $P \to \cdot (M) \,/\, ;,,,)$ $P \to \cdot \mathbf{a} \,/\, ;,,,)$	$P \Rightarrow 11$ $(\Rightarrow 12$ $\mathbf{a} \Rightarrow 17$
11	$E \to E,P \cdot \,/\, ;,,,)$	$\#E \to E,P$
12	$P \to (\cdot M) \,/\, ;,,,)$ $M \to \cdot \,/\,)$ $M \to \cdot L \,/\,)$ $L \to \cdot L;E \,/\, ;,)$ $L \to \cdot E \,/\, ;,)$ $E \to \cdot E,P \,/\, ;,,,)$ $E \to \cdot P \,/\, ;,,,)$ $P \to \cdot (M) \,/\, ;,,,)$ $P \to \cdot \mathbf{a} \,/\, ;,,,)$	$M \Rightarrow 15$ $\#M \to \Lambda$ $L \Rightarrow 7$ $E \Rightarrow 13$ $P \Rightarrow 14$ $(\Rightarrow 12$ $\mathbf{a} \Rightarrow 17$
13	$L \to E \cdot \,/\, ;,)$ $E \to E \cdot ,P \,/\, ;,,,)$	$\#L \to E$ $, \Rightarrow 10$
14	$E \to P \cdot \,/\, ;,,,)$	$\#E \to P$
15	$P \to (M \cdot) \,/\, ;,,,)$	$) \Rightarrow 16$
16	$P \to (M) \cdot \,/\, ;,,,)$	$\#P \to (M)$
17	$P \to \mathbf{a} \cdot \,/\, ;,,,)$	$\#P \to \mathbf{a}$
18	$P \to (M \cdot) \,/\, \dashv,;,,$	$) \Rightarrow 19$
19	$P \to (M) \cdot \,/\, \dashv,;,,$	$\#P \to (M)$
20	$P \to \mathbf{a} \cdot \,/\, \dashv,;,,$	$\#P \to \mathbf{a}$
21	$E \to P \cdot \,/\, \dashv,;,,$	$\#E \to P$
22	$L \to E \cdot \,/\, \dashv,;$ $E \to E \cdot ,P \,/\, \dashv,;,,$	$\#E \to E,P$ $, \Rightarrow 4$

Figure 5.1.1. LR(1) Item Sets for G_1(continued)

Item Set	Items	Successors
0	$L \rightarrow \cdot L;E \ / \ \dashv,;$ $L \rightarrow \cdot E \ / \ \dashv,;$ $E \rightarrow \cdot E,P \ / \ \dashv,;,,$ $E \rightarrow \cdot P \ / \ \dashv,;,,$ $P \rightarrow \cdot (M) \ / \ \dashv,;,,$ $P \rightarrow \cdot \mathbf{a} \ / \ \dashv,;,,$	$L \Rightarrow 1$ $E \Rightarrow 8$ $P \Rightarrow 9$ $(\Rightarrow 6$ $\mathbf{a} \Rightarrow 12$
1	$L \rightarrow L \cdot ;E \ / \ \dashv,;$	$; \Rightarrow 2$
2	$L \rightarrow L; \cdot E \ / \ \dashv,;,)$ $E \rightarrow \cdot E,P \ / \ \dashv,;,,)$ $E \rightarrow \cdot P \ / \ \dashv,;,,)$ $P \rightarrow \cdot (M) \ / \ \dashv,;,,)$ $P \rightarrow \cdot \mathbf{a} \ / \ \dashv,;,,)$	$E \Rightarrow 3$ $P \Rightarrow 9$ $(\Rightarrow 6$ $\mathbf{a} \Rightarrow 12$
3	$L \rightarrow L;E \cdot \ / \ \dashv,;,)$ $E \rightarrow E \cdot ,P \ / \ \dashv,;,,)$	$\#L \rightarrow L;E$ $, \Rightarrow 4$
4	$E \rightarrow E, \cdot P \ / \ \dashv,;,,)$ $P \rightarrow \cdot (M) \ / \ \dashv,;,,)$ $P \rightarrow \cdot \mathbf{a} \ / \ \dashv,;,,)$	$P \Rightarrow 5$ $(\Rightarrow 6$ $\mathbf{a} \Rightarrow 12$
5	$E \rightarrow E,P \cdot \ / \ \dashv,;,,)$	$\#E \rightarrow E,P$
6	$P \rightarrow (\cdot M) \ / \ \dashv,;,,)$ $M \rightarrow \cdot /)$ $M \rightarrow \cdot L /)$ $L \rightarrow \cdot L;E \ / \ ;,)$ $L \rightarrow \cdot E \ / \ ;,)$ $E \rightarrow \cdot E,P \ / \ ;,,)$ $E \rightarrow \cdot P \ / \ ;,,)$ $P \rightarrow \cdot (M) \ / \ ;,,)$ $P \rightarrow \cdot \mathbf{a} \ / \ ;,,)$	$M \Rightarrow 10$ $\#M \rightarrow \Lambda$ $L \Rightarrow 7$ $E \Rightarrow 8$ $P \Rightarrow 9$ $(\Rightarrow 6$ $\mathbf{a} \Rightarrow 12$
7	$M \rightarrow L \cdot /)$ $L \rightarrow L \cdot ;E \ / \ ;,)$	$\#M \rightarrow L$ $; \Rightarrow 2$
8	$L \rightarrow E \cdot \ / \ ;,),\dashv$ $E \rightarrow E \cdot ,P \ / \ ;,,),\dashv$	$\#L \rightarrow E$ $, \Rightarrow 4$
9	$E \rightarrow P \cdot \ / \ ;,,),\dashv$	$\#E \rightarrow P$
10	$P \rightarrow (M \cdot) \ / \ \dashv,;,,$	$) \Rightarrow 11$
11	$P \rightarrow (M) \cdot \ / \ \dashv,;,,$	$\#P \rightarrow (M)$
12	$P \rightarrow \mathbf{a} \cdot \ / \ ;,,),\dashv$	$\#P \rightarrow \mathbf{a}$

Figure 5.1.2. LALR(1) Item Sets for G_1

It may be suspected that such a merger will sometimes introduce parsing conflicts in the LALR parser which are absent in the corresponding LR parser. This is indeed the case, as is shown by the trivial example in Figure 5.1.3. Here, states 6 and 12 distinguish between the cases where an a or a b was the initial symbol of the input. If the former, then an e is to be reduced to A if a c follows ($S \to aAc$) but to a B if a d follows ($S \to aBd$), whereas the reverse applies in state 12 (using $S \to bBc$ and $S \to bAd$). In producing an LALR(1) automaton, these two states are merged to give the item set

$$A \to e \cdot \ / \, c, d$$
$$B \to e \cdot \ / \, c, d$$

and the grammar is not LALR(1).

Before describing algorithms for constructing LALR(k) parsers without first building the full LR(k) parser, the theory of Chapter 4 must be applied to the LALR(k) definition in order to verify that a parser constructed in this manner will behave correctly. The theory can also be used to give some idea of the additional restrictions on grammars imposed in return for the smaller parsers.

It can easily be shown that the construction of the LALR(k) automaton ensures that $\delta^{l*}(q_0^l, \alpha) = \text{LAC}(\delta^{0*}(q_0^0, \alpha))$ for all α. Thus, by definition of LAC, $[A \to \alpha \cdot \beta, u] \in \delta^{l*}(q_0^l, \alpha)$ iff $\exists q \in Q : [A \to \alpha \cdot \beta, u] \in q \wedge \text{core}(q) = \text{core}(\delta^*(q_0, \alpha))$. This is always true if $[A \to \alpha \cdot \beta, u] \in \delta^*(q_0, \alpha)$, of course, but not only if: in the example of Figure 5.1.3, for example, $[B \to e \cdot, c] \in \delta^{l*}(q_0^l, ae)$, but $[B \to e \cdot, c] \notin \delta^*(q_0, ae)$. This is sufficient to guarantee that if $\psi u \in \text{LRC}(A \to \beta)$ then $[A \to \beta \cdot, u] \in \delta^{l*}(q_0^l, \psi)$ and if $\exists x : x \neq \Lambda \wedge \psi u x \in \text{LRC}(G)$ then $\exists [A \to \alpha \cdot a\beta, v] \in \delta^{l*}(q_0^l, \psi) : u \in \text{first}_k(a\beta v)$. i.e., the implications of Lemma 4.10 hold in one direction only. Thus, using the definition of the canonical LR(k) parser's moves relation, it will be the case that

$(\psi, aw, \Pi) \vdash_c (\psi a, w, \Pi)$

$\quad\quad$ implies $\exists [A \to \alpha \cdot a\beta, v] \in \delta^{l*}(q_0^l, \psi) : k : aw \in \text{first}_k(\alpha\beta v)$

$\quad\quad$ implies $(\psi, aw, \Pi) \vdash_{LALR} (\psi a, w, \Pi)$

and

$(\alpha\beta, uw, \Pi) \vdash_c (\alpha A, uw, (A \to \beta) \cdot \Pi)$

$\quad\quad$ implies $[A \to \beta \cdot, u] \in \delta^{l*}(q_0^l, \alpha\beta)$

$\quad\quad$ implies $(\alpha\beta, uw, \Pi) \vdash_{LALR} (\alpha A, uw, (A \to \beta) \cdot \Pi)$.

However, these unidirectional implications allow for the possibility that $[A \to \beta \cdot, u] \in \delta^{l*}(q_0^l, \alpha\beta)$ when the canonical parser would not make a

$$S \to aAc \quad S \to bAd \quad A \to e$$
$$S \to bBc \quad S \to aBd \quad B \to e$$

Item Set	Items	Successors
0	$S \to \cdot aAc, \dashv$ $S \to \cdot aBd, \dashv$ $S \to \cdot bBc, \dashv$ $S \to \cdot bAd, \dashv$	$a \Rightarrow 1$ $b \Rightarrow 7$
1	$S \to a \cdot Ac, \dashv$ $S \to a \cdot Bd, \dashv$ $A \to \cdot e, c$ $B \to \cdot e, d$	$A \Rightarrow 2$ $B \Rightarrow 4$ $e \Rightarrow 6$
2	$S \to aA \cdot c, \dashv$	$c \Rightarrow 3$
3	$S \to aAc \cdot, \dashv$	$\#S \to aAc$
4	$S \to aB \cdot d, \dashv$	$d \Rightarrow 5$
5	$S \to aBd \cdot, \dashv$	$\#S \to aBd$
6	$A \to e \cdot, c$ $B \to e \cdot, d$	$\#A \to e$ $\#B \to e$
7	$S \to b \cdot Bc, \dashv$ $S \to b \cdot Ad, \dashv$ $B \to \cdot e, c$ $A \to \cdot e, d$	$B \Rightarrow 8$ $A \Rightarrow 10$ $e \Rightarrow 12$
8	$S \to bB \cdot c, \dashv$	$c \Rightarrow 9$
9	$S \to bBc \cdot, \dashv$	$\#S \to bBc$
10	$S \to bA \cdot d, \dashv$	$d \Rightarrow 11$
11	$S \to bAd \cdot, \dashv$	$\#S \to bAd$
12	$B \to e \cdot, c$ $A \to e \cdot, d$	$\#B \to e$ $\#A \to e$

Figure 5.1.3. A grammar that is LR(1) but not LALR(1)

reduce move, as has just been seen. The LALR(k) parser will reduce, however. The moves of the canonical parser are a subset of those possible in the LALR parser, which is sufficient to guarantee the correctness of the latter, but means that it is deterministic in fewer cases. If there is a state in the LALR parser for which a reduction is appropriate, it will make it. If it is inappropriate, then the state will also indicate the correct action (a shift or some other reduction), so there must be a parsing conflict in that state.

For the particular case $k = 1$, if merging states introduces new conflicts, they will be reduce-reduce ones.

Lemma 5.1. *The LALR(1) automaton for G has a shift-reduce conflict if and only if the LR(1) automaton for G does.*

Proof. If the LALR(1) automaton has a shift-reduce conflict, there is a state $q^l \in Q^l$ such that $[A \rightarrow \alpha \cdot a\beta, b] \in q^l$ and $[B \rightarrow \delta \cdot, a] \in q^l$. In the LR(1) automaton there is some state q with $\text{core}(q) = \text{core}(q^l)$ and $[B \rightarrow \delta \cdot, a] \in q$. But, by definition of core, there is also an item $[A \rightarrow \alpha \cdot a\beta, c] \in q$ for some c (which may or may not be equal to b), so q also has a shift-reduce conflict on a.   □

This result cannot be extended to $k \geq 2$.

The lookahead sets produced using the lookahead completion are, however, the smallest sets with which the LR(0) parser can be annotated to produce a correct LALR parser, so the LALR grammars defined thereby constitute the largest class that can be parsed using this technique. This is easily seen by considering an automaton obtained by augmenting the LR(0) automaton with lookahead sets smaller than those given by LAC, or equivalently, as in the statement of the next theorem, omitting some items from LAC.

Theorem 5.2. *Let* $LALRA' = (Q', N \cup T, P, \delta', q_0', \text{Reduce}')$ *be an automaton for* $G = (N, T, P, S)$ *with* $Q' \subseteq 2^{I_k}$, $\text{core}(q_0') = q_0^0$ *and* $\forall q' \in Q' : \text{core}(\delta'(q', X)) = \delta^0(\text{core}(q'), X)$ *where* q_0^0 *and* δ^0 *are the initial state and transition function respectively of G's LR(0) automaton. Let* Q *be the set of states of G's canonical LR automaton. Then* $\vdash_{LALRA'}$ *is a parsing relation iff* $\forall q' \in Q', q \in Q : \text{core}(q) = \text{core}(q')$ *implies* $\forall [A \rightarrow \beta \cdot, u] \in q : [A \rightarrow \beta \cdot, u] \in q'$.

Proof. Suppose $\exists q \in Q, q' \in Q' : \text{core}(q) = \text{core}(q') \wedge \exists [A \rightarrow \beta \cdot, u] \in q : [A \rightarrow \beta \cdot, u] \notin q'$. Now, by (4.2.8), $(\alpha\beta, uy, \Pi) \vdash_c (\alpha A, uy, (A \rightarrow \beta) \cdot \Pi)$, but, since $[A \rightarrow \beta \cdot, u] \notin q'$, $(\alpha\beta, uy, \Pi) \nvdash_{LALRA'} (\alpha A, uy, (A \rightarrow \beta) \cdot \Pi)$, so $\vdash_{LALRA'} \nsubseteq \vdash_c$ and hence cannot be a parsing relation.   □

Examples have been cited above to show that the LALR(1) grammars are a proper subset of the LR(1) grammars but include some grammars which are not SLR(1). These inclusions apply for all $k \geq 0$ so, for any k, the LALR(k) grammars are an intermediate class lying between the SLR(k) and LR(k) grammars. It is frequently asserted that the class of LALR(1) grammars is large enough to include grammars for most programming languages. (This does not mean that the reference grammars for most programming languages are LALR(1): they are often ambiguous.)

Since the most popular alternative parsing method is recursive descent, which requires LL(1) grammars, it is useful to compare LL(1) and LALR(1) grammars. It has often been claimed (e.g., [AhJo74], [Horn76]) that every LL(1) grammar is SLR(1) and thus LALR(1), but this is not true; counterexamples can be found in [Heil77] and [HuSz78]. In fact, the classes LL(1) and LALR(1) are incomparable, and Hunt and Szymanski show that it is undecidable whether an arbitrary LL(1) grammar is SLR(k) for any $k \geq 0$. Their proof is easily extended to show that the equivalent problem for LALR(k) is also undecidable.

Beatty [Beat82] shows that the desired result does hold for certain restricted LL(1) grammars. A grammar is said to be *p-reduced* if $\forall A \in N : \exists t \in T^+ : A \Rightarrow^* t$, i.e., every nonterminal derives some non-empty string. Every p-reduced LL(1) grammar is LALR(1), whereas there are some LL(1) grammars containing variables deriving only Λ which are not LALR(1).

5.2   Practical LALR Constructor Algorithms

The definition of an LALR state as the lookahead completion of some state of the LR(0) automaton is a good way of discovering which items belong in it, but it does not directly provide a constructor algorithm for LALR(k) parsers, because it requires the prior construction of the entire LR(k) and LR(0) automata. The obvious thing to do about this is to merge LR(k) item sets on the fly as they are generated. That is, after computing a successor, I say, to some item set, the existing collection of item sets should be examined to determine whether there is an item set I' already present, with an identical core (rather than one that is completely identical, as in the full LR(k) case). If so, then I' should be replaced by $I' \cup I$. Extra items may be introduced by this union, and their successor items should be propagated into any successors of I' which may already have been computed, giving extra items in the successors, differing only in lookahead components from those originally present. The unioned set is therefore marked in some way, or put in a queue. After the computation of item sets is complete, another pass is made in which all item sets which are marked have their successors recomputed so that the lookaheads are correctly propagated. This may lead to new item sets becoming marked, so the process must be iterated until all marks are removed.

The algorithm just described, which is that devised by Anderson et al. [AnEH73] is shown as Algorithm 5.1. If the set C is kept as some indexed data structure and indices are used as the values of δ, the recomputation of δ after I' has been replaced by I'' will be unnecessary. The algorithm does not guarantee that an item set will only ever be marked once; lookaheads may be propagated from more than one predecessor or they may have to be propagated around loops in the LR(0) automaton in a way that requires more than one 'trip' around the loop. This algorithm then, although it is space efficient and produces a parser with the same number of states as the LR(0) parser, still contains inefficiencies in its lookahead computation.

A number of improved algorithms for lookahead computation have been developed, notably the one used in Yacc (see Chapter 10) which is described at length in [AhUl77,section 6.9], and recently published algorithmsby Kristensen and Madsen [KrMa81] and DeRemer and Pennello [DePe82] (see also [DePe79]). The last of these is claimed to be optimal in the sense of performing the least number of lookahead unions necessary. It is also instructive because it computes lookaheads using the structure not of the grammar but of the LR(0) automaton. Following its original description, it will be described only for the special case $k = 1$; the generalization to $k > 1$ is claimed in the references to be easy. To simplify notation, in the rest of this section the superscripts on states and components of automata will be omitted, except for emphasis, as it should be obvious which automaton is meant.

In contrast to the previous algorithm, this one computes $LA(q, A \to \beta)$ directly, making no use at all of LR(1) items. The reasoning which enables lookahead sets to be computed from the LR(0) automaton's structure is simple. The lookahead symbols for which a reduction is the correct action are the terminal symbols which may be read in the first shift move following the reduction, and these can be found by tracing the intervening moves through the parser. The computation is only nontrivial, in fact, because of the possibility of extra reductions occurring before a shift because the subject of the reduction occurs on the right hand side of a production followed at most by some nullable nonterminals.

DeRemer and Pennello in fact *define* the lookahead set as the symbols which may be shifted after a reduction, a definition made easier by considering the moves of an LR(0) automaton which stacks states defined

Algorithm 5.1. LALR(k) parser construction

let $G = (N, T, P, S)$

let $C = \emptyset$

let $\delta = \emptyset$

proc successors(I)

  for $X \in N \cup T$ **do**

  { **let** XsuccI $=$ closure(succ(I, X))

    unless XsuccI$= \emptyset$ **do**

      test $\exists I' \in C$: core(I') $=$ core(XsuccI) **then**

      { **test** $I' =$ XsuccI **then** $\delta(I, X) := I'$

        else

        { **let** $I'' = I' \cup$ XsuccI ; $C := C \cup \{I''\}$

          $\delta(I, X) := I''$

          for all $X \in N \cup T$ **do** $\delta(I'', X) := \delta(I', X)$

          for all $J \in C$: $\delta(J, X) = I'$ **do** $\delta(J, X) := I''$

          mark(I'') ; $C := C \setminus \{I'\}$

        }

      }

      else { $C := C \cup \{$XsuccI$\}$

         $\delta(I, X) :=$ XsuccI

         successors(XsuccI)

      }

  }

$\left.\begin{array}{l} \text{closure}(I) \\ \text{succ(I,X)} \end{array}\right\}$ as before in section 4.2.

successors(closure($\{\ [S \rightarrow \cdot\alpha, \perp]\ |\ S \rightarrow \alpha \in P \}$))

while $\exists I \in C$:marked(I) **do**

  for all $I \in C$: **marked**(I) **do**

  { unmark(I) ; successors(I) }

by (4.2.9) and (4.2.10). The DeRemer/Pennello lookahead set is

$DPLA(q, A \rightarrow \beta) =$

$$\{\, a \in T \mid ([q_0 : \alpha\beta], az, \Pi) \vdash'_{LRA0} ([q_0 : \alpha A], az, (A \rightarrow \beta) \cdot \Pi) \wedge$$
$$\text{Top}[q_0 : \alpha\beta] = q \,\}$$

where $\vdash'_{LRA0}$ is the moves relation defined by (4.2.9) and (4.2.10) for the LR(0) automaton for G. (c.f. [DePe82], p620. Since $\vdash_{LRA0}$ is a parsing relation, the additional condition that the reduction leads to an accepting configuration is superfluous, and the implication that a is to be shifted is immediate.)

This is the same lookahead set as that computed by using the lookahead completion definition.

Theorem 5.3. Let $LRA0 = (Q^0, N \cup T, P, q_0^0, \delta^0, \text{Reduce}^0)$ be the $LR(0)$ automaton for $G = (N, T, P, S)$. For all $q^0 \in Q^0$, $[A \to \beta\cdot, a] \in \text{LAC}(q^0)$ if and only if $a \in DPLA(q^0, A \to \beta)$.

Proof. . 'Only if' is immediate from Theorem 5.2 and the definition of $DPLA$. If $a \in DPLA(q^0, A \to \beta)$ and $A \to \beta\cdot \in q^0$ then $([q_0^0 : \alpha\beta], az, \Pi) \vdash'_{LRA0} ([q_0^0 : \alpha A], az, (A \to \beta) \cdot \Pi)$ and $\text{Top}([q_0^0 : \alpha\beta]) = q^0$. By definition of a path, $q^0 = \delta^{0*}(q_0^0, \alpha\beta)$ so $\alpha\beta \in LR0C(A \to \beta)$, meaning that $S \perp \Rightarrow^* \alpha A y \Rightarrow \alpha\beta y$, for some y, in particular for $y = az$ (since $\alpha\beta az$ is known to be a sentential form), so $\alpha\beta a \in LR1C(A \to \beta)$ whence, in G's LR(1) automaton, $[A \to \beta\cdot, a] \in \delta^*(q_0, \alpha\beta)$. Now, $\text{core}(\delta^*(q_0, \alpha\beta)) = \delta^{0*}(q_0^0, \alpha\beta) = q^0$ so that $[A \to \beta\cdot, a] \in \text{LAC}(q^0)$. $\square$

To identify the symbols which may be shifted after the reduction by $A \to \beta$ in q, one considers the possible states which could be exposed on top of the stack by the reduction, and their A-successors. The former are called the *lookback states* for the reduction by $A \to \beta$ in q, and are defined as

$$LB(q, A \to \beta) = \{ p \mid \delta^*(p, \beta) = q \land \delta(p, A) \neq \emptyset \}$$

It is easy to see that after a reduction the state entered is $\delta(p, A)$ for some $p \in LB(q, A \to \alpha)$, so the lookahead symbols are the terminals which may be read following the transition under A. Let these be denoted $\text{Follow}(p, A)$ (not to be confused with the FOLLOW sets of section 3.3), then $DPLA(q, A \to \beta) = \bigcup_{p \in LB(q, A \to \beta)} \text{Follow}(p, A)$. The follow sets may be defined as

$$\text{Follow}(p, A) = \{ a \in T \cup \{\dashv\} \mid ([q_0 : \alpha A], az, \Pi) \vdash'^*_{LRA0} ([q_0 : \varphi], \dashv, \Pi') \land$$
$$\text{Top}([q_0 : \alpha]) = p \land S \to \varphi \in P \} \qquad (5.2.1)$$

Notice that it is *not* correct to define them as $\{ a \in T \cup \{\dashv\} \mid ([q_0 : \alpha A], az, \Pi) \vdash_{LRA0} ([q_0 : \alpha Aa], z, \Pi) \}$ because of the possibility of intermediate reductions. However, the correctness of $LRA0$ ensures that a will be shifted eventually, so (5.2.1) is an adequate definition.

Consider the moves that could be made before it is shifted. If A appears on the right hand side of a production of the form $B \to \rho A a \sigma$, then the shift *is* immediate. All the symbols which could be shifted in this manner are available in the LR(0) machine: they are the terminals that can be read from p's A-successor, $DR(p, A) = \{ a \in T \mid \delta^*(p, Aa) \neq \emptyset \}$. A special case arises if there is an item $S \to \alpha\cdot \in \delta(p, A)$, when

⊣ is obviously a valid next symbol, but it will never be shifted. This possibility must be specially dealt with by using the set

$$DR'(p, A) = \begin{cases} DR(p, A) \cup \{\dashv\}, & \text{if } \exists \alpha \colon S \to \alpha \in \text{Reduce}(\delta(p, A)) \\ DR(p, A), & \text{otherwise.} \end{cases}$$

(Using the LR(0) Reduce function to identify the special case means there is no need to retain item sets especially for the purpose.) This special treatment is avoided if augmented grammars are used, as described in section 3.4, in which case the ⊣-transitions appear in the LR(0) automaton.

It may be the case that A occurs in a production $B \to \rho\gamma A\sigma$ where $\gamma \Rightarrow^* \Lambda$. Reductions of the empty string may thus occur and the required symbols will be found in the corresponding nonterminal successors to the A-successor of p. This may be made clearer by Figure 5.2.1, where $C_i \Rightarrow^* \Lambda$ for $0 < i \le m$, $(\gamma = C_1 \dots C_m$ above).

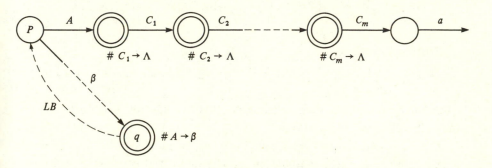

Figure 5.2.1. The reads *Relation*

The relationship embodied here may be expressed as a relation reads $\subseteq$ $(Q \times N)^2$, where (p, A)reads(r, C) iff $C \Rightarrow^* \Lambda \wedge \delta^*(p, AC) \ne \emptyset$. The terminals that can be read following the A-transition are therefore

$$\text{Read}(p, A) = \bigcup \{ DR'(r, C) \mid (p, A)\text{reads}^*(r, C) \} \qquad (5.2.2)$$

The final source of complications arises when A occurs in a production $B \to \rho A\gamma$ with $\gamma \Rightarrow^* \Lambda$. The sequence of events following the original reduction will then be that, after the A-transition from $p \in LB(q, A \to \beta)$, the reductions of the null string to γ and the corresponding transitions will take place, until the reduction by $B \to \rho A\gamma$. This sequence corresponds to the reverse of the derivation $\psi B y \Rightarrow \psi\rho A\gamma y \Rightarrow^* \psi\rho A y \Rightarrow \psi\rho\beta y$. Follow$(p, A)$ must then include Follow(p', B), for some $p' \in LB(q', B \to \rho A\gamma)$, where q' is the state in which the B-reduction occurs. B may of course occur on the right hand side of productions of the form $B' \to \rho' B \gamma' a' \sigma'$ and also $B'' \to \rho' B \gamma'$ with $\gamma' \Rightarrow^* \Lambda$, i.e., the above reasoning must be repeated for B.

The relationship between transitions corresponding to the reductions is expressed by another relation includes $\subseteq (Q \times N)^2$ where the transition (p, A)includes(p', B) if and only if $B \to \rho A \gamma \wedge \gamma \Rightarrow^* \Lambda \wedge p = \delta^*(p', \rho)$. The final part of the condition results from the fact that $p' \in LB(q', B \to \rho A \gamma)$, since q' must be $\delta^*(p, A\gamma)$ if the sequence of moves just described takes place.

Thus, Follow$(p', B) \subseteq$ Follow(p, A) if (p, A)includes(p', B) Also, naturally, Read$(p, A) \subseteq$ Follow(p, A), Read$(p', B) \subseteq$ Follow(p', B) and there may be $p'', B'' \ldots r, C$ so

$$\text{Follow}(p, A) = \bigcup \{ \text{Read}(r, C) \mid (p, A)\text{includes}^*(r, C) \} \qquad (5.2.3)$$

A bit of manipulation shows that

$$\text{Follow}(p, A) = \bigcup \{ DR'(r, C) \mid (p, A)\text{includes}^* \cdot \text{reads}^*(r, C) \}$$

so

$$DPLA(q, A \to \beta) =$$
$$\bigcup_{p \in LB(q, A \to \beta)} \bigcup \{ DR'(r, C) \mid (p, A)\text{includes}^* \cdot \text{reads}^*(r, C) \}$$

(Formal proofs of theorems leading to this formulation can be found in [DePe82].)

DR', LB and the two relations reads and includes can be found by inspection of the LR(0) automaton, so the lookahead sets can be computed by two RTC computations. The main problem, once the required sets have been cast in this form, is that of efficiently computing these closures for the relations found in realistic grammars.

The set $Q \times N$ on which includes and reads are defined will typically have thousands of members so a straightforward use of bit matrices is impractical. Even if only the (p, A) pairs for which transitions are defined are used, the space demands are excessive: DeRemer and Pennello give an example of a grammar for which each of the relations requires a matrix of nearly five million bits. Even if the space is available, the time required to process such a matrix becomes excessive. In any case, the relations are typically sparse, except in contrived examples. A simple iterative algorithm would suffer from the drawback of the algorithm for merging LR(1) item sets on the fly, namely that the order in which elements are considered, which is essentially random, does not guarantee that each will only be processed once. The technique of Eve and

Algorithm 5.2. Computation of Follow sets

let $G = (N, T, P, S)$ be a CFG
let $LRA0 = (Q, N \cup T, P, q_0, \delta, \text{Reduce})$ be G's LR(0) automaton
let $R \subseteq (Q \times N)^2$ be a relation
let $F': Q \times N \to 2^T$ be a function
let $F = \emptyset$
let $N: Q \times N \to \text{int}$ be an array of 0, indexed by $Q \times N$
let $S: (Q \times N)^*$ be a stack of (state, nonterminal) pairs

proc *traverse*$(q: Q, A: N, k: int)$
{

    $push(S, (q, A))$
    $N(q, A) := k$; $F(q, A) := F'(q, A)$
    for all $(p, B) \in Q \times N: (q, A)R(p, B)$ **do**
    {   **if** $N(p, B) = 0$ **then** *traverse*$(p, B, k + 1)$
         $N(q, A) := \min(N(q, A), N(p, B))$
         $F(q, A) := F(q, A) \cup F(p, B)$
    }
    if $N(q, A) = k$ **then**
    repeat $N(top(S)), F(top(S)) := \infty, F(q, A)$
    until $pop(S) = (q, A)$

}

for all $(q, A) \in Q \times N: N(q, A) = 0$ **do** *traverse*$(q, A, 1)$

Kurki-Suonio [EvKS77] does guarantee this and uses a data structure suitable for sparse relations; it is therefore the method of choice for computing the $DPLA$ sets. (The various RTC algorithms are described in the appendix.)

It is convenient to calculate the Follow sets on the run during the closure computations, so the composition of relations is not needed; instead, the calculation is carried out in accordance with (5.2.2) and (5.2.3) using the procedure of Algorithm 5.2, with $F'(p, A)$ first set to $DR(p, A)$ so that application of the algorithm to $R = $ reads gives $F = \text{Read}(p, A)$. These values are then used as F' in a second application with $R = $ includes, computing $F = \text{Follow}(p, A)$. The Follow sets can then be combined according to LB to give the required lookahead sets.

A number of interesting optimizations to this algorithm are proposed in [DePe82], which minimize the amount of computation required by ensuring that only the parts of the closure that are actually needed for the lookahead sets are computed; furthermore, in an important improvement, lookback and lookahead sets are only computed for reductions in

LR(0) states with parsing conflicts (see the reference for full implementation details).

A useful observation is that a similar approach permits the computation of SLR(1) lookahead sets (FOLLOW sets for nonterminals) from the LR(0) automaton, since

FOLLOW$(A) =$

$$\bigcup \{ \operatorname{Read}(p, B) \mid \exists \beta \in (N \cup T)^* \colon B \Rightarrow^* \beta A \gamma \wedge \gamma \Rightarrow^* \Lambda \wedge \delta(p, B) \neq \emptyset \}$$

In the notation of section 3.3

$$\operatorname{FOLLOW}(A) = \bigcup \{ \operatorname{Read}(p, B) \mid B \gg^* A \wedge \delta(p, B) \neq \emptyset \}.$$

Thus, applying the closure algorithm a second time to the $\gg$ relation instead of to includes will give the SLR(1) lookaheads. A sensible strategy is thus to build the LR(0) automaton, check for consistency and if no inconsistent states are present, do no lookahead computation. Otherwise, compute Read and then the SLR(1) lookahead sets; if the grammar is SLR(1) this will be sufficient to resolve conflicts, otherwise, the includes relation, or as much of it as necessary, is computed and the LALR(1) lookaheads are obtained for those reductions which cannot be resolved by the SLR(1) sets.

5.3   A Practical General Method

It is widely believed that the context free syntax of programming languages can easily be described by LALR(1) or SLR(1) grammars (cf. [Horn76], [AhJo74] or [AhUl77]) and most parser generators that are available are based on one or other of these algorithms. It is, however, the case that there are grammars which are LR(1) but not LALR(1), such as the one exhibited in Figure 5.1.3; loosely speaking, in such grammars, distinct left contexts, which are kept separate in the construction of the canonical LR(k) automaton, get merged in the LALR(k) automaton. It has been asserted [Spec81] that such situations do arise in practical parsers, especially if incremental changes are being made to a grammar. There are, in any case, aesthetic reasons for wishing to be able to produce deterministic bottom-up parsers for all the grammars for which this is theoretically possible. Further, if it is desired to use LR techniques for applications, such as natural language parsing, where the grammars are not LR, so that it is necessary to make use of semantic information to assist with parsing decisions, it is helpful to confine the situations calling for such assistance to those where the LR approach genuinely fails, without introducing more conflicts by using an algorithm that only works for a subset of the LR grammars.

The canonical LR parser has too many states and its construction as described in section 4.2 requires too much time and memory for it to be considered as a practical proposition. Pager has devised algorithms that produce parsers of a manageable size for any LR(1) grammar in an efficient manner [Page77, Page77a]. The simpler of these methods, that of [Page77], has been used in a successful parser generator called LR (see Chapter 10) which is reported as having acceptable running times for 'Pascal size' grammars. Acceptable running times for parser generation using this algorithm have also been reported by Heilbrunner [Heil81].

The basic idea is the same as that employed in Algorithm 5.1: states of the canonical parser are merged on the fly as they are created, and lookaheads are propagated from merged states. The difference is the criterion used for deciding whether two states should be merged. Lemma 5.1 showed that, for $k = 1$ (the only case being considered here) merging items with identical cores could only ever introduce reduce-reduce conflicts. It is necessary to identify those item sets whose merger will lead to their successors under some string having a reduce-reduce conflict. Say a set of items q has a potential conflict, $PC(q)$ if $\exists \psi : (closure \cdot succ)^*(q, \psi)$ has a reduce-reduce conflict, where closure and succ are defined by (4.2.3) and (4.2.4). Item sets with identical cores should not be merged if their union has a potential conflict but the separate states did not. In Algorithm 5.1 the test $core(I') = core(X succ I)$ should be replaced by $I' \, R \, X succ I$ where R is some relation on item sets satisfying

$$qRq' \text{ implies } core(q) = core(q') \wedge$$
$$(\neg PC(q) \wedge \neg PC(q') \text{ implies } \neg PC(q \cup q')) \qquad (5.3.1)$$

How can a relation R with this property be efficiently computed? Pager provides two answers. Two states q_1 and q_2 are *weakly compatible*, $q_1 R_w q_2$ iff $core(q_1) = core(q_2)$ and

$$\neg \exists [A \rightarrow \alpha \cdot \beta, a] \in q_1, [B \rightarrow \rho \cdot \sigma, a] \in q_2:$$
$$[A \rightarrow \alpha \cdot \beta] \neq [B \rightarrow \rho \cdot \sigma] \wedge \neg \exists i \in \{1, 2\}, \exists c: [A \rightarrow \alpha \cdot \beta, c] \in q_i \wedge$$
$$[B \rightarrow \rho \cdot \sigma, c] \in q_i$$

That is, two items with the same lookahead symbol and different cores from separate states should not be put together in a merged state unless there are already two items in one of the states with those cores and a common lookahead.

The intuition behind this definition is simple: suppose $[A \to \alpha \cdot \beta, c] \in q_1$ and $[B \to \rho \cdot \sigma, c] \in q_1$. Then there are strings ψ_1 and ψ_2 such that $[A \to \alpha \cdot \beta, c] \Rightarrow^* \psi_1[C \to \gamma \cdot, c]$ and $[B \to \rho \cdot \sigma, c] \Rightarrow^* \psi_2[D \to \delta \cdot, c]$ for some productions $C \to \gamma$ and $D \to \delta$, because of the way the item grammar is defined. The construction of the LR automaton means that $[C \to \gamma \cdot, c] \in \delta^*(q_1, \psi_1)$ and $[B \to \delta \cdot, c] \in \delta^*(q_1, \psi_2)$. Since $\neg PC(q_1)$, $\psi_1 \neq \psi_2$ and the items $[C \to \gamma \cdot, c]$ and $[B \to \delta \cdot, c]$ are in different states. If, in addition, $[A \to \alpha \cdot \beta, a] \in q_1$ then $[C \to \gamma \cdot, a] \in \delta^*(q_1, \psi_1)$. It will be safe to merge an item $[B \to \rho \cdot \sigma, a]$ into q_1 since its lookahead symbol will be propagated into $\delta^*(q_1, \psi_2) \neq \delta^*(q_1, \psi_1)$, so that no conflict will result. If, however, there are no pairs of items $[A \to \alpha \cdot \beta, c]$ and $[B \to \rho \cdot \sigma, c] \in q_1$ this cannot be guaranteed, unless there are such items in q_2 when a symmetrical argument follows. Formal proofs that R_w satisfies (5.3.1) are available in [Page77] and [Heil81].

It is only a little more difficult to test for the condition $q_1 R_w q_2$ than for $\text{core}(q_1) = \text{core}(q_2)$. In fact, it is only necessary to test items in the nuclei of q_1 and q_2: since $\text{core}(q_1) = \text{core}(q_2)$ the lookahead components of closure items in both states will be identical unless there is an item of the form $[A \to \alpha \cdot B, a]$ in the core; but in that case any conflict introduced in closure items derived from it will also show up as a conflict with some item $[B \to \rho \cdot \sigma, a] \in \text{core}(q_2)$. Thus the additional overhead incurred by this test may be very small.

It may be the case, though, that this weak merging criterion is unnecessarily pessimistic, and an algorithm based on it will fail to merge some item sets which could safely be combined. A more restrictive criterion, called *strong compatibility*, may be derived from the above argument. States q_1 and q_2 are strongly compatible, $q_1 R_s q_2$, iff $\text{core}(q_1) = \text{core}(q_2)$ and

$$\neg \exists [A \to \alpha \cdot \beta, a] \in q_1, [B \to \rho \cdot \sigma, a] \in q_2:$$
$$[A \to \alpha \cdot \beta] \neq [B \to \rho \cdot \sigma] \land \exists [C \to \gamma \cdot] \neq [D \to \delta \cdot], \psi, \forall c:$$
$$[A \to \alpha \cdot \beta, c] \Rightarrow^* \psi[C \to \gamma \cdot, c] \land [B \to \rho \cdot \sigma, c] \Rightarrow^* \psi[D \to \delta \cdot, c]$$

This is just a restatement of the conditions under which merging two states which are not weakly compatible would, in fact, lead to a reduce-reduce conflict.

Evidently, R_s cannot be computed directly. It can be obtained indirectly via a relation μ defined on pairs of LR(0) items as follows:

$$\begin{pmatrix} A & \to \alpha \cdot X\beta \\ B & \to \rho \cdot X\sigma \end{pmatrix} \mu \begin{pmatrix} A & \to \alpha X \cdot \beta \\ B & \to \rho X \cdot \sigma \end{pmatrix} \quad \text{for all } X$$

$$\begin{pmatrix} A & \to \alpha \cdot C\beta \\ B & \to \rho \cdot \sigma \end{pmatrix} \mu \begin{pmatrix} C & \to \cdot\gamma \\ B & \to \rho \cdot \sigma \end{pmatrix} \quad \text{if } \beta \Rightarrow^* \Lambda$$

$$\begin{pmatrix} A & \to \alpha \cdot \beta \\ B & \to \rho \cdot D\sigma \end{pmatrix} \mu \begin{pmatrix} A & \to \alpha \cdot \beta \\ D & \to \cdot\delta \end{pmatrix} \quad \text{if } \sigma \Rightarrow^* \Lambda$$

It can be shown by induction that

$$\begin{pmatrix} A & \to \alpha \cdot \beta \\ B & \to \rho \cdot \sigma \end{pmatrix} \mu^* \begin{pmatrix} C & \to \gamma \cdot \\ D & \to \delta \cdot \end{pmatrix}$$

if and only if

$$\forall a, \exists \psi \colon [A \to \alpha \cdot \beta, a] \Rightarrow^* \psi[C \to \gamma \cdot, a] \wedge [B \to \rho \cdot \sigma, a] \Rightarrow^* \psi[D \to \delta \cdot, a].$$

Thus a standard RTC procedure can be used to check strong compatibility. In the case of strong compatibility, the implication in (5.3.1) can be tightened to 'if and only if', so an algorithm based on R_s will merge as many states as it is possible to, without introducing conflicts.

If strong compatibility is used, the number of states will be as small as possible for a deterministic parser. Pager reports that, for most grammars, using the weak criterion is sufficient to produce the minimal parser, and that a significant improvement is only obtained by using strong compatibility in contrived grammars invented for the purpose. This being so, it would appear unnecessary for practical purposes to go to the expense of computing and storing R_s, when the much simpler test for R_w suffices.

The generalization of these algorithms for values of $k > 1$ also seems unnecessarily complex. It is claimed in [Page77] that this generalization is straightforward, but this cannot be entirely true, since Lemma 5.1 does not apply for $k > 1$ so it would be necessary to consider potential shift-reduce conflicts also. Additionally, it would no longer be sufficient to consider nucleus items only. [†] It appears, once again, that practical parsers should only consider a single symbol of lookahead. For that purpose, the algorithm described in this section should be seriously considered as an alternative to the conventionally accepted LALR(1) methods.

[†] I am told that the generalization has been done in: Schmitz, L. *Theorie Kettenfreier LR-Zerteiler*, Ph.D. Thesis, Fachbereich Informatik, Hochschule der Bundeswehr, Munich, and it is indeed not straightforward.

6

Implementation of LR Parsers

6.1   Data Structures and Code

All LR parsers, irrespective of the parser generating algorithm used to produce them, make only two types of move, shifts and reductions, each of which is defined as a certain transformation of the stack contents, input and output. In all practical parsers, the stack will be a stack of parser states, not symbols, of course. The choice of move to make at any point in the parse is controlled by the functions δ and Reduce. Whereas these functions are dependent on the grammar for which the parser has been built, the nature of the moves is independent of it. Because of this fact, LR parsers are well suited to implementation in a *table driven* fashion: the parser is constructed as a set of routines to implement the shift and reduce moves, with an interpreter to select the move to make by consulting a set of tables containing some representation of the δ and Reduce functions. Only the tables have to be changed to produce a parser for a new grammar. The typical arrangement of software in a system of this sort is shown in Figure 6.1.1.

Such an arrangement has a number of advantages for a programmer wishing to implement a parser, either as part of a compiler or for one of the less conventional applications mentioned in section 1.1. Given the correctness of the parser generator and the fixed part of the parser, correctness is automatically guaranteed. Verifying that a parser conforms to a syntactical definition is trivial, since that definition can itself be the grammar used as input to the parser generator. There is no need to write entirely new parsers for new applications, all that is required is a new grammar; this makes it much easier to modify the parser if the syntax of the language is changed, as is often the case with a new language under development. There is also nothing *ad hoc* about the construction process, so the situation where special tricks are developed for each new application does not arise; the user need only learn how to use a parser generating system and all applications implemented using it can be done with the same knowledge.

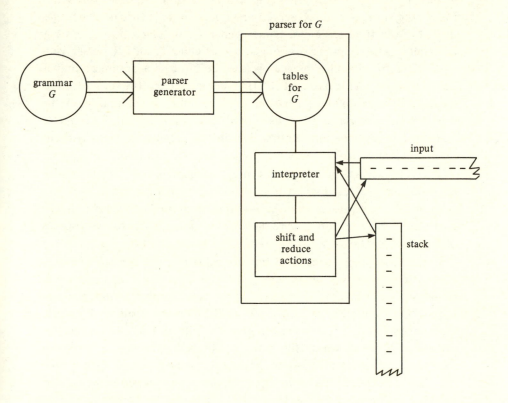

Figure 6.1.1. Parser Generator and Table Driven Parser

There are some disadvantages. The main one is that, although the LR(k) grammars form a very large set, there are occasional language features which are convenient and reasonable that cannot be described using such a grammar; nevertheless, it is possible, using tricks in conjunction with handwritten parsers, to implement them in a perfectly satisfactory way. An example is the convention followed in several languages of allowing the programmer to omit semicolons if they occur at the end of a line. This is easily done in a compiler based on recursive descent (see [RiWS79]). It can also be done in an LR(1) parser, but only by modification of the tables and parsing action functions, not by using an automatic system in the way it is intended. Some languages simply have grammars which are so unsystematic (Fortran, Cobol) or complicated (Algol68) that it is easier to use *ad hoc* techniques, either wholly or partly, to cope with their idiosyncrasies. Another disadvantage of the automatic approach to parser generation is that it encourages users to view the parser and parser generator as black boxes. This is fine, unless something goes wrong. In particular, if an LR parser generator fails to produce a parser because its input is a grammar that is not LR(1) (or LALR(1) or SLR(1)) it is difficult for the user to know what to do to rectify the situation without some understanding of the way the parser works and is constructed. It is quite difficult for a parser generator to produce information relating to parsing conflicts without making reference to item sets and lookahead computation.

There are several possible ways of representing δ and Reduce and a choice of physical data structures to be employed in storing them in a computer. The representation and storage structure will determine the particular form the shift and reduce actions take, so these two aspects of the implementation must be considered in conjunction.

In the most common case, of parsers using a single symbol of lookahead, the obvious representation of the two functions is as two-dimensional arrays, or vectors of vectors. For δ, this requires an array of size $|Q| \times |N \cup T|$, for Reduce, only $|Q| \times |T|$ since the domain of Reduce does not include N. The matrices produced for an LALR(1) parser for grammar G_1 are shown in Figure 6.1.2. States are represented by small integers; symbols should also be mapped by some input procedure to a contiguous range of integers so that the matrix can be directly indexed by state and symbol (see section 7.1.). All codes for terminals should be less than those for nonterminals since the latter are not required for Reduce. In the Reduce matrix, productions are represented by numbers, corresponding to the order they appear in the grammar. (These remarks apply to implementation languages without enumerated types; if these are allowed they provide a neat way of representing states and symbols. A mapping to small integers is performed by the compiler for the implementation language.) Blank entries correspond to arguments for which the function is undefined. These tables should be compared with Figure 5.1.2.

Given this representation of the parser tables, it is very easy to write the rest of the parser. The existence of some auxiliary functions will be taken for granted for the moment. Since the parsing algorithm uses a stack, one must be supplied. The specific concrete data structure employed is irrelevant, the stack will be treated as an occurrence of an abstract data type with the usual operations, push(S,x) which adds x to the top of the stack S, pop(S) which removes the top element

delta

	;	,	a	(	)	⊣	L	E	P	M
0			12	6			1	8	9	
1	2									
2			12	6				3	9	
3		4								
4			12	6					5	
5										
6			12	6			7	8	9	10
7	2									
8		4								
9										
10					11					
11										
12										

Reduce

	;	,	a	(	)	⊣
0						
1						
2						
3	1				1	1
4						
5	3	3			3	3
6					7	
7					8	
8	2				2	2
9	4	4			4	4
10						
11	6	6				6
12	5	5			5	5

Figure 6.1.2. LALR(1) Parser Tables for G_1

of S, top(S) which returns the top element. In addition, a predicate holds(S,x) returns true if x is the only element on S. It will be assumed that overflow is dealt with by the stack manipulation functions. Underflow will never occur. The function nextsym is assumed to return the small integer representing the next symbol of the input; error(q,x) is called when an error is detected in state q on symbol x. Details of what may happen inside this routine are given in Chapter 8.

The entries in the Reduce matrix are production numbers; in order to perform the reduction the parser needs to know the length of the right hand side of the production and its subject. These are found in the vectors `plength` and `psubj` respectively. The information is available to the parser generator so it can easily produce these extra tables as part of its output. The parser will also need to know the sentence symbol and the start state; again, these are easily passed on by the parser generator. The value **undefined** corresponds to the blank entries in the tables in Figure 6.1.2.

Under these assumptions, the BCPL code shown in Figure 6.1.3 provides a parser. It works for any set of tables based on one symbol lookahead.

Making **shift** and **reduceby** into functions that return the successor state is done only for convenience. The value **accept** can be any number that is not a state and is used simply to indicate to the **parse** routine that a successful parse has been completed; **sym** is a global variable that holds the lookahead symbol. In practice, one would probably put the code for **shift** and **reduceby** in line to avoid the overhead of a procedure call on every move the parser makes. The loss of clarity is here probably outweighed by the efficiency gain, because of the number of times the loop of **parse** is executed.

In BCPL, and several other languages, it is not possible to declare vectors with initial values that are not compile-time constants. Since **delta** and **Reduce** are vectors of vectors some code would be required to set these up, if they are to be indexed as shown (although the individual rows can be set up by declarations). This code can be incorporated into the fixed part of the compiler. Alternative approaches are possible, including representing the tables as a one dimensional vector and using a simple mapping function to compute an index from q and **sym**, or actually reading the tables from a file, and performing all the table building at run time. This last scheme, although inefficient, does provide the maximum flexibility. If it is not adopted, the material produced by the parser generator may be merged with the parsing routines either textually or by whatever linkage mechanism is supplied by the implementation language. In this case, global declarations could be made for **psubj**, **plength**, **delta**, **Reduce**, q0 and **sentence**, and written into a header file accessed by the different parts of the parser. All a program using the parser needs to do is set up the stack, call the table initializing routine, if necessary, and then call **parse**.

Although this implementation illustrates many of the practical features of an LR parsing program, it is not a very good implementation.

```
Let shift(q, t) = Valof
$(
    Let succ = delta!q!t
    sym := nextsym()
    Test succ = undefined
    Then error(q, t)
    Or $(  push(stack, succ)  ;  Resultis succ  $)
$)

Let reduceby(p) = Valof
$(r
    Let s, n = psubj!p, plength!p
    For i = 1 To n Do pop(stack)
    Test s = sentence /\ sym = eof /\ holds(stack, q0)
    Then Resultis accept
    Or
    $(
        Let q = delta!top(stack)!s
        push(q)
        Resultis q
    $)
$)r

Let parse() Be
$(
    Let q = q0
    sym := nextsym()  ;  push(q0)
    Until q = accept Do
    $(
        Let r = Reduce!q!sym
        q := r = undefined -> shift(q, sym),
                              reduceby(r)
    $)
$)
```

Figure 6.1.3. Simple Implementation of the Parsing Functions

In particular, the chosen representation of δ and Reduce is extremely wasteful of space. There are two aspects to this. Firstly, if the parser is deterministic, entries in the two matrices must be mutually exclusive, so if delta!q!t is not equal to undefined then Reduce!q!t must be, and vice versa. Secondly, most of the entries in the delta matrix are

	;	,	a	(	)	⊣	L	E	P	M
0			s12	s6			s1	s8	s9	
1	s2									
2			s12	s6				s3	s9	
3	r1	s4			r1	r1				
4			s12	s6					s5	
5	r3	r3			r3	r3				
6			s12	s6	r7		s7	s8	s9	s10
7	s2				r8					
8	r2	s4			r2	r2				
9	r4	r4			r4	r4				
10					s11					
11	r6	r6				r6				
12	r5	r5			r5	r5				

Figure 6.1.4. LALR(1) Parsing Table for G_1

undefined and correspond to errors.

Because of the first of these aspects, the values for Reduce and δ may both be stored in a single parsing table, providing a mechanism is supplied to distinguish between the meanings of the two different sorts of entry. Abstractly, this implies the existence of a function action: $Q \times T \rightarrow \{shift, reduce\}$, and the LR parsing algorithm is quite often described using such a function, in the literature. It is easy to see how action may be constructed from the LR automaton as previously described. For implementation, representing action as an array in order to allow δ and Reduce to share storage is apparently silly, since it requires exactly the same number of entries as the Reduce function. However, action only needs to distinguish between two values, so it may be represented as an array of single bits. Better still, the action values can be stored in the same array as the parsing functions; a simple convention is to represent a reduction by the pth production by the entry $-p$, and a shift to state q by $+q$. The parsing table for G_1 obtained in this way is shown in Figure 6.1.4, where a shift to state q is indicated as sq and a reduction by rp. The entries for nonterminals are conveniently shown as shifts, although they are not actually used by **shift**. The main loop of the procedure **parse** now becomes

```
Until q = accept Do
$(
    Let pa = parsetable!q!sym
    q := pa < 0 -> reduceby(-pa), shift(q, sym, pa)
```

```
$)
```

The procedure `shift` is modified to take an extra parameter, the successor state, and no longer has to look this up. The parameter `sym` is retained for error reporting. If the code for parsing moves were performed in line this would be unnecessary. The `reduceby` procedure is unchanged, except that it looks up the successor state in the combined table `parsetable`, not `delta`, which is no longer distinguished.

This simple modification of the parse table format saves $|Q| \times |T|$ entries. For LALR(1) parsers for most programming languages $|Q|$ is between about 200 and 450, and $|T|$ is around 50. (These figures are based on experience and statistics published in a number of papers, notably [AnEH73] and [DePe82].) For complex languages the figures may be higher. Assuming most machines' memories to be byte-organized, at least two bytes are required for each table entry, so up to 4500 bytes may be saved. This still leaves around 9 kilobytes being occupied by parse tables (since $|N|$ is also typically about 50). This may or may not be acceptable, but since most of the entries correspond to errors there is considerable scope for further table compaction.

The running example being used here is not typical in the proportion of error entries. Realistic grammars will produce tables with between 80% and 95% error entries. This is because the syntax of languages is often organized in a partitioned way. For example, in a programming language, declaration syntax may have nothing in common with expression syntax. This means that states concerned with parsing expressions will have error actions for all the symbols involved in declarations. This suggests that sparse matrix techniques will be appropriate for the parsing tables. The well known, general purpose sparse matrix structures (see [Knu73]) may be used, but, by considering the properties of the parsing table, it is possible to devise better representations.

One of the commonest storage structures for sparse matrices is based on the use of lists. The storage structures suitable for holding LR parser tables can be understood best if they are considered to be based on the abstract data type *list*. Specific parsers may implement lists as linked list structures using pointers, or as contiguous areas of storage. Such variations at the concrete implementation level will be discussed later, since the same basic representation is being used in all varieties of list based representation. For the moment, examples will use linked lists of nodes with a pointer field `link` and further data fields, as appropriate.

There is a considerable difference between the columns of the parsing table labelled with nonterminals and those labelled with terminals. The former never include reductions and are only ever consulted by the function **reduceby**, which does not consult the latter. Furthermore, because of the correctness of the LR automaton, it is impossible for an error to be detected on a nonterminal symbol. This strongly suggests that the parsing table should be split into terminal and nonterminal columns, and the two parts should be treated differently.

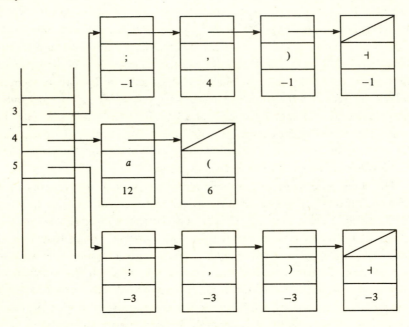

Figure 6.1.5. Lists for States 3, 4 and 5

Consider first the terminal columns. It is preferable to have a lot of short lists rather than a few long ones, since this cuts down lookup time, so this part of the table may be stored as a vector of lists, one list per state. Each list element contains a symbol code, in the field **psym** and the value from the parsing table, in **paction**. The lists should be kept sorted in order of symbol codes; this is easily arranged. Figure 6.1.5 shows part of the vector of lists for the running example. The main loop of **parse** is again modified.

```
Until q = accept Do
$(
        Let p = ptable!q        || ptable is the vector of lists
```

```
Until p = nil \/ psym!p >= sym Do p := link!p
Test p = nil \/ psym!p > sym
Then error(q, sym)
Else
$(
    Let act = paction!p
    Test act < 0
    Then q := reduceby(-act)      || reduction as before
    Or
    $(                            || shift
        q := act
        push(q)
        sym := nextsym()
    $)
$)
$)
```

Since the function **shift** has become almost trivial it has been incorporated into the loop.

In states where there is a reduction the action for many symbols will be the same, as here in states 3 and 5. Space might be saved by allowing the **psym** fields to point to lists of symbols, but this complicates the list searching. An easier alternative is to make the commonest reduction in any such state into a *default action*. Nodes for symbols with this action are omitted from the lists. Instead, a node is added to the end, with **psym** set to some dummy value **deflt**, say, indicating the default action. States with only shift actions are stored as before. The modified lists for states 3, 4 and 5 are shown in Figure 6.1.6. Now the main loop is as follows.

```
Until q = accept Do
$(
    Let p = ptable!q
    Until p = nil \/ psym!p = deflt \/ psym!p = sym Do
        p := link!p
    Test p = nil Then error(q, sym)
    Else
    ....
    ||  as before
```

The lists must now always be searched to the end, so there is no advantage in their being sorted. Most readers should be able to devise variations on this representation that could still take advantage of sorting the lists.

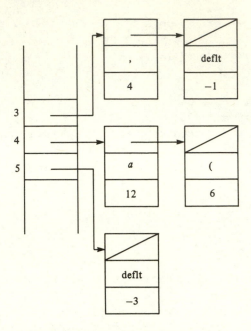

Figure 6.1.6. Use of Default Nodes in Lists

It may be the case that using default actions in this way will cause
the parser to make a reduction when the following symbol is not legal
and an error should really be reported. This probably will not matter.
Certainly, an error will be announced when an attempt to shift the
offending symbol is finally made. Intervening reductions will only affect
the stack contents at the time the error is detected, and this may, in
fact, permit a better recovery from it. This subject will be discussed in
Chapter 8.

In this example, which is typical in this respect, the parsing action
entries for terminal symbols are identical in several states. Further space
may thus be saved by sharing lists. In this example, the entries for
states 0, 2, 4, and 6 would all point to the same list.

The parser generating algorithm used will affect the space required
for storing parse tables in list form. Since SLR(1) lookahead sets may
be larger than LALR(1) ones there may be fewer error entries in the
tables for an SLR(1) parser than for an LALR(1) parser for the same
grammar.

Now consider the columns of the parsing table headed by nonterminals. At first sight, these do not present the same opportunities for
storage optimization as the terminal columns did: in the absence of re-

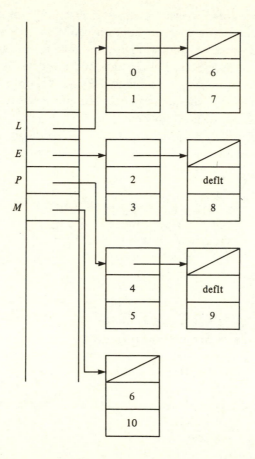

Figure 6.1.7. Lists for Nonterminals

ductions, even though no errors can occur, no space can be saved by
the use of defaults, and it is less common to find states with identical
sets of entries. However, looking down the columns, instead of along the
rows, it is seen to be the case that there are relatively few different values in each column. The reason for this is that the parser construction
algorithm guarantees that each state in the automaton is entered after
some transition under a unique *accessing symbol.* The number of states
accessed by a transition under a symbol X is usually small, certainly
much smaller than the total number of states. (If X occurs n times on
the right hand side of productions, theoretically there are $2^n - 1$ possible states that might be accessed by X. In practice, the structure of
grammars usually leads to few more than n.) If, therefore, nontermi-

nal columns are stored as lists, one per nonterminal, of nodes holding
a state and its successor for that nonterminal, then, because there can
be no errors detected on nonterminals, the default mechanism can be
used for the most popular successor state and more space can be saved.
The code for the nonterminal can be used to index the vector of pointers
to these lists. Lists for the nonterminal columns of the example parser,
using this scheme, are shown in Figure 6.1.7.

The code needed to perform a reduction is modified to handle this
storage scheme as follows.

```
Let reduceby(p) = Valof
$(
    Let s, n = psubj!p, plength!p
    For i = 1 To n Do pop(stack)
    Test s = sentence /\ sym = eof
                      /\ holds(stack, q0)
    Then Resultis accept
    Else
    $(
        Let q = top(stack)
        Let t = transitions!(s-nt0)
        || transitions is a vector of lists,
        || nt0 the lowest nonterminal code

        Until state!t = q \/ state!t = deflt Do
            t := link!t
        q := successor!t
        push(q)
        Resultis q
    $)
$)
```

It should be understood that, as mentioned previously, any concrete
representation of the abstract type list may be used instead of the simple
linked lists of these examples. Because the length of the list is known
to the parser generator, it will often be more sensible to store the values
in contiguous locations. Searching the list then only requires updating
a pointer, not following a chain of indirections. The vector of pointers
to states can be dispensed with if all the table entries are stored in
a contiguous vector, with entries for different states separated by nils,
and states are renumbered non-consecutively so that the first entry for a
state numbered q can be found at the offset q from the base of the vector.

Figure 6.1.8 shows the part of the vector of terminal actions for states 3, 4 and 5, with a suitable renumbering. A similar trick may be applied to the lists for nonterminals by reassigning their symbol codes. Further, more elaborate, variants on the implementation of lists, aimed at saving more space by overlapping shared sublists are described in [AnEH73] and [AhUl77].

State	Renumbering		
old	new		
0	0		
1	5		
2	8		
3	13		
4	18		
5	23		
6	26		
7	31		
8	36		
9	41		
10	44		
11	47		
12	50		

Right-hand column listing:

13	,
	18
	deflt
	−1
18	*a*
	50
	(
	26
23	deflt
	−3

Figure 6.1.8. Contiguous Representation of the Lists

A somewhat different approach to representing the parsing tables results from observing that entries for most states of an LALR(1) parser consist entirely of shift actions or a reduction by a unique production (i.e., these states correspond to consistent states of the LR(0) automaton). This suggests that states should be typed, by defining a function *type*: $Q \rightarrow \{shift, reduce, look\}$. States of type *shift* can be represented as lists of symbols and successors, those of type *reduce* need only the production number. Those of type *look* need lists of both sorts, just as before. The main effect of choosing this representation, besides the necessity to tag states somehow with their types, is to change the parsing code slightly. The details are left as an exercise. This arrangement does not have much to commend it, even though look states will be rare. It is, however, quite often found in the literature and presumably, therefore, in practical parsers.

The descriptions of LR(k) style parsers given in this section has been exclusively for the case $k = 1$. This is by far the most common case to arise in practice. Although the theory for $k > 1$ is interesting, its practical application is seldom found. In principle, there is no particular problem in using larger values of k, and the list representation of parsing tables could be adapted in a straightforward way. However, it appears to be the case that the substantial additional complications involved in generating parsers which use more than a single symbol of lookahead, combined with the extra space inevitably required by the parser, and the necessity to buffer lookahead strings, outweighs the slight increase in the size of the class of grammars for which deterministic parsers may be constructed. It is usually easier to make the slight modification required to produce an LR(1) grammar than it is to use an LR(k) parser for some $k > 1$. (See section 10.2.)

6.2   Language Dependent Implementations

All the representations described so far are essentially independent of the implementation language used for the parser. It is sometimes the case that a particular programming language will provide (or lack) features to make one implementation strategy preferable, easier, or more efficient. Although taking advantage of language dependent feature, or even compiler features, is perhaps a little unscrupulous, the possibilities are interesting. Two examples will be given.

Figure 6.2.1 is a BCPL program which comprises an LALR(1) parser for G_1. Here, the 'tables' are actually part of the code, the lists of previous arrangements being replaced by case statements and conditional expressions. The format of the tables is really the same as the list representations described in the previous section, with default reductions being employed and successors to reductions being arranged by symbol instead of by state. Now, additionally, it has been possible to overlap state 6 with 0, 2 and 4. It is easy enough for a parser generator to produce these statements instead of code to initialize a list data structure. With most BCPL compilers, it is also an efficient table representation. This is because a language restriction that the labels for each case be compile time constants enables the compiler to perform substantial optimization on case statements.

It is not unreasonable to expect any production compiler for the language to make the optimization, which consists in selecting an optimum code sequence according to the number of cases and their density in the range which they cover. The large case statement in the main loop of **parse**, in which there is a case for every possible value of q would almost certainly be implemented as a vector of machine addresses, pointing to the code for each case, and the selection would be done by an indexed jump. The short statements for each individual state would be implemented in the obvious way as a sequence of tests, resembling a linked list in the code. A parser generator can easily spot the states where there are only two actions and produce conditional expressions, as in state 1, for example. This is slightly more compact than a case statement. Larger case statements where a relatively small proportion of the range of values is actually used for case labels can be implemented as a binary search. On some machines, special machine instructions for performing case selections are available, and their use may further speed up execution. Whether the code occupies more space than an implementation using pointers will depend on factors such as the quality of the code generator and the instruction set of the machine on which the parser is being run. In this respect, using 'compiled' tables is less advisable as good software engineering practice.

The features of functional languages provide scope for interesting implementations of the parser tables, and the novel implementation techniques being developed for such languages (see [PeyJ87]) can provide unusual optimizations.

Sasl [Turn76] is a typical modern functional language. The distinctive feature of these languages is the total absence of an assignment statement; this in turn eliminates the possibility of side effects and makes for a very clean semantics, without any concept of 'state' or 'store'. Reasoning about, proving and transforming programs is much more straighforward than in conventional imperative languages. In contrast to some newer functional languages, which support data abstraction, Sasl's only data structures are provided by lists, but, as Lisp has shown over many years, these can form the basis of an extremely powerful general data

```
|| Declare program-wide variables as 'static'
Static $( sp = 0 ;  sym = ?  ;  stack = ?
             plength = ?  ;  psubj = ?
          $)


|| Declare some constants
Manifest $( accept = 999  ;  stacksize = 50  $)


|| Stack handling, input and error handling procedures
|| go in here
|| push, pop, top, holds, nextsym, eof, synerror

Let shift(q) = Valof
$(
    sym := nextsym()
    Resultis q
$)


Let reduceby(p) = Valof
$(
    Let n, s = plength!p, psubj!p
    If p <= 2 /\ eof() /\ holds(stack, 0)
        Resultis accept
    For i = 1 To n Do pop(stack)
    $(
        || Select the nonterminal transition
        Let q = top(stack)
        Switchon s Into
        $(
        Case 'L':  Resultis q = 0 -> 1, 7
        Case 'E':  Resultis q = 2 -> 3, 8
        Case 'P':  Resultis q = 4 -> 5, 9
        Case 'M':  Resultis 10
        $)
    $)
$)
```

Figure 6.2.1. A Parser Implemented as BCPL Code

structuring facility, provided they are used in a disciplined manner.

The considerable expressive power of functional languages is derived from their treatment of functions as 'first class objects'. This means that functions may be handed as arguments to other functions, returned as

```
Let parse() Be
$(
    Let q = 0
    sym := nextsym()
    Until q = accept Do
    $(
        push(q)
        q := Valof Switchon q Into
        $(
        Case 0: Case 2: Case 4: Case 6:
            Switchon sym Into
            $(
            Case 'a':  Resultis shift(12)
            Case '(':  Resultis shift(6)
            Default:   Test q = 6 /\ sym = ')'
                       Then Resultis reduceby(7)
                       Else synerror(q, sym)
            $)
        Case 1:  Test sym = ';' Then Resultis shift(2)
                                    Else synerror(q, sym)
        Case 3:  Resultis sym = ',' -> shift(4),
                                        reduceby(1)
        Case 5:  Resultis reduceby(3)
        Case 7:  Resultis sym = ';' -> shift(2),
                                        reduceby(8)
        Case 8:  Resultis sym = ',' -> shift(4),
                                        reduceby(2)
        Case 9:  Resultis reduceby(4)
        Case 10: Test sym = ')' Then Resultis shift(11)
                                    Else synerror(q, sym)
        Case 11: Resultis reduceby(6)
        Case 12: Resultis reduceby(5)
        $)
    $)
$)


||  The main program must set up the stack and
||  the vectors psubj and plength
```

Figure 6.2.1. A Parser Implemented as BCPL Code (continued)

the values of other functions, stored in lists, and generally used in any sensible context where values of any other type may be used. In the particular example of LR parsers this permits the parse table to be implemented as a function which returns, for each pair of arguments comprising a state and a symbol, a function which transforms configurations into new configurations. A configuration naturally consists of a list with three elements: a stack, an input string, and an output string.

It would be possible to define a separate function for each parse table entry, but the entries fall into only two types, shifts and reductions. All the shifts are generically similar and differ only in the new state which is pushed on top of the stack; similarly, all reductions perform the same sort of stack manipulation, differing only in details determined by the production being used in any particular reduction. This suggests that shift and reduce functions, parameterized in successor state and production respectively, should be defined to transform configurations, in accordance with (4.2.9) and (4.2.10).

Figure 6.2.2 shows a possible definition of these functions; some of the syntactical details require explanation for the sake of readers unfamiliar with the language. Function application is denoted by simple juxtaposition, although brackets are often necessary to make operators in arguments bind properly – function application is more binding than any other operation. The operator : sticks its left hand operand on to the front of the list which is its right hand operand (i.e., it performs the Lisp **cons** operation); it is the major constructor for lists. Lists may also be constructed by enumerating their elements, separated by commas. In function definitions, pattern matching is used to eliminate the need for selector operations being applied to arguments which are lists. Thus, **reduce** takes two arguments, the first must be a list of length two, the second a list of length three. When **reduce** is applied, the name A is associated with the first component of the first argument, **beta** with its second, and so on. If the arguments do not match the pattern, a runtime error occurs. The definition of **shift** shows a more general form of pattern matching: the second component of the configuration is a list, and **a** will be its first element, **z** the rest of it. Thus, the notation used here is closely related to the abstract definitions of moves in section 4.2. Because of the way the : operator works, both as a list constructor and a selector in pattern matching, it is convenient to put the top of the state stack at the left, not, as previously, at the right. The function **bottom** is assumed to return the appropriate sublist of **gamma** with **length beta** items removed. The functions **length** and

```
||  shift:: state -> configuration -> configuration

    shift q1 (gamma, a:z, Pi) = (q1:gamma, z, Pi)

||  reduce:: production -> configuration -> configuration

reduce (A, beta) (gamma, z, Pi)
        = (q1:gamma1, z, (A, beta):Pi)
    where gamma1 = bottom (length beta) gamma
          q1 = nonttransitions (hd gamma1) A
```

Figure 6.2.2. Sasl definitions of parsing functions

hd are standard Sasl library functions, returning the number of elements in a list, and its first element, respectively.

The preceding description is slightly misleading in referring to **shift** and **reduce** as functions with two arguments. In fact, **shift** is a function of *one* argument, a state, which returns another function, which in turn can be applied to one argument, a configuration. Similarly, **reduce** is a function of a production which returns a function. The type of these functions is thus as indicated in the comments. This is the usual way of defining functions of more than one argument in Sasl, hence the way the syntax allows the definitions to be collapsed into a single one, as here. However, it does mean that, if **q** is a state, then **shift q** is a legitimate expression, whose value is a function that takes a configuration and returns the new configuration obtained by shifting a symbol and stacking **q**. But this is exactly what is required as the parse table entries for shift actions. Similarly **reduce (A, beta)** gives suitable functions for the reduce entries. The parse table, or parsing action function, for G_1 is shown in Figure 6.2.3. (In Sasl **%x** denotes the character x, strings are written between ' and ".)

The pattern matching mechanism has been used as a way of implementing some of the storage optimizations previously described. When a function is applied, each of the separate clauses of its definition is examined to see whether it matches the arguments supplied. If the formal parameters in the definition are literals, they will only match themselves, so a table lookup is in effect being performed. Variable parameters, however, match anything, so use of clauses such as **paction 3 x** provide the default actions for states where this is appropriate. The function **nonttransitions** provides the values in the nonterminal columns of the parse table to be used by **reduce** and the same technique has been

```
qf = (3,3), (8,1) ||  final states
q0 = 0             ||  initial state

nonttransitions 0 %L = 1
nonttransitions 6 %L = 7
nonttransitions 2 %E = 3
nonttransitions X %E = 8
nonttransitions 4 %P = 5
nonttransitions X %P = 9
nonttransitions 6 %M = 10

paction 0 %( = shift 6
paction 0 %a = shift 12
paction 1 %; = shift 2
paction 2 x = paction 0 x
paction 3 %, = shift 4
paction 3 x  = reduce (%L, 'L;E")
paction 4 x  = paction 0 x
paction 5 x  = reduce (%E, 'E,P")
paction 6 %) = reduce (%M, '")
paction 6 x  = paction 0 x
paction 7 %; = shift 2
paction 7 %) = reduce (%M, 'L")
paction 8 %, = shift 4
paction 8 x  = reduce (%L, 'E")
paction 9 x  = reduce (%E, 'P")
paction 10 %) = shift 11
paction 11 x = reduce (%M, '(L)")
paction 12 x = reduce (%P, 'a")
paction q x  = error
```

Figure 6.2.3. The Parsing Action Functions

used here. Some function **error** must be supplied to deal gracefully with syntax errors.

Remembering that the top of the state stack is always the current state, a move of the parser is given by a function from configurations to configurations which applies the correct paction function to its argument.

```
move (q:gamma, a:z, Pi) =
              (paction q a) (q:gamma, a:z, Pi)
```

To perform a parse, **move** must be applied to the initial configuration, then applied to its result and so on, until an accepting configuration is reached. This is done in the following way.

```
parse input = until accepting move ((0,), (), input++'!")
  where accepting (q:gamma, z, Pi) = z = '!" &
                                     final (q:gamma)
```

(0,) is the singleton list consisting of 0, the initial state, () is the empty list, ++ denotes concatenation, the character ! is being used instead of ⊣. The function `final` uses `qf`, a list of pairs, consisting of a state with a reduction by a production with the sentence symbol as its subject, and the length of its right hand side, to check whether the stack is of the right form for an accepting configuration. The built-in Sasl function `until` is defined as follows:

```
until f g x = f x -> x; until f g (g x)
```

The semicolon separates the then and else parts of a conditional expression (like the comma in BCPL), so `until` achieves the effect of iteration using tail recursion.

The efficiency of this implementation is dependent on the efficiency of the Sasl compiler being used. Any respectable compiler for a functional language would certainly remove the tail recursion and implement the parser iteratively. The pattern matching is the main source of inefficiency, but fairly sophisticated algorithms now exist for the compilation of definitions of this sort.

Peyton-Jones [PeyJ85] has described a similar implementation of LR parsers in Sasl. In his scheme, each state is a function taking the stack and input as arguments and passing a new stack and input to its successor. A general higher order function `state` is used, parameterized by the parsing action information for each state. The pattern matching overhead is thereby decreased, and the cost of using a higher order function is minimized by the fact that the Sasl system does not apply `state` every time a state is entered, but instead creates a customized copy of it for each state with the fixed parameter bound the first time it is called for that state. Further self optimizing properties result from this implementation method; the shift-reduce optimization (see section 6.3) occurs automatically.

The novel language implementation techniques that are being developed for functional languages affect the efficiency of particular representations of parsers in sometimes unexpected ways, as this last example shows. Efficiency considerations in the use of functional languages may be expected to change drastically as new hardware and machine architectures are developed for their execution. This will mean that the implementations just described will become attractive, practical alternatives to more conventional ones, instead of just being entertaining curiosities.

6.3   Optimizing the Parser Tables

In section 6.1, data structuring techniques for minimizing the space required to store LR tables were discussed. Further improvements in storage requirements and increases in parsing speed can be made by modifying the data in the parsing tables themselves, independently of their concrete representation. Two important modifications of this type will be described.

Most grammars have LR parsers with many states for which the only permissible move for any lookahead symbol is a reduction by one particular production. If a representation of the action table with default actions is used, then the parser will never consult the lookahead symbol when it is in one of these states. Such states, where the parser's move may be determined independently of the lookahead, are accordingly referred to as *LR(0) reduce states*. They may be completely removed from the parser by introducing a new type of move: *shift-reduce*. As its name signifies, this move comprises a shift followed by a reduction. If q is an LR(0) reduce state for a production $A \rightarrow \beta$, then the parser tables can be modified in the following way. For all states p, such that, for some symbol X, $\delta(p, X) = q$, make the action for X in p shift-reduce by $A \rightarrow \beta$. The effect of this action is to read the next symbol and stack p, pop the stack $|\beta|$ times and change state to the A-successor of the state exposed on the stack top. The state q can now be left out of the parsing tables. It is necessary to stack p because $\beta = \Lambda$ is possible in an LR(0) reduce state.

Figure 6.3.1 shows the effect of this modification on the tables for G_1 given in Figure 6.1.4; shift-reduce actions are indicated as **sr**n. A second bit is now required to encode the action type but this is unlikely to cause difficulties. States 5, 9, 11 and 12 have been eliminated from the original table and the states have been renumbered accordingly. The list representations of the tables, discussed in section 6.1 may still be used. Since, though, the actions for nonterminals are no longer exclusively shifts, the lists corresponding to the columns of the table headed by nonterminals must accomodate shift-reduce entries as well, and **reduceby** must be modified appropriately. This does not interfere with the space optimizations obtained by using default nodes in these lists.

	;	,	a	(	)	⊣	L	E	P	M
0			sr5	s5			s1	s7	sr4	
1	s2									
2			sr5	s5				s3	sr4	
3	r1	s4			r1	r1				
4			sr5	s5					sr3	
5			sr5	s5	r7		s6	s7	sr4	s8
6	s2				r8					
7	r2	s4			r2	r2				
8					sr6					

Figure 6.3.1. Parsing Table for G_1 with shift-reduce Actions

Groening [Groe84] has published some experimental results on the efficacy of this modification. For the grammars of five modern programming languages, between 37% and 48% of the states of an LALR(1) parser were LR(0) reduce states and could be deleted. This had the effect of reducing the number of entries in parsing tables represented as lists with default actions by between 5% and 12%. (In the absence of defaults, the percentage saving in table entries would be much higher, of the same order as the saving in states.)

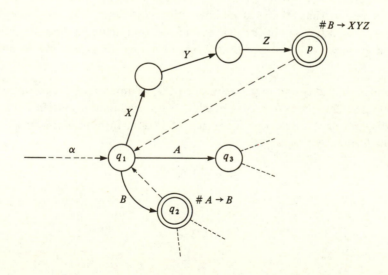

Figure 6.3.2. Unit Reduction

A more complex optimization, which has received considerable attention, is the elimination of reductions by productions of the form $A \to X$, where X is a single symbol. Such productions are referred to as *unit productions*, the corresponding reductions are *unit reductions*. Unless some semantic action is associated with it, a unit reduction is a waste of time, but unit productions are often required in a grammar to impose the correct structure on sentences. Suppose a grammar includes productions $A \to B$ and $B \to XYZ$ and that an LR(1) parser has been constructed for it. If this parser is presented with an input string $w_1 XYZ w_2$, such that $S\dashv \Rightarrow^* \alpha A w_2 \Rightarrow \alpha B w_2 \Rightarrow \alpha XYZ w_2 \Rightarrow^* w_1 XYZ w_2$, for some α, then it will behave as follows. After reading and parsing the prefix w_1 and reading XYZ its stack contents will be $[q_0 : \alpha XYZ]$. In its current state, p say, it will reduce by $B \to XYZ$, exposing some state q_1 on top of the stack. It now pushes $q_2 = \delta(q_1, B)$ and changes state to it. If the assumed derivation is possible, the lookahead symbol will be in $LA(q_2, A \to B)$ and a reduction by $A \to B$ is immediate, so q_2 is popped, q_1 exposed again, and $q_3 = \delta(q_1, A)$ is pushed; parsing now proceeds. This is illustrated in Figure 6.3.2.

The wasteful unit reduction would be avoided if the B-transition from q_1 were made to q_3 directly. The problem is to find a way of modifying the parser so that it avoids making unit reductions, but still accepts exactly the same set of strings as before, producing derivation trees differing only in the lack of branches and nodes corresponding to unit reductions.

Unit reductions are very common in the grammars of programming languages. One particular area in which they are found is in defining the binding power of operators. This is normally done by a set of productions of the form

$$E_0 \to E_0 o_1 E_1$$
$$E_0 \to E_1$$
$$E_1 \to E_1 o_2 E_2$$
$$E_1 \to E_2$$
$$\vdots$$
$$E_{n-1} \to E_{n-1} o_n E_n$$
$$E_{n-1} \to E_n$$
$$E_n \to P$$

$$P \to X_0$$

$$\vdots$$

$$P \to X_m$$
$$P \to (E_0)$$

where the o_i are operators in increasing order of binding power and the X_i are the atomic components of expressions (cf. the productions for ; and , in G_1). There are sometimes 12 or more different levels of binding, leading to chains of unit reductions taking place during the parsing of expressions. The optimization can, therefore, be well worth while. Correctly eliminating unit reductions is not, however, without its pitfalls. A survey of various published attempts at devising an elimination algorithm may be found in [Toku81].

Before any algorithms are described, it will be helpful to formalize the notion of unit reduction elimination, even though the subsequent treatment will be largely informal in nature. Let $G = (N, T, P, S)$ and let $U \subseteq P$ be a set of unit productions to be eliminated. Define $H: P^* \to P^*$ by

$$H(\Lambda) = \Lambda$$

$$H(A \to \beta) = \begin{cases} A \to \beta & \text{if } A \to \beta \notin U \\ \Lambda & \text{if } A \to \beta \in U \end{cases}$$

$$H(\pi \cdot \Pi) = H(\pi) \cdot H(\Pi).$$

H erases unit productions. If $\vdash_U$ is the moves relation of an LR automaton with reductions by productions in U eliminated, it is necessary that

$$(\Lambda, z, \Lambda) \vdash_U^* (S, \bot, H(\Pi)) \text{ if and only if } (\Lambda, z, \Lambda) \vdash_c^* (S, \bot, \Pi). \quad (6.3.1)$$

This is actually quite a weak condition: it specifies that the modified parser must correctly parse all and only the sentences in $L(G)$, except for omitting unit productions. It does not specify what is to happen in the case of erroneous input, not even that the parser will halt. Of course, one would like the parser to stop and announce error at the earliest possible opportunity and to parse correctly the input up to that point. Remembering the conventions of chapter 4, this can be expressed as

$$(\Lambda, xy, \Lambda) \vdash_U^* (\psi, y, \Pi) \text{ implies } \exists \Pi_1, \Pi_2, z: \Pi\Pi_1 = H(\Pi_2) \wedge S \stackrel{\Pi_2}{\Rightarrow} xz.$$
$$(6.3.2)$$

A parser satisfying (6.3.2) is said to be *prefix correct*. Eliminating unit reductions to produce prefix correct parsers is quite difficult and it may be necessary to settle for parsers satisfying only (6.3.1) or to refrain from eliminating certain unit reductions.

A simple algorithm of the latter type is obtained by considering only the particularly easy case that arises when the state in which the unit reduction takes place is an LR(0) reduce state (in Figure 6.3.2, q_2 has no outgoing transitions or other reductions). If this is so, then it is obvious that the transition under the right hand side of the unit reduction may be rerouted to the successor state under its subject as just described. This can have no effect other than to eliminate the unit reduction provided the parser was making use of default reductions. If it was not, then error detection might be delayed as it is when default reductions are used. This is the case whether the parser is canonical or constructed by the LALR(1) or SLR(1) methods or that of section 5.3.

A little care is needed to deal efficiently and correctly with chains of unit reductions such as $E_0 \to E_1$, $E_1 \to E_2$, $E_2 \to E_3 \ldots$. For suppose some state q has an E_1 successor q_1 in which a reduction by $E_0 \to E_1$ is made, and an E_2 successor q_2 in which a reduction by $E_1 \to E_2$ is made, and also an E_0 successor q_0. If $E_1 \to E_2$ is eliminated first, the E_2 transition to q_2 will be rerouted to q_1, so q will have two transitions to q_1, both of which will have to be redirected to q_0 when $E_0 \to E_1$ is eliminated. If, on the other hand, $E_0 \to E_1$ is eliminated first, the E_1 transition will be rerouted to q_0 and when $E_1 \to E_2$ is eliminated this propagates automatically so that the E_2 transition is made directly to q_0 and both reductions will be short circuited when an E_2 is found. It is best therefore to arrange the unit productions according to an ordering $\prec$ such that $A \to B \prec C \to D$ if $C = B$.

The elimination of these special unit reductions may be done very simply if the shift-reduce optimization has already been performed, since the actions to be changed are all shift-reduce by $A \to B$. In this case, Algorithm 6.1 will eliminate unit reductions that would have occurred in LR(0) reduce states. Notice that it is never possible to eliminate a unit reduction by a production with the sentence symbol as its subject.

If this algorithm is applied to the table of Figure 6.3.1 it eliminates reductions by $P \to \mathbf{a}$ and $E \to P$, producing the table shown as Figure 6.3.3. This small change has quite a dramatic effect on the speed of the parser. Consider the derivation of the sentence $\mathbf{a,a;a,a}$ in G_1 (shown in section 2.1). The sequence of productions used in this derivation is $\Pi = L \to L;E, E \to E,P, P \to \mathbf{a}, E \to P, P \to \mathbf{a}, L \to E, E \to E,P, P \to \mathbf{a}, E \to P, P \to \mathbf{a}$. With $U = \{P \to \mathbf{a}, E \to P\}$ eliminated, the new sequence is $H(\Pi) = L \to L;E, E \to E,P, L \to E, E \to E,P$,

Algorithm 6.1. Elimination of Unit Reductions in LR(0) Reduce States

let $G = (N, T, P, S)$ be a CFG
let $U = (u_1, u_2, \ldots, u_n)$ be a set of unit productions
                     to eliminate, partially ordered by $\prec$
let Q be the set of states of G's LR(1) parser
let *action* be the parsing table for G

for $i = 1$ to n **do**
{   **let** $A \to X = u_i$
     unless $A = S$ **do**
     for $q \in Q$ **do**
         if $action(q, x) = \mathbf{sru}_i$
           then $action(q, X) := action(q, A)$
}

	;	,	a	(	)	⊣	L	E	P	M
0			s7	s5			s1	s7	s7	
1	s2									
2			s3	s5				s3	s3	
3	r1	s4			r1	r1				
4			sr3	s5					sr3	
5			s7	s5	r7		s6	s7	s7	s8
6	s2				r8					
7	r2	s4			r2	r2				
8					sr6					

Figure 6.3.3. Modified Parsing Table for G_1

a reduction in length of 60%. The combined effect of this optimization and the use of shift-reduce moves is to cut the number of moves made in parsing the sentence from 17 to 9.

In general, as in this example, Algorithm 6.1 will fail to eliminate some unit reductions, those that take place in states which also have shift actions or other reductions. A naive strategy for dealing with these is to add these other actions to the state to which the transition is rerouted. Referring to Figure 6.3.2, this means that any shifts or reductions made from q_2, apart from the unit reduction by $A \to B$, should be transferred to q_3. This modification is shown as Algorithm 6.2.

At first sight this algorithm is satisfactory. Consider Figure 6.3.2 again. For a canonical parser to have the structure shown, there must be items of the form $[C \to \alpha \cdot A\beta, a] \in q_1$, giving rise, by closure, to items

Algorithm 6.2. Elimination of Unit Reductions

let $G = (N, T, P, S)$ be a CFG
let $U = (u_1, u_2, \ldots, u_n)$ be a set of unit productions
$\qquad\qquad\qquad\qquad$ to eliminate, partially ordered by $\prec$
let Q be the set of states of G's LR(1) parser
let *action* be the parsing table for G

for $i = 1$ **to** n **do**
$\{$ $\quad$ **let** $A \to X = u_i$
$\quad$ **unless** $A = S$ **do**
$\quad$ **for** $q_2 \in Q$ **do if** $\exists t \in T$: $action(q_2, t) = \mathbf{r}i$ **Do**
$\quad\quad$ **for** $q_1 \in Q$ **do if** $action(q_1, X) = \mathbf{s}q_2$ **do**
$\quad\quad\quad\{$
$\quad\quad\quad\quad$ **let** $q_3 =$ the A successor of q_1, found from *action*
$\quad\quad\quad\quad$ **for** $Y \in N \cup T$ **do**
$\quad\quad\quad\quad\quad$ **unless** $action(q_2, Y) = \mathbf{r}u_i$ **do**
$\quad\quad\quad\quad\quad\quad$ $action(q_3, Y) := action(q_2, Y)$
$\quad\quad\quad\}$
$\}$

of the form $[A \to \cdot B\gamma, b]$ for symbols $b \in \text{first}_1(\beta a)$. The nucleus of state q_2 comprises all items of the form $[A \to B \cdot \gamma, b]$, and its closure all items that may be derived from them. There is at least one nucleus item with $\gamma = \Lambda$. Since q_2 is consistent, no other item in q_2 causes a conflict on any symbol $b \in \text{first}_1(\beta a)$ for any β and a such that $[C \to \alpha \cdot A\beta, a] \in q_1$. Therefore, there can be no conflict with any of the items derived from any of the $[C \to \alpha A \cdot \beta, a] \in q_3$ (all the symbols following the dot, or lookahead symbols for items with the dot at the end must be in $\text{first}_1(\beta a)$ for some βa because of the way the parser is constructed) so Algorithm 6.2 cannot produce an inadequate state. It will be shown in Chapter 8 that canonical LR parsers can only detect errors in states accessed by a terminal symbol so the canonical parser's ability to detect syntax errors is not affected by the modification and it satisfies (6.3.1).

Informally, the reason no error can be detected in a state accessed by a nonterminal is that such a state can only be entered following a reduction. Because of the structure of the canonical parser, any symbol that was erroneous could not have been the first symbol in the lookahead string when the reduction occurred, so any error would have been detected in the state with the reduction. For noncanonical parsers, this is not so. An LALR(1) parser will reduce by $A \to X$ in state q for any lookahead symbol in $LA(q, A \rightarrow X)$; these symbols are the followers of *any* state that might be entered after the reduction, not just the specific one that will be entered when the reduction is made in some particular context. Thus, there is no guarantee that a symbol causing a reduction is not, in fact, erroneous in its actual context. Figure 6.3.4 shows an LALR(1) automaton for $G_7 = (\{S, A, B\}, \{a, b, c, d\}, P_7, S)$ with P_7 containing the following.

$$S \rightarrow Aa \qquad A \rightarrow B$$
$$S \rightarrow Bb \qquad A \rightarrow c$$
$$S \rightarrow aAb \qquad B \rightarrow d$$

(lookahead sets for reductions are shown in braces). The string cb is not accepted, but the error on b is detected in state 1, accessed by the nonterminal A. Applying Algorithm 6.2 with $U = \{A \rightarrow B\}$ produces an automaton that accepts this erroneous string. [†]

Although SLR(1) lookahead sets are larger than LALR(1) sets, and one might expect the situation to be accordingly worse, this is not so. Suppose Figure 6.3.2 represents part of an SLR(1) parser. Then it will only announce error in q_3 if the erroneous symbol is in FOLLOW(A), for if it is not, no reduction to A could have been made and q_3 would not have been entered. In q_2, the unit reduction takes place for any symbol in FOLLOW(A); since the parser is consistent, in q_2 other actions are only defined for symbols not in FOLLOW(A). Modifying the parser so that $\delta(q_1, B)$ becomes q_3 and these actions are transferred to q_3 cannot therefore compromise the parser's error detecting powers: any symbol in FOLLOW(A) that would have caused an error will still do so. (Remember, since $A \rightarrow B$, FOLLOW(A) $\subseteq$ FOLLOW(B).)

Parsers using default reductions may never consult the lookahead symbol at all so it is not possible to make the same sort of assertions about when an error will be detected. At best, it will be known that there is a set of symbols to which an erroneous symbol cannot belong – those for which actions other than the default are defined. Eliminating unit reductions by Algorithm 6.2 may lead to parsers accepting erroneous input, as with the LALR case. Parsers produced by the method of section 5.3 also behave like LALR parsers when unit reductions are eliminated.

The preceding discussion considered only the removal of one unit reduction, whereas Algorithm 6.2 purports to remove an entire set of them.

[†] This example first appeared in [SoiS77].

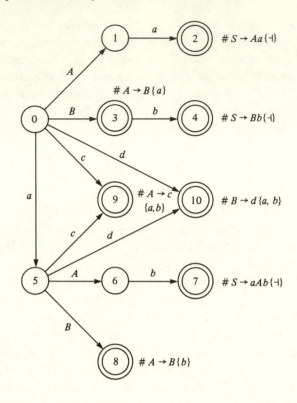

Figure 6.3.4. LALR(1) Automaton for G_7

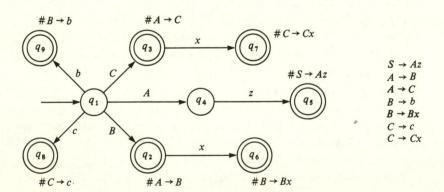

Figure 6.3.5. Two Unit Reductions

If more than one is to be removed, it is possible for the removals to interact, so as to invalidate the arguments presented so far. Figure 6.3.5 exemplifies one sort of difficulty that can arise. Here, q_1 has two successors with unit reductions. Removing that by $A \rightarrow B$ requires q_1 to have an x-transition to q_7; removing that by $A \rightarrow C$ requires it to have an x-transition to q_8. Clearly, Algorithm 6.2 cannot be used to eliminate both. Figure 6.3.6 shows a more subtle difficulty. The algorithm is applied to the grammar $G_8 = (\{S, A, B\}, \{x, y, z\}, P_8, S)$ where P_8 contains

$$S \rightarrow Ax$$
$$A \rightarrow z \qquad B \rightarrow By$$
$$A \rightarrow B \qquad B \rightarrow y$$

Reductions are eliminated for $U = \{A \rightarrow B, A \rightarrow z, B \rightarrow y\}$. A similar construction to that in the previous example leads to the modified parser accepting erroneous strings (e.g., zyx). Once $A \rightarrow z$ is eliminated, since the original A-successor to q_0 can now be accessed by a terminal, it can announce error, in particular on the symbol y, so it is not legitimate to give it a new action for y when $A \rightarrow B$ is eliminated. In effect, an action is already defined, as in the previous example. In the original presentation of Algorithm 6.2, [AhUl72a], the special case of grammars with two or more unit reductions with the same subject was identified as one the algorithm could not handle. Unfortunately, this special case often occurs in grammars for programming languages, particularly with productions defining the atomic components of expressions.

Some of the difficulties can be avoided by eliminating unit reductions by modifying the parser construction process instead of modifying the tables it produces. The successor and closure functions can be redefined so that transitions are rerouted to avoid unit reductions, and these are omitted from the parser.

If I_k is the set of LR(k) items for a grammar G and U is a set of unit reductions to be eliminated, then UFI$_k$, the set of U-free LR(k) items for G is

UFI$_k$ =

$$I_k \setminus (\{[A \rightarrow X\cdot, u] \mid A \rightarrow X \in U\} \cup \{[A \rightarrow \cdot B, u] \mid A \rightarrow B \in U\}).$$

Note that $X \in N \cup T$ whereas $B \in N$, so UFI$_k$ may include items of the form $[A \rightarrow \cdot a, u]$ with $a \in T$. The U-free LR(k) automaton for G is $(Q_{uf}, N \cup T, P, q_{uf0}, \delta_{uf}, \text{Reduce}_{uf})$ where $Q_{uf} = 2^{\text{UFI}_k}$, $q_{uf0} =$

Canonical LR(1) Parser

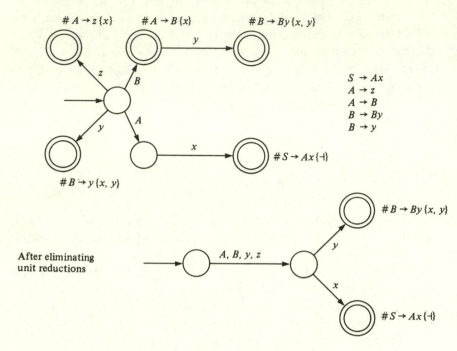

Figure 6.3.6. Parser for G_8 without Unit Reductions

$\text{UFI}_k \cap \text{closure}(\{ [S \to \cdot\alpha, \perp] \mid S \to \alpha \in P \})$ and

$$\delta_{uf}(q, X) = \text{UFI}_k \cap \text{closure} \left(\bigcup_{Y \in \text{CHAIN}(X)} \text{succ}(q, Y) \right)$$

where $\text{CHAIN}(X) = \{ Z \mid Z \overset{\Pi}{\Rightarrow} X \wedge \Pi \in U^* \}$.

It is not hard to see that, for the special case where Algorithm 6.2 works, this construction produces the same automaton. In cases where the table modification procedure fails, this modified construction will succeed because it produces extra states in the automaton, effectively creating 'copies' of those states for which elimination of more than one unit reduction requires incompatible actions. Figure 6.3.7 shows this construction applied to the troublesome grammar G_8. Because A is the subject of only unit reductions the transitions under it could have been entirely removed from the automaton – they can never be made. This removal can be extended to any symbol that is the subject of a unit reduction, as first noted in [Deme75]. In general, this can lead

State	Items	Successors
0	$S \to \cdot Ax \, / \dashv$ $A \to \cdot z \, / \dashv$ $B \to \cdot By \, / \, x, y$ $B \to \cdot y \, / \, x, y$	$z, A \Rightarrow 1$ $B, y \Rightarrow 3$
1	$S \to A \cdot x \, / \dashv$	$x \Rightarrow 2$
2 3	$S \to Ax \cdot \, / \dashv$ $B \to B \cdot y \, / \, x, y$ $S \to A \cdot x \, / \dashv$	$\#S \to Ax$ $y \Rightarrow 4$ $x \Rightarrow 2$
4	$B \to By \cdot \, / \, x, y$	$\#B \to By$

X	CHAIN(X)
S	S
A	A
B	B, A
x	x
y	A, B, y
z	A, z

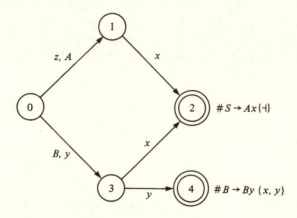

Figure 6.3.7. U-free Item Set Construction Applied to G_8

to a substantial decrease in the size of the parser tables, and may also permit the elimination of some states. Performing the necessary extra rerouting correctly is very complicated, however, see [Schm84] and [Heil85].

Like the table modification algorithm, the modified construction relies on the fact that errors cannot be detected in certain states of canonical or SLR(1) parsers. Schmitz [Schm84] proves that the construction as described correctly eliminates unit reductions from canonical LR(1), LALR(1) and SLR(1) parsers. If the transitions under the subjects of unit reductions are also to be removed, the optimization can be performed correctly for canonical LR(1) parsers and SLR(1) parsers without nullable nonterminals (and some with, but the precise restriction is somewhat technical). In the worst case, unfortunately, the elimination of unit reductions in this way can lead to a quadratic increase in the number of states [SoiS80].

Entertainingly, if unit reductions are eliminated from SLR(1) parsers during their construction, by building a U-free LR(0) automaton and then computing FOLLOW sets, consistent parsers may be produced for grammars that are not SLR(1). This is illustrated by the example in Figure 6.3.8 (taken from [KoSS79]). The grammar, G_7, is not SLR(1), but this shows up in its SLR(1) automaton as a shift-reduce conflict involving the unit production $A \rightarrow B$. (The LR(0) parser is shown in Figure 6.3.4; if SLR(1) lookahead sets are used instead of LALR(1) state 3 is inconsistent, since FOLLOW$(A) = \{a, b\}$.) The U-free SLR(1) parser is free of conflicts, but it accepts illegal strings, such as da. If all unit reductions are to be eliminated from an SLR(1) parser, therefore, it is necessary to check beforehand that the grammar is SLR(1).

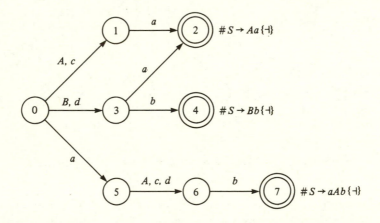

Figure 6.3.8. U-free SLR(1) Automaton Constructed for G_7

Two approaches have been devised to the elimination of unit reductions from other noncanonical LR parsers. Pager modified his construction, described in section 5.3, to permit additional merging of states so that unit reductions would be avoided; this is essentially the same as the constructive algorithm just described, but, in order to preserve the parser's error detecting properties special 'exception items'[†] must be added to item sets. These are used to prevent certain mergers, by indicating lookahead symbols with which the item is not compatible, even though it may be so according to the merging criterion. Heilbrunner has subsequently refined this algorithm and provided a rigorous proof that the refined version produces prefix-correct parsers for all LR(1) grammars [Heil85].

An alternative, avoiding some of the complications, is to leave some unit reductions intact. This is done by identifying those productions whose elimination would cause the loss of error detection and then modifying the definition of UFI_k and the CHAIN function to consider only the remaining members of U (see [SoiS77]). The advantage of this approach is that it deals with all parsers performing default reductions, as well as with LALR(1) parsers. It is difficult to see how such a technique could be combined with the DeRemer and Pennello algorithm for computing lookahead sets.

It may be tempting to conclude that the difficulties of eliminating all unit reductions correctly, particularly from useful, noncanonical parsers, entail an unjustified amount of effort and that the simple solution of eliminating only those in LR(0) reduce states is to be preferred. (This was argued in [Joli76], for example, where it was reported that an SLR(1) parser for the programming language XPL was speeded up by 50% by eliminating just 8 unit productions from the LR(0) reduce states.) The trouble is that the most important cause of unit reductions is the chains of productions used to define operator precedence, as exhibited earlier. Only the unit productions for P and E_n will be eliminated in LR(0) reduce states. When parsing an expression consisting of a single atomic value, $n + 2$ unit reduce moves will be made; of these, 2 will be eliminated, so the percentage of moves saved is less than 50 if the number of precedence levels exceeds 2. For expressions with a single binary operator of precedence class o_{i+1} the number of unit redcutions made is $2n + 3 - i$ (see Figure 6.3.9). Assuming, perhaps unjustifiably, that the probability of an operator of precedence class o_i is $1/n$ for $1 \leq i \leq n$, the total number of unit reduce moves made in parsing N such expressions is $\frac{N}{n}\Sigma_{i=0}^{n}2n + 3 - i = \frac{N}{2n}(4n^2 + 9n + 6)$. Of these, $4N$ are eliminated, so the proportion eliminated is $8/(4n^2 + 9n + 6)$, which is only greater than one half for $n = 1$. For expressions involving more operators these

[†] Called 'error items' in [Page79]

figures would be improved, as shown by the example and reference given earlier. It still seems fair to conclude that elimination of unit reductions in LR(0) reduce states is the least a parser generator should attempt to do, and it will often be worthwhile going to the trouble of using the more elaborate elimination algorithms to get rid of more.

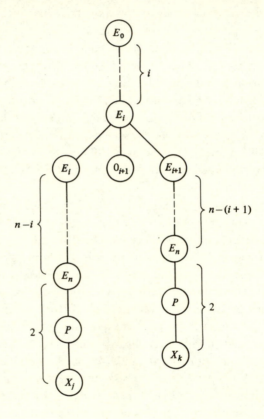

Figure 6.3.9. Unit Reductions Made in Parsing a Binary Expression

7

Using LR Parsers

7.1 Supplying the Input

A syntax analyser is never used in isolation, it is invariably part of a larger system and needs to interact with other parts. There are three areas of interaction: input, output, and errors. The subject of error handling is sufficiently complex to warrant a chapter to itself; the remaining two interactions may be dealt with relatively briefly.

The terminals of the string to be parsed must be supplied to the parser, one at a time, in left to right order, as they are consumed by shift moves. In the examples given so far, the terminals have been single characters, which can be found in any computer character set, so all that is required is a function to read a character from an input stream. In this respect, though, these examples are unrealistic.

Applications of parsers may usefully be divided into textual and non-textual, as far as their input is concerned. In textual applications, the input is built out of characters from some writable alphabet, often the Latin alphabet augmented with numerals and a few additional symbols. Textual input corresponds to our usual idea of a language, based on our experience of written natural languages and mathematical notations. The most common textual application of LR parsers is in compilers for programming languages. There is a well developed technology associated with the input phase of compilers; this will be reviewed briefly, to see how it interacts specifically with LR parsers.

Usually, the terminal alphabet of a programming language's grammar comprises compound symbols made up of more than one character from an available character set, such as Ascii. The terminals are often referred to as *basic symbols* and include things like names, numbers, operators and keywords. The input may include white space, in the form of spaces, tabs and newlines, which will be considered irrelevant by the syntax analyser, and comments, which must also be disregarded.

The input to the syntax analyser is supplied in the form of *tokens*, values, usually small integers or the values of an enumerated type, corresponding arbitrarily to the basic symbols. A routine, called a *lexical analyser*, is required to identify basic symbols and convert them to tokens, and also to discard white space and comments. Lexical analysers are usually based on finite state techniques, because the simple structure of basic symbols does not require more elaborate recognition algorithms. Descriptions of the construction of lexical analysers may be found in any of the standard textbooks on compiler construction, such as [AhUl77]. All that will be considered here is the interface between lexical and syntax analysis.

A minor point, but one which can cause irritating problems, is that, since the association between basic symbols and token values is arbitrary, it is necessary to make sure that the lexical analyser and the parser are using the same values. This becomes a problem if the two are compiled separately. The grammar used as the input to a parser generator will have a terminal alphabet denoting the basic symbols; the parser generator will have had to perform a mapping from these terminals to token values in order to produce the tables to be used by the parser. The problem, therefore, is to ensure that the mapping used by the parser generator is the same as that implemented by the lexical analyser. The usual way this is done is for both to use symbolic names for tokens – most modern languages provide some means of giving names to constant values. The parser generator can write out a set of definitions for all the symbolic names corresponding to tokens and these definitions are then used by both analysers, often by accessing a common header file, if the implementation language permits this. A common consequence of this arrangement is that, in order to maintain consistency, the lexical analyser must be re-compiled every time a new parser is generated. This is easily overlooked and mysterious bugs can appear as a result.

Only a little thought is required to realize that basic symbols are of two types. There are those such as + or := which are unique symbols, standing only for themselves, but there are also things such as names or integers, which are syntactically equivalent sets of symbols, usually infinite sets. A parser for arithmetic expressions does not need to distinguish between 123 and 567, they are both integers syntactically and should be treated in the same way. When it comes to evaluating expressions, though, the difference is obviously crucial. For symbols of this sort the lexical analyser must produce two values: a token corresponding to the basic symbol class and also a representation of the particular instance that has been encountered. So, if the input contained the characters 123, the values required would be the token for integer, which would be used by the parser to determine its next move, and the number one hundred and twenty three. The question of what the parser would do with the second value will be answered later in this chapter.

It may be objected that this device of using a single token to represent whole sets of symbols is unnecessary. For example, if the decimal digits $0 \ldots 9$ were used as basic symbols, they would be of the first type, standing only for themselves, and a number could be defined syntactically by productions such as the following.

$$
\begin{array}{ll}
N \to D & L \to 1 \\
N \to L\,N & \\
D \to 0 & \vdots \\
D \to L & L \to 9
\end{array}
$$

(N stands for number, D for digit and L for leading digit.) This is the case, but the approach is rarely used because it leads to large grammars and hence to large parsers, while the sets of symbols being defined are invariably regular languages and can therefore be recognized efficiently using FSMs without requiring the full mechanics of an LR parser performing stack manipulations.

For most classes such as integers, strings or characters, it is obvious what the value passed by the lexical analyser in addition to the token should be. For names, however, it is not so obvious. One possibility is to pass a string containing the characters of the name, and leave it to other parts of the system to determine any of its attributes that may be useful. A more common arrangement is to give the lexical analyser access to a *symbol table* in which are recorded all the names encountered and any attributes they may be known to possess. The lexical analyser will look up names in this table, making a new entry if necessary, and pass back a pointer to the symbol table entry. This may simplify things in implementation languages with poor string handling facilities; it also has some other advantages. Firstly, many languages make use of *reserved words* (such as If, Then etc.), which are syntactically identical to names but have special significance and may not be used as identifiers. By putting entries for these into the symbol table, a cheap method whereby a lexical analyser may identify reserved words and produce the correct token for them is provided. Secondly, if other parts of the system also have access to the symbol table it is possible for them to pass information back to the lexical analyser which may make parsing easier. An example will illustrate this.

Suppose in a programming language array subscripting is denoted by following the array name by a list of subscripts, separated by commas, enclosed in parentheses, as in A(i, j). Suppose also that the same syntax is used for function calls, as in f(x, y). The following productions would seem suitable to distinguish the two usages. (This example introduces a new notational convention, which is more appropriate for the implementation oriented material in this chapter. Symbols now have descriptive names, nonterminals in italics, terminals in boldface. Productions with the same subject are combined, with the different right hand sides separated by a |.)

$$exp \rightarrow fncall \,|\, arrayref \,|\, \textbf{name}$$
$$fncall \rightarrow fnname \,(\, explist \,)$$
$$arrayref \rightarrow arrayname \,(\, explist \,)$$
$$explist \rightarrow exp \,|\, explist \,,\, exp$$
$$fnname \rightarrow \textbf{name}$$
$$arrayname \rightarrow \textbf{name}$$

This is ambiguous, but can be disambiguated by making use of type information in declarations, since presumably it is possible to determine from a declaration that a name refers to an array or a function. Suppose then that in addition to the preceding productions there are also the following.

$$declaration \rightarrow arraydecl \,|\, fndecl \,|\, vardecl$$
$$arraydecl \rightarrow \textbf{array name}$$
$$fndecl \rightarrow \textbf{function name}$$
$$vardecl \rightarrow \textbf{var name}$$

and that **fnname** and **arrayname** are now *terminals* in the expression syntax, the last two productions of which are dropped. Now consider the following fragment.

```
function f
array A
var i
var j
    .
    .
    .
f(a(i, j))
```

When the lexical analyser first encounters the name f it will create a symbol table entry and pass back the token for **name** with a pointer into the table. When the declaration is being processed, the module which does this will have access to this pointer (the way in which this can be arranged will be described shortly). Since it knows it is processing a function declaration it can mark the symbol table entry suitably. Similarly, when processing the declaration of A the symbol table will be marked to show that A is the name of an array. The entries for i and j will not be marked. When the lexical analyser next encounters the name f, on looking it up in the symbol table it will discover that f has been declared as a function and return the token for **fnname**. If something like i(j) were encountered, since the token for i still corresponds to **name** a syntax error would be detected by the parser. In this way, it is possible to incorporate some context sensitive features of syntax into a parser, albeit in a rather *ad hoc* way. Another useful application of this trick, that the reader might like to investigate, is in handling the precedence of user defined operators in 'extensible' languages.

The structure of basic symbols usually gives little opportunity to the lexical analyser for detecting errors. The most common type of error is the presence of completely illegal characters, that cannot appear as part of any basic symbol. The best response to such an error is for the lexical analyser to return a special token that does not correspond to any symbol in the parser's terminal alphabet. The parser will then detect a syntax error, and the mechanisms to be described in Chapter 8 can be invoked to deal with it.

Non-textual applications such as syntax based pattern recognition systems require a different sort of input processing. Often, the original input will not be in digital form, so some analogue to digital conversion will be required: images will be converted to matrices of dots or grey-scale levels, continuous waveforms will be sampled at suitable intervals and so on. The values produced by this conversion may provide suitable input symbols for the parser, but it is more likely that some additional processing will be required. One form of input processing, which can never arise in textual applications, consists of filtering and enhancement – removing noise and interference. This is required, for example, with signals being received from space probes. Whereas this may be quite a simple process, carried out by special hardware, it may also be extremely complex and require a great deal of computing power.

Just as the basic symbols of a programming language are built from primitive characters, so the analogous components of a pattern, often called 'pattern primitives' can be built out of the elements of the digitized input, and it is necessary to carry out a process similar to lexical analysis to identify these primitives. This will require the identification of line ends and edges in image processing, or the isolation of phonemes in speech recognition. This identification is usually done using statistically based techniques. In order to arrive at the pattern primitives a classification of the elements isolated in this way may also be necessary. For example, lines may be classified into long lines, short lines and medium lines. Criteria for this classification will have been devised by the writer of the grammar describing the patterns being recognized.

For further details on techniques of input processing for pattern recognition see [Fu82] and [Pavl77].

7.2   Including Semantic Actions

The real job of a parser is to pass the structural information it extracts from the input on to another part of the system where some useful work based on it will be done. For the example grammar G_1, which describes lists, the useful work might be to build linked list structures corresponding to the input string. The terms *semantic routine* and *semantic action* are in wide use to describe those parts of a system making use of the structural information. Often, these routines are not concerned with semantics at all, but with such non-context-free syntactical matters as type checking. Nevertheless, the terms will be used in their accepted sense. In theory, a sequence of productions used in the reverse of a rightmost derivation contains all the information required by the semantic routines, but it is not then in a very tractable form. It is quite easy to provide a much more convenient interface between the parser and the semantic routines.

The grammar itself can be used to provide the structure of this interface. One particular semantic action is associated with each production; it will be performed whenever a reduction by that production is made. The action may be specified by the user in some abstract form, perhaps using attribute grammars (see section 7.3), or it may be necessary to write some code in a conventional programming language to carry it out. The latter alternative will be considered first.

The association between actions and productions may be made in several different ways. The easiest of these to implement is to have the parser call a routine `action` whenever it performs a reduction, passing it some value to identify the production concerned; it is up to the user to supply a definition of `action`. This is a rather error-prone arrangement and many parser generators allow the user to specify the code for each action in the grammar, and the parser generator takes care of the

$$prog \rightarrow \textbf{type}\ decls\ \textbf{in}\ list$$
$$decls \rightarrow decls\ decl\,|\,decl$$
$$decl \rightarrow \textbf{name} = typespec$$
$$typespec \rightarrow \textbf{*}\ typespec\,|\,stype$$
$$stype \rightarrow \textbf{i}\,|\,\textbf{c}$$
$$list \rightarrow list\ \textbf{;}\ element\,|\,element$$
$$element \rightarrow element\ \textbf{,}\ prim\,|\,prim$$
$$prim \rightarrow \textbf{name}\,|\,\textbf{number}\,|\,\textbf{character}\,|\,\textbf{(}\ list\ \textbf{)}$$

Figure 7.2.1. A Grammar for Typed Lists

book-keeping necessary to ensure that the appropriate piece of code is executed at each reduction. Such an arrangement is useful for a wide range of applications. In the jargon, schemes where actions are associated with productions are referred to as *syntax directed*. They provide a convenient structuring method for programs that deal with structured input.

Consider the task of building a derivation tree for a sentence. Parsing is proceeding in a bottom up fashion, so the tree will have to be built by starting at the leaves and collecting up subtrees according to the definition of derivation tree. This means that whenever a reduction is performed, the `action` routine must have access to the trees already produced for each of the nonterminals on the production's right hand side. This can be arranged by giving the parser a second stack, the *action stack*. Whenever a shift move is performed the symbol shifted is pushed on the action stack; whenever a reduction by $A \rightarrow \beta$ is performed, the top $|\beta|$ entries on the action stack will be subtrees or terminals (i.e., leaves of the derivation tree) corresponding to the symbols of β. These can be unstacked by `action` and replaced by a new tree whose root is A and whose descendants are the items just removed from the stack. In this way, items on the action stack correspond to the grammar symbols that would be stacked by an LR automaton making moves defined by $\vdash$ instead of $\vdash'$. It is therefore guaranteed that the top $|\beta|$ elements of the action stack will indeed correspond to β in the required sense. The same mechanism can be used to pass information between routines performing arbitrary semantic actions.

For a detailed example, consider the grammar shown in Figure 7.2.1. This is based on G_1 but has been extended in a couple of ways. The elements of lists are allowed to be names, numbers or characters, and a system of type declarations has been added: types integer and character are denoted i and c respectively, and these may be preceded by *s to indicate a list of that type. Thus, *i is a list of integers, ***i is a list of lists of lists of integers. It is to be a requirement that lists contain only values of the same type, so

```
type x = *i
     y = i
  in (1,y), x
```

is legal, whereas

```
type x = *i
     y = i
  in 1, y, x
```

is not. All isolated values are lists: 1 is a list of integers with a single element, not a number. If a list of type t is enclosed in brackets, it is treated as a single value of type *t. The empty list has been omitted from the grammar, as the need for it to be compatible with lists of anything somewhat obscures the example. It will be assumed, for simplicity, that a name can be associated with a value of its declared type when it is used in a list (perhaps the value is read from some input device).

The grammar is SLR(1), so a parser may easily be constructed. Semantic actions are required to build a list structure and to check that the type of all its elements is the same. There are many ways of doing this, the following is a fairly low level implementation, designed primarily to show how the syntax directed organization works at the lowest implementation level.

First, the parsing functions must be modified so that they update the action stack. As explained in the previous section, **nextsym** will be returning a value in addition to the token; this must be pushed onto the action stack at the same time as the state is pushed onto the parse stack when a shift move is made. The code for a reduction is augmented in the following way.

```
Let reduceby(p) = Valof
$(
    Let s, n = psubj!p, plength!p
    Let rhs = Vec maxprodlength
    || Vectors must be fixed length, so a maximum must
    || be imposed.
    For i = 0 To n-1 Do
    $(
        rhs!(n-1) := top(actionstack)
        pop(actionstack)
```

```
$)
push(actionstack, action(p, rhs))

||  Carry on with a reduction as before.
```

The vector **rhs** provides a way of passing the elements of **actionstack** corresponding to the symbols of the production's right hand side into **action** where they can be accessed as **rhs!1**, **rhs!2** and so on. In this way, the integrity of **actionstack** is preserved.

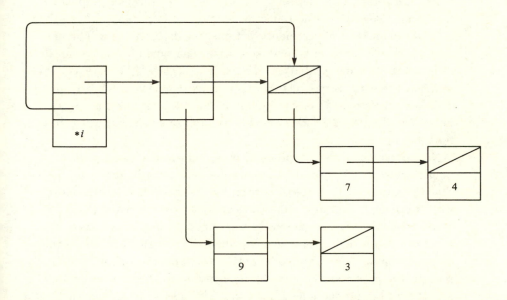

Figure 7.2.2. List structure built for (9,3),(7,4)

The actions themselves are naturally dependent on the representation chosen for lists. The left recursive productions that have been used mean that, if the lists are built as the expression is parsed, successive elements must be added to the end. This suggests that a list should be represented by a pointer to its start and a pointer to its end; the standard insertion algorithm for this representation (see [Knu73]) can then be used. A list should carry an indication of its type but since the constraint that all the elements of a list be of the same type is being enforced, the elements themselves do not need to record their type once they have been inserted. The two simple types may be represented by the characters i and c. A

simple way of recording the level of list nesting (the number of *s) is
to represent the type $*^n$s by $2^n s$, where s is a simple type code. A list
structure with a head pointer, tail pointer and type field can thus be
used, with the values held in nodes with a single link field and the value
itself (see Figure 7.2.2). The function **node** takes a simple value and its
type and makes it into a list of one element; **append** removes the header
from one list and inserts its elements at the end of another.

Names are most conveniently dealt with using a symbol table. The
lexical analyser can find or create a table entry whenever it encounters a
name, and return a pointer to it, together with the token corresponding
to **name**. Because of the order in which an LR parser performs its
reductions, and hence its semantic actions, the declarations will all have
been processed before list building starts. The type of a name can be
recorded in its symbol table entry when it is declared. When it is used
in a list, the entry is passed to a function **eval**, which obtains a value.
This is then passed to **node** to be put into a form suitable for insertion
into a list. Figure 7.2.3 shows a possible definition of **action** using these
functions.

Notice that there are unit productions for which semantic actions must
be performed. Reductions by these productions must be made, in order
that the corresponding call to **action** occurs, they cannot be removed
if the optimization of unit reduction elimination is carried out.

In systems where the actions are specified with the grammar, it is
usual to provide some syntactical expedient for referring to the elements
of the action stack. In Yacc, for example, the pseudo-variables $1, $2,...
refer to the action stack entries corresponding to the first, second, ...
elements of the production's right hand side. The value assigned to the
pseudo-variable $$ will be pushed onto the action stack following the
reduction (see section 10.1 for an example).

Using the grammar in this way, to structure the actions performed by
the system, can require a larger grammar than is necessary simply for
syntactical purposes. Consider again the grammar used as an example
in section 7.1.

$$exp \rightarrow fncall \mid arrayref \mid \textbf{name}$$

$$fncall \rightarrow fnname \ (\ explist \ )$$

$$arrayref \rightarrow arrayname \ (\ explist \ )$$

$$explist \rightarrow exp \mid explist \ , \ exp$$

$$fnname \rightarrow \textbf{name}$$

$$arrayname \rightarrow \textbf{name}$$

```
Let action(n, rhs) = Valof Switchon n Into
$(
Case 1:              || prog -> type decls in list
    Resultis rhs!4   || only want the list
Case 4:              || decl -> name = typesepc
    type!(rhs!1) := rhs!3
    Endcase          || discard result
Case 5:              || typespec -> * typespec
    Resultis (rhs!2)<<1
Case 9:              || list -> list ; element
Case 11:             || element -> element , prim
    Unless type!(rhs!1)=type!(rhs!3)
        Do type.error()
    Resultis append(rhs!1, rhs!3)
Case 13:             || prim -> name
    $(
        Let name = rhs!1
        Resultis node(eval(name), type!name)
    $)
Case 14:             || prim -> number
    Resultis node(rhs!1, 'i')
Case 15:             || prim -> character
    Resultis node(rhs!1, 'c')
Case 16:             || prim -> ( list )
    $(
        Let list = rhs!2
        Resultis node(list, (type!list)<<1)
    $)
Default:
    Resultis rhs!1
$)
```

Figure 7.2.3. Semantic Action Function

The same language can be generated by

$$exp \rightarrow subsexp \,|\, \textbf{name}$$

$$subsexp \rightarrow \textbf{name} \,(\, explist \,)$$

$$explist \rightarrow exp \,|\, explist \,,\, exp$$

This is not only smaller, it is unambiguous, and would not require the trickery involving symbol tables needed to parse the modified version of the original grammar. In a syntax directed compiler, though, this distinction is necessary because of the very different nature of the code to be generated for array references and for function calls. It is possible to generate code if the second grammar is used, but in that case the action corresponding to *subsexp* → **name** (*explist*) would need to determine whether **name** was a function or an array name and then generate code accordingly; the structuring principle of syntax directed schemes would thereby be lost.

A more serious example is the following. Suppose a grammar for a programming language includes the following productions.

$$functiondecl \rightarrow \textbf{function name} \ (\ namelist \ )$$

$$readstatement \rightarrow \textbf{read} \ namelist$$

$$namelist \rightarrow \textbf{name} \,|\, namelist \ \textbf{, name}$$

The meaning to be associated with the *namelist* in each of the first two productions is very different: in the first, it is a list of names of formal parameters, in the second, a list of variables into which values from the input are to be read. The different meaning only becomes apparent when a reduction to *functiondecl* or *readstatement* is made, so nothing could be done with the names until then; it would be necessary to actually build a list structure to hold the names, to be unpicked by the actions for those reductions. The grammar can be rewritten.

$$functiondecl \rightarrow \textbf{function name} \ (\ formallist \ )$$

$$readstatement \rightarrow \textbf{read} \ readlist$$

$$formallist \rightarrow \textbf{name} \,|\, formallist \ \textbf{, name}$$

$$readlist \rightarrow \textbf{name} \,|\, readlist \ \textbf{, name}$$

Now actions can be associated with the productions for *formallist* and *readlist* to generate the appropriate code sequence for either sort of name. New productions and nonterminals have had to be introduced to get round the fact that when an action is performed the only context available is that supplied by the production being reduced by. This is a typical situation, and it leads to extra states in the parsing automaton and new table entries for the new symbols.

If actions could be performed during shift moves as well as reductions the rewriting of the grammar could be avoided: as soon as the symbol **function** has been read it is known that the parser is processing a function definition. It would therefore be possible to set some flag, so that, when the list of names was being processed they would be correctly treated as formal parameter names. Similarly, the flag could be set to an alternative value after shifting the symbol **read**. Associating semantic actions with shifts in this way is undesirable, though, since it requires a knowledge of the structure of the parsing automaton and cannot be based on the grammar, as actions associated with reductions can.

A way of achieving the same effect is to force the parser to make a reduction after reading the initial keyword. This can be done by inserting a nullable nonterminal at the point where the action is required so that it can be performed when the empty string is reduced there. The productions for the function and read example become

$$functiondecl \rightarrow \textbf{function } fx \textbf{ name (} namelist \textbf{)}$$

$$readstatement \rightarrow \textbf{read } rx \; namelist$$

$$namelist \rightarrow \textbf{name} \mid namelist \textbf{ , name}$$

$$fx \rightarrow \Lambda$$

$$rx \rightarrow \Lambda$$

This produces a marginally smaller parser than the previous modification, but its main advantage is that it is a general purpose method for forcing the parser to perform reductions and so to allow actions at arbitrary places in the grammar.

There is a risk in all these tricks of modifying the grammar to fit in the actions, that the modified grammar will not be LR(k) (or, as is more likely to be necessary, LR(1) or LALR(1)) even though the original grammar was. In practice, trial and error is usually employed to find a modified grammar that is suitable for structuring the necessary actions, but is still parsable. This can be a time consuming and frustrating process. For the modification employing nullable nonterminals it is possible to deduce a little bit about the effects of modification from theoretical considerations.

The dot notation for LR(0) items already provides a convenient way of referring to positions in the grammar. The problem is to identify those items where the dot can be safely replaced by a nullable nonterminal. These items are said to be free, according to the following definition.

An LR(0) item $A \rightarrow \alpha \cdot \beta$ of an LR(k) grammar $G = (N, T, P, S)$ is *LR free for X* iff the grammar $G' = (N \cup \{X\}, T, P \cup \{A \rightarrow \alpha X \beta, X \rightarrow \Lambda\} \setminus \{A \rightarrow \alpha\beta\}, S)$ is also LR(k). Similar definitions may be made of LALR free and SLR free.

If the grammar happens to be LL(k) to begin with, then all of its LR(0) items are LR free for all $X \notin N$: consideration of the LL(k) definition shows that inserting a new nullable nonterminal into an LL(k) grammar leaves it LL(k), and all LL(k) grammars are LR(k). Thus it is possible to insert any number of nullable nonterminals into an originally LL(k) grammar and keep it LR(k). However, because a grammar into which a nullable nonterminal has been added in this way has nonterminals that do not derive any non-empty terminal string, this argument cannot be extended to LALR free (see section 5.1).

In any case, one of the reasons for preferring LR parsing algorithms is that they work for many grammars that are not $LL(k)$, and in these there may be items which are not free for all X. Two possibilities exist: an item may be *forbidden*– not free for any X – or it may be contingent, that is, free for some choice of X and not for others.

If a grammar is $LR(0)$, all its items are forbidden, since introducing a nullable nonterminal immediately introduces a shift-reduce conflict. In $LR(1)$ grammars, forbidden items occur in left recursive productions.

Suppose a grammar G has a production $A \to A\alpha$, then there must also be a production $A \to \beta$, otherwise A is useless. If $A \to A\alpha$ is replaced by $A \to XA\alpha$ and $X \to \Lambda$, suppose there is some state q in the automaton for the modified grammar, such that $[A \to \cdot XA\alpha, u] \in q$. State q also includes $[A \to \cdot\beta, u]$ and, for all $u' \in \text{first}_k(A\alpha u)$, $[X \to \cdot\Lambda, u']$. It also includes all items $[C \to \cdot\sigma, v]$ such that $[A \to \cdot\beta, u] \Rightarrow^* [C \to \cdot\sigma, v]$. It follows by Lemma 4.8 that $\exists w: \beta u \Rightarrow^* \sigma vw$, so $\text{first}_1(\sigma v) \subseteq \text{first}_1(\beta u) \subseteq \text{first}_1(A\alpha u)$. There must be some $C \to \sigma$ such that either $\sigma = \Lambda$ or $\sigma = a\rho$ for some $a \in T$. In the first case, there is a reduce-reduce conflict, in the second a shift-reduce conflict.

Contingent items are free only for some $X \in N$. This apparently strange situation can occur if several nullable nonterminals are being inserted successively at different places in the grammar. Inserting some nonterminal X at a particular place may mean that other items become forbidden for all nonterminals except X. This may be seen in the $LR(1)$ grammar with the following productions.

$$S \to A \qquad A \to B$$
$$A \to Bx \qquad B \to y$$

$A \to \cdot Bx$ and $A \to \cdot B$ are both free for all X, so suppose the grammar is modified to

$$S \to A$$
$$A \to XBx \qquad X \to \Lambda$$
$$A \to B \qquad B \to y$$

Now $A \to \cdot B$ is contingent, because, if some nullable nonterminal Y is added there, the initial $LR(1)$ item set becomes

$$S \to \cdot A/\dashv$$
$$A \to \cdot XBx/\dashv \qquad Y \to \cdot\Lambda/y$$
$$A \to \cdot YB/\dashv \qquad X \to \cdot\Lambda/y$$

which is inconsistent unless $X = Y$.

The reason for introducing nullable nonterminals in this way was to permit actions to be associated with reductions to them. If an item is contingent, a nonterminal can only be inserted there if the action to be performed on reducing to it in whatever other place it occurs in the grammar is also appropriate in this position, otherwise the exercise is pointless.

Purdom and Brown [PuBr80] have devised an algorithm for classifying the items of a grammar into free, forbidden and contingent, thereby informing the user where actions can be inserted in the manner described.

The existence of forbidden and contingent items may make it impossible to perform semantic actions at a suitable point in the parse. In any case, a semantic routine only has access, through the action stack, to values associated with symbols on the right hand side of the production being reduced by when it is called. These two problems can mean that it is not possible for a system incorporating an LR parser to be organized in a purely syntax directed way. A popular, simple solution to this is for the semantic actions to build a parse tree, or a simplified version of one that only retains essential structural information, and for this to be passed on to some other part of the system. This latter module is free to traverse the tree in any convenient order, as many times as necessary, so that arbitrary actions may be performed. In the world of compiler writers, such an arrangement would be described as a multi-pass organization, and it is common to find compilers using LR parsers organized in this way.

7.3   Attribute Grammars

One way of looking at a grammar, when it is the input to a parser generator, is as an abstract specification of a syntax analyser. It would be useful to be able to write a similarly abstract specification of the semantic actions of a system and avoid the mixture of levels and the confusion of specification with implementation that occurs when actions can only be written explicitly in some programming language. Currently, the most popular and successful means of achieving this end are based on systems known as *attribute grammars (AGs)*, originally proposed by Knuth in [Knu68]. AGs can be used to describe or specify many applications based, implicitly or explicitly, on traversals of a parse tree. Much of the popularity of AGs results from the fact that they are a simple extension of context free grammars. This means that they are fairly readable, being based on a familiar notation, and also that they can be easily integrated with the highly developed technology of context free syntax analysis.

An attribute grammar is a means of associating nodes in a derivation tree with values in some semantic domains. This is done in a systematic way by giving each symbol in the terminal and nonterminal alphabets of a CFG a collection of *attributes* which map derivation tree nodes labelled with that symbol to attribute values in the corresponding domain. In the extended example of the previous section, the nonterminal *list* could have a pair of attributes giving the corresponding linked list and its type, and the terminal **number** could have an attribute giving the integer value it denotes. The productions of the CFG are augmented with *evaluation rules* and *predicates*; the former show how certain attributes may be evaluated as functions of others, and the latter impose constraints on the values attributes may take. The evaluation rules and predicates associated with a particular production may only involve attributes of the symbols appearing in that production; the attributes provide a means of conveying information from one part of the tree to another.

The attributes of nonterminals are partitioned into two sorts: *synthesized* and *inherited*. If A is a nonterminal and $A \Rightarrow^+ \omega$ then the synthesized attributes of A convey information from ω while the inherited attributes convey information about its context. The evaluation rules will have the effect of passing inherited attributes downwards in the tree (from the root towards the leaves) and synthesized attributes upwards. This distinction has no formal significance but it is generally agreed to make AGs easier to understand; it also has important implications for implementing systems described in this way. To emphasize this flow of attribute values, the positions where attributes may occur in a production are also classified: inherited attributes of the subject and synthesized attributes of the symbols of the right hand side are said to be in *defining* positions, the others are in *applied* positions. The evaluation rules are restricted to functions giving the values of attributes in applied positions in terms of those in defining ones. Terminal symbols cannot have inherited attributes: they could never appear in a defining position, so no use could be made of them. Terminals may, however, have synthesized attributes; these correspond to the values produced by a lexical analyser.

A neat notation for AGs has been devised by Watt and Madsen [WaMa83]. The symbols in productions of a CFG are replaced by *at-*

tributed symbol forms, comprising a symbol followed by a set of attribute expressions, one for each attribute of the symbol; synthesized attributes are preceded by $\uparrow$, inherited ones by $\downarrow$. Attribute expressions may consist of names, constants or the application of a semantic function to an attribute expression. The use of expressions in this way, in conjunction with a systematic substitution rule for names, permits evaluation rules and predicates to be defined implicitly in a way reminiscent of vanWijngarden grammars. A formal definition of the notation and a demonstration that it is equivalent to more conventional AGs where evaluation rules and predicates are added explicitly to the grammar may be found in [WaMa83] together with a lengthy example.

To make the way this notation works clearer, the typed list example has been reworked as an AG in Figure 7.3.1. The basic domains Char, Int and Name are taken as given. They are used to build up structured domains: Value is the discrimated union[†] of Char and Int. List is a sequence of Values. The domain Type is recursively defined so it comprises the basic types and lists of any type. An Environment is a map from names to their types; an Entry is just a pair, suitable for adding to an environment.

The meaning of the attributed productions should be mostly self-evident. The synthesized attributes of *decl* and *decls* are used to build up a symbol table, which is then passed down in the inherited attributes of the nonterminals used in the list expression syntax. Symbol table manipulations appear explicitly in the attribute grammar, instead of being relegated to the lexical analysis. The semantic functions are used in the same way as in the BCPL version. Type checking is done implicitly. For example, the production

$list \uparrow$ append(VAL, VALUE) $\uparrow$ TYPE $\downarrow$ ENV $\rightarrow$

$list \uparrow$ VAL $\uparrow$ TYPE $\downarrow$ ENV ; *element* $\uparrow$ VALUE $\uparrow$ TYPE $\downarrow$ ENV

specifies that the type of the list corresponding to *element* must be the same as that of the list to the left of the ; and that the type of the list formed by appending the two will also be the same. This is because the

---

[†] If $T_1 \ldots T_n$ are domains and $g_1 \ldots g_n$ are distinct names, then $U = (g_1(T_1)| \ldots |g_n(T_n))$ denotes the discriminated union of $T_1 \ldots T_n$ with selectors $g_1 \ldots g_n$; $g_i(\emptyset)$ is abbreviated g_i. For all $1 \le i \le n$, $a \in T_i$, $g_i(a) \in U$. Thus, the discriminated union is like a set union that 'remembers' the domain its members are from. It is rather like a variant record structure.

Domains

Value = char(Char) | int(Int)
List = Value*
Type = (character | integer | list(Type))
Environment = Name → Type
Entry = Name × Type

Semantic Functions

add : Environment × Entry → Environment
append : List × List → List
node : Value → List
eval : Entry → Value

Symbols

decl ↑ Entry
decls ↑ Environment
element ↑ List ↑ Type ↓ Environment
list ↑ List ↑ Type ↓ Environment
name ↑ NAME
prim ↑ List ↑ Type ↓ Environment
prog ↑ List
stype ↑ Type
typespec ↑ Type

Figure 7.3.1. Example attribute grammar

same value must be substituted for the name TYPE wherever it appears in the production.

The correspondence between the specification in the attribute grammar and the implementation in section 7.2 is quite close. It should be obvious that the use of an action stack in the manner described is sufficient to directly evaluate synthesized attributes: if $A \uparrow a \rightarrow X_1 \uparrow x_1 \ldots X_n \uparrow x_n$ is a production, then $x_1 \ldots x_n$ can be available on the action stack. Since a must be a function of these only, it can be evalu-

Productions

prog ↑ VAL
    → type *decls* ↑ ENV in *list* ↑ VAL ↑ TYPE ↓ ENV
decls ↑ add(ENV, ENTRY)
    → *decls* ↑ ENV *decl* ↑ ENTRY
decls ↑ add(∅, ENTRY) → *decl* ↑ ENTRY
decl ↑ (NAME, TYPE)
    → **name** ↑ NAME = *typespec* ↑ TYPE
typespec ↑ list(TYPE) → * *typespec* ↑ TYPE
typespec ↑ TYPE → *stype* ↑ TYPE
stype ↑ integer → i
stype ↑ character → c
list ↑ append(VAL, VALUE) ↑ TYPE ↓ ENV
    → *list* ↑ VAL ↑ TYPE ↓ ENV ;
            element ↑ VALUE ↑ TYPE ↓ ENV
list ↑ VALUE ↑ TYPE ↓ ENV
    → *element* ↑ VALUE ↑ TYPE ↓ ENV
element ↑ append(VAL, VALUE) ↑ TYPE ↓ ENV
    → *element* ↑ VAL ↑ TYPE ↓ ENV ,
            prim ↑ VALUE ↑ TYPE ↓ ENV
element ↑ VALUE ↑ TYPE ↓ ENV
    → *prim* ↑ VALUE ↑ TYPE ↓ ENV
prim ↑ eval(node(NAME)) ↑ ENV(NAME) ↓ ENV
    → **name** ↑ NAME
prim ↑ node(VALUE) ↑ integer ↓ ENV
    → **number** ↑ VALUE
prim ↑ node(VALUE) ↑ character ↓ ENV
    → **character** ↑ VALUE
prim ↑ node(VALUE) ↑ list(TYPE) ↓ ENV
    → (*list* ↑ VALUE ↑ TYPE ↓ ENV)

Figure 7.3.1. Example attribute grammar (continued)

ated when an LR parser for the CFG produced by removing all attribute information from the AG reduces by $A \to X_1 \ldots X_n$, and can be pushed on the action stack to be used subsequently. If all the productions of the AG are of that form, then all attributes can be evaluated in parallel with a bottom up parse. (If symbols have more than one synthesized attribute the same applies, but the action stack must be able to hold multiple values.) For such AGs a straightforward translation into semantic routines that make no use of global data is possible.

Although any specification given as an attribute grammar with both synthesized and inherited attributes can also be given using synthesized attributes alone (see [Knu68]), most AGs make use of inherited attributes. The distinction between the two sorts is often claimed to be a major advantage of the AG formalism and to lead to much simpler productions that are easier to understand and manipulate than those using only synthesized attributes. Any system for implementing AGs must therefore be able to deal with inherited attributes.

Since AGs are based on derivation trees, a feasible method of evaluating attributes is to use a multi-pass organization and build a tree, allocating space in the nodes for attribute values. Once the tree is built, the attributes at each node may be evaluated according to the evaluation rules. There is a problem, though, and that is the order in which attributes must be evaluated, since, in general, attributes may depend on each other in arbitrarily complicated ways. In the extreme, it is possible to write *circular* AGs, where the value of some attribute of a node depends indirectly on itself. In that case, there is no order in which all the attributes may be evaluated †. It is possible to test for circularity, but the test has a time complexity that is exponential in the size of the grammar, and the problem of testing for circularity has been shown to be NP-complete, implying that this is probably the best that can be done.

Most efficient attribute evaluators work by visiting the nodes in some specific order (e.g., left to right across the tree) one or more times. Usually, these evaluators only work for a restricted set of AGs but they are more general than the evaluation using an action stack, that only works for synthesized attributes.

Between these two approaches lies the possibility of evaluating some inherited attributes using an action stack. When a reduction by $A \to \beta$ is made, the inherited attributes of A may be required, but they can only be evaluated during a reduction by a production of the form $B \to \gamma A \alpha$, with A in an applied position, which will take place later. Suppose A has an inherited attribute a, then, provided the evaluation of a does not require any synthesized attributes of α it could be performed in the

---

† It is possible sometimes to make an assignment of values to all the attributes in a circular AG (see [Mads80]), but it is not clear when such an assignment exists, so it is customary to equate circularity with ill-formedness of AGs.

parser state q containing items with the core $B \to \gamma \cdot A\alpha$. One way of doing this is to evaluate the inherited attributes of all such As during the shift move that causes the parser to enter q and to store them in the parse stack with q – the required attribute values will be in the action stack, below its top. Since there may be more than one such nonterminal, some of this computation may prove redundant, but the extent of this is unlikely to be serious. Instead of evaluating attributes during shifts, extra nullable nonterminals may be inserted before A, as described in section 7.2 and the attribute evaluation may be performed during the reduction of Λ.

It is possible that q contains items with cores $B \to \gamma_1 \cdot A\alpha_1$ and $B \to \gamma_2 \cdot A\alpha_2$ with $\gamma_1 \neq \gamma_2$, such that the values defined for a would be different for each case. If this does not happen and the evaluation can be performed as described, the AG is said to be *LR attributed* [JoMa80] and all its attributes can be evaluated during parsing by an LR parser, without building a derivation tree. The typed list AG is LR attributed. For grammars that are not LR attributed, the preceding discussion demonstrates which attributes can be evaluated; a system can evaluate these as it goes along, deferring evaluation of the remainder until after parsing is complete. It may then only be necessary to build part of a derivation tree, or some simpler structure.

A lot of work has been done to devise efficient attribute evaluators and to build systems incorporating them (see the bibliography [Rai80a] for an indication of the extent of this work). Recent accounts, [KoRS82], [Rai80], [Farr82] suggest that such systems have progressed beyond the experimental stage, although they have not yet achieved the same widespread use as LR parser generators. There are still problems with efficiency, especially in respect of space requirements: a large amount of workspace may be consumed storing the values of attributes. Handwritten semantic routines often avoid this overhead by using global data; some attempts have been made to extend AGs by allowing 'global attributes' in a similar way, but this tends to obscure the specifications. New storage management techniques seem to offer a better alternative.

An interesting postscript to the material on functional languages in section 6.2 is provided by an attribute evaluation scheme suggested in [John86]. This scheme is entirely dependent on the ability that is only available in functional languages to pass around functions in the same way as other objects. A transformation is applied to a conventional

AG so that each symbol has exactly one attribute, a function taking its inherited attributes (in the original AG) as arguments, and returning a list of its synthesized attributes as its result. For example, if an AG included the production

$$A \downarrow I_1 \downarrow I_2 \uparrow f(s_1, s_2) \rightarrow B \downarrow f_2(I_1) \uparrow s_1\ C \downarrow f_3(I_2, s_1) \uparrow s_2$$

the single attribute of A would become the function `Af` defined by

```
Af I1 I2 = f(s1, s2) where s1 = $1 (f2(I1))
                           s2 = $2 (f3(I2, s1))
```

where the pseudofunctions `$1` and `$2` are the attributes of B and C, respectively (cf., Yacc's pseudovariables). When the attributes take this form they can be passed around on an action stack, just like a single synthesized attribute in a conventional implementation. The pseudofunctions `$1` and `$2` can simply be replaced by references to corresponding elements of this stack. When a reduction by $A \rightarrow \beta$ is made, **reduce** should replace the top $|\beta|$ elements of the action stack by the attribute function defined for A in the AG production corresponding to $A \rightarrow \beta$ – the functions for the symbols of β will be bound in to its definition.

Functions must be provided to evaluate predicates explicitly. The production

$list \uparrow$ append(VAL, VALUE) $\uparrow$ TYPE $\downarrow$ ENV $\rightarrow$

   $list \uparrow$ VAL $\uparrow$ TYPE $\downarrow$ ENV ; $element \uparrow$ VALUE $\uparrow$ TYPE $\downarrow$ ENV

where the type constraint is implicit would have to be transformed to give

```
listf ENV = ((append VAL VALUE),
                     typecheck(TYPE1, TYPE2))
          where (VAL, TYPE1) = $1 ENV
                (VALUE, TYPE2) = $2 ENV
typecheck T T = T
typecheck T U = error
```

(Type errors propagate upwards. This is probably too simple minded, but the question of error handling by attribute evaluators is a vexed one, and is really outside the scope of this book.)

The evaluation of attributes is started by applying the attribute function for the sentence symbol to any inherited attributes it may have (such as an initial environment) to produce its synthesized attributes when they are required. This scheme will work for all AGs, not just LR attributed ones, provided the implementation language uses *lazy evaluation*, a mechanism commonly used for modern functional languages.

The essence of this mechanism is that expressions are not evaluated until their value is needed. Conversely, they are evaluated when it is, so inherited attributes that are needed by a function will be evaluated (by starting off the application of further attribute functions) at the point it is applied, whatever the dependencies in the grammar. In contrast to most conventional evaluators, which use a fixed order of evaluation, the order is demand driven. It is important that the input grammar be tested for circularitybefore it is transformed, because a lazy evaluator would otherwise attempt to evaluate the circularly defined attributes.

8

Errors

8.1   Detection, Diagnosis and Correction of Errors

A complete account of the behaviour of a parser must provide
an answer to the question: 'What happens when it is presented with a
string that is *not* in the language it recognizes?' An LR parser will not
accept any such string, but will announce that it contains an error. It is
often asserted that LR parsers possess 'good' error detecting properties.
This is because they are *correct prefix parsers*: they will only continue to
read input as long as there is some possible way of extending the string
read so far to give a sentence in the language. More precisely, a parser
possesses the correct prefix property if and only if

$$(\Lambda, yw, \Lambda) \vdash^* (\psi, w, \Pi) \text{ implies } \exists z \colon S \perp \Rightarrow^* yz.$$

(The notational conventions introduced in Chapter 4 are used throughout this chapter; all derivations are rightmost.) If the stack contents is
a prefix of some LR(0) context, then the existence of a suitable contin-
uation is guaranteed.

Lemma 8.1.

$(\Lambda, yw, \Lambda) \vdash^* (\psi, w, \Pi) \wedge \exists \sigma \colon \psi\sigma \in LR0C(G)$ *implies* $\exists z \colon S \perp \Rightarrow^* yz.$

Proof.   Induction on the number of moves shows that $(\Lambda, yw, \Lambda) \vdash^*$
(ψ, w, Π) implies $\psi \Rightarrow^* y$. If $\exists \sigma \colon \psi\sigma \in LR0C(G)$ then, by definition,
$\exists w, A \to \beta \colon S \perp \Rightarrow^* \alpha A w \Rightarrow \alpha\beta w \wedge \psi\sigma = \alpha\beta$, whence $S \perp \Rightarrow^* \psi z$, where
$z = z'w$ and $\sigma \Rightarrow^* z'$. Thus $\exists z \colon S \perp \Rightarrow^* yz$.   □

The stack is bound to have this form when the moves are those of the
canonical LR(0) parser.

Lemma 8.2.   Let $\vdash_0$ *denote the moves relation of the canonical LR(0)*
parser. $(\Lambda, yw, \Lambda) \vdash_0^* (\psi, w, \Pi)$ *implies* $\exists \sigma \colon \psi\sigma \in LR0C(G)$.

Proof.   When the configuration (Λ, w, Π) is reached, the parser is in
the state $q = \delta^{0^*}(q_0^0, \psi)$. If the item $A \to \alpha \cdot \beta \in q$ then, in the LR(0)
item grammar, $[S] \Rightarrow^* \psi[A \to \alpha \cdot \beta]$, so, by its construction, $[S] \Rightarrow^*$

$\psi\beta[A \rightarrow \alpha\beta\cdot]$. By Theorem 4.9, this means that $\psi\beta \in LR0C(A \rightarrow \beta)$, i.e., $\exists\sigma: \psi\sigma \in LR0C(G)$. $\qquad\square$

This is sufficient to show that parsers produced by any of the construction algorithms described in Chapters 3 to 5 possess the correct prefix property.

Theorem 8.3. *For $k \geq 0$, all LR(k), LALR(k) and SLR(k) parsers are correct prefix parsers.*

Proof. For all of these parsers, if $[A \rightarrow \alpha \cdot \beta, u] \in \delta^*(q_0, \psi)$ then $A \rightarrow \alpha \cdot \beta \in \delta^{0^*}(q_0^0, \psi)$ from the properties of the function *core* (section 5.1). The proof of Lemma 8.2 can thus be used to show that its result holds for all the types of parser, so, from Lemma 8.1, they all possess the correct prefix property. $\qquad\square$

(Here LR(k) parsers include both canonical parsers and those produced by the practical algorithm of section 5.3.) Because this proof is independent of lookahead strings, it is apparent that the use of default reductions as described in Chapter 6 will not impair the correct prefix property. Furthermore, because of the properties of paths, Theorem 8.3 applies to parsers stacking states instead of symbols, given the obvious interpretation of 'correct prefix' for that case.

If $(\Lambda, yuw, \Lambda) \vdash^* (\psi, uw, \Pi)$ and there is no z such that $S \perp\Rightarrow^* yuz$ then a canonical parser will be unable to make any further move. Obviously, no correct prefix parser can shift, but a reduction is only forbidden by the definition of the canonical moves.

Lemma 8.4.

$\quad (\Lambda, yuw, \Lambda) \vdash^*_c (\alpha A, uw, (A \rightarrow \beta) \cdot \Pi)$ *implies* $\exists z: S \perp\Rightarrow^* \alpha Auz$

Proof. The automaton can only enter the latter configuration by a reduction $(\alpha\beta, uw, \Pi) \vdash (\alpha A, uw, (A \rightarrow \beta) \cdot \Pi)$. By the definition of the canonical parser's reduction (4.1.7), $\alpha\beta u \in LRC(A \rightarrow \beta)$, i.e., $\exists z: S \perp\Rightarrow^* \alpha Auz \Rightarrow \alpha\beta uz$. $\qquad\square$

As a corollary, it follows that, for $k > 0$, for all states $q \neq q_0$ of the canonical LR(k) automaton, if $\exists q', A: q = \delta(q', A)$ no error can be detected in q. This fact was used in section 6.3 to justify the transformations used to eliminate unit reductions. Clearly, the proof of Lemma 8.4 is not valid for noncanonical automata, including those using default reductions. These may make additional reductions before announcing the error and, as already discussed, their optimization is more complex.

Correct prefix parsers are only good at detecting errors in comparison with parsers, such as those using operator precedence, that do not even possess this property; they do not guarantee to detect an error at the point it actually occurred. This can be seen from a commonplace example. Pascal programmers learning BCPL are apt to forget that the two way conditional is introduced by the keyword **Test** and write **If** *condition* **Then** *statement* **Else** *statement*. A correct prefix parser will not detect any error until it tries to read **Else**, since **If** *condition* **Then** *statement* is a perfectly good one way conditional.[†] Since the statement following **Then** may be compound, the error may be detected an arbitrary distance from where it occurred.

The point at which a correct prefix parser detects an error is sometimes referred to as a *parser defined error*. Even for simple languages, a parser defined error may be an arbitrary distance from the location of an actual error. Worse, for an arbitrary deterministic CFL it is undecidable whether a parser defined error is guaranteed to lie within k characters of an actual error, for all $k \geq 1$ (see [Weth78]), so no attempt at imposing language restrictions to guarantee this can be verified.

If $(\Lambda, yuw, \Lambda) \vdash^* (\psi, uw, \Pi)$ and $\psi uw \neq S \perp$ but no further move can be made, then (ψ, uw, Π) is an *error configuration* since there is no z such that $S \perp \Rightarrow^* yuz$. If $q = \delta^*(q_0, \psi)$, then q will have neither a reduction nor a shift defined for u; q is referred to as the *error state* and, in the usual case that $k = 1$, u consists of the single *error symbol*. Conversely, whenever the parser finds no action defined for its current state and lookahead it must be in an error configuration and can announce that its input string is not a member of $L(G)$. If it is being used as a simple recognizer, as might be the case in pattern recognition applications, it can then halt. For most applications, particularly for compilers, a more sophisticated response is usually required.

Users will expect a system to issue an informative message to help them identify and correct the error. At the least, the user should be told where the error was detected; this is best done by printing the text of the relevant line with a flag of some sort identifying the current symbol, although a line number and the symbol may sometimes be considered adequate. Any additional message should attempt to indicate the nature of the error. At first sight, LR parsers should be able to give a lot of helpful information, since the current state and the parsing action tables

---

[†] Remember that **Do** and **Then** are synonyms.

can be used to find all the terminals that would have been acceptable at this point. Thus, an error message of the form 'X was found where A, B or C was expected' can easily be produced. This may not always be very helpful, though.

Consider the parsing tables for G_1, as shown in Figure 6.1.4. If an error were detected in state 6, say on the input $(,a)$, the message produced would be ', was found where $(,)$ or a was expected'. While not actually misleading, this does not really capture the essence of the problem, that is, that a left bracket must be followed by a list, possibly the empty one. This information can only be conveyed by a message that refers to the nonterminals for which actions are defined in the state where the error is detected. If all possibilities are included, then the number of alternatives becomes bewildering. (Consider state 6 in the example, and imagine what would happen if a language required 13 levels of operator precedence.) Given the way the parser is constructed, it seems that the 'important' symbols will be those following the dot in nucleus items, since the closure items are all derived from these. In the state just considered the only nucleus item has the core $L \rightarrow (\cdot M)$ so, putting 'possibly empty list' for M, a message of the form ', was found where the beginning of a possibly empty list was expected' may be produced. If the dot precedes a terminal then the form of message originally considered – 'X was found where Y was expected' – will be appropriate. Naturally, if there is more than one nucleus item the messages should be combined.

If an error is detected in a state whose nucleus includes items of the form $[A \rightarrow \alpha\cdot, a]$ then such a message cannot sensibly be produced. Even listing the lookahead symbols may be misleading, since, except for canonical parsers, these may not be valid next symbols in the context of the error. When default reductions are being used, they may not even be available in the parse tables. Under these circumstances, it is better to use the state's accessing symbol in the error message. Thus, if the input was $a()$, an error would be detected in state 12 and the message 'a cannot be followed by (' would be produced. This is fairly weak, but might be augmented by further messages produced when the parser attempts to recover from the error (see section 8.2).

Provided the designer of the grammar uses meaningful mnemonic names for nonterminals, or is given a means of associating short descriptive phrases with them specifically for the purpose, messages of this sort may be produced automatically by the parser generator (see [SiSS83]). Their usefulness will vary with the structure of the grammar. For applications where the quality of messages is important, such as compilers used for introductory programming courses, it is preferable to design messages for each combination of state and error symbol, using knowledge of likely language idioms and common errors. This does require some understanding of the way the parser works.

Further advice and conventional wisdom on what error messages should say and how they should be laid out can be found in [Horn76a].

It might be hoped that, at least under some restrictions, a parser would have enough information available to permit an error to be corrected by somehow changing the erroneous input, in much the same way as errors occurring during data transmission can sometimes be corrected. This sort of correction is not possible, but the reasons for this are quite interesting. A useful model of the desired correction process helps explain matters.

An *error corrector* C for a language L is a function from Σ^* to L, taking arbitrary strings into members of the language. The mapping performed by C, whatever it is, can be expressed as a series of primitive editing operations on single symbols. Usually the operations are taken to be the deletion or insertion of a symbol, and the replacement of one symbol by another. Strictly the last of these is redundant, but intuitively replacement is a single operation and not a deletion followed by an insertion. The *error distance* $d(x, y)$ between two strings x and y is the smallest number of such operations required to change x into y (or vice versa). C is a *minimum distance* error corrector if, for every string $y \in \Sigma^*$ if $\exists x \in L: d(x, y) = k$, then $d(y, C(y)) = k$. Such a C will map y back into some string in L using as few editing operations as possible.

For true error correction to be possible on strings with fewer than k errors it is necessary that every minimum distance error corrector maps a string y with fewer than k errors to a unique $x \in L$. Obviously, this implies certain restrictions on the strings allowed in L. In fact, it can be shown that it requires that the minimum value of $d(x, y)$ for any pair of strings $x, y \in L$ with $x \neq y$ be greater than or equal to $2k + 1$. Unfortunately, for an arbitrary CFG G, it is undecidable whether $L(G)$ satisfies this condition (see [Weth78]). This makes it futile to try and devise languages that can be corrected, and means there is no point in trying to look for general algorithms for performing true error correction.

It might be thought that, despite this result, minimum distance error correction is worthwhile, since it allows a parser to carry on parsing, and the minimum distance correction is quite likely to be close to the intended string. Unfortunately, such an approach has to be ruled out on efficiency grounds, since the best algorithms for performing a minimum distance correction to a string of length n have a time complexity of n^3 (see [Back79]). This cannot really be considered acceptable for correcting errors in computer programs, which usually have a lot of tokens in them. Anyway, it is not acceptable for the time spent on error correction to be dependent not on the number of errors, but on the length of the program.

8.2 Recovery from errors

Because it is not usually feasible to correct errors, most parsers attempt to do something else, namely *recover*, in the sense of transforming the error configuration into some other, from which parsing can proceed. This is done mainly in order to find as many errors as possible in a single scan of the input. A recovery can be made by changing the remaining input, the stack, or both. It is usual to confine these changes to the first few symbols of the input or the top few elements of the stack, thus localizing the changes to the vicinity of the point where the error was detected. This may well be unjustified, since the actual location of the error may be an arbitrary distance away. Nevertheless, on practical grounds, it is a sensible strategy. In particular, almost no recovery schemes attempt to undo the effect of reductions, both because it is an awkward operation, similar to the backtracking of section 2.2, and because it might invalidate semantic actions already performed. Because dealing with errors is a practical matter, in this section only parsers using single symbol lookahead will be considered.

Several proposed recovery schemes are based on the idea of a *phrase level* recovery. This assumes that the input in the region of the error detection point is a mangled version of some string that can be derived from a nonterminal. The recovery simulates the shifting of some symbols, followed by a reduce-like move, in which the top stack elements are replaced by a nonterminal. That is, an error configuration having the form $(\psi\rho, yz, \Pi)$ is transformed into $(\psi A, z, \Pi')$, for some A, Π', that is not an error configuration.

For some sorts of error, it may be possible to effect a phrase level recovery by the simple expedient of adding extra productions to the grammar, defining the form of erroneous input. The transformation from the error configuration to a new one is achieved by normal parser moves, culminating in a reduction by $A \to \rho y \in P$. At this point, a semantic routine may issue an error message. For example, the BCPL grammar could be augmented by productions defining **If-Then-Else** as a two way conditional; when a reduction using these productions is made, the message 'the form of a two way conditional is **Test-Then-Else**' could be issued. Productions of this sort can only be added to deal with common errors, and considerable skill is required to avoid grammatical ambiguity. When they are used, an excellent recovery can be made and a good diagnostic issued; examples taken from Pascal are given in [FiMa80].

In general, the number of ways a user can mangle any language construct is too great for it to be possible to devise productions to describe them all. It is still possible to make a similar recovery using special *error productions* taking the form $A \rightarrow \alpha?\beta$ where $\alpha, \beta \in (N \cup T)^*$ and $? \notin N \cup T$ is a special *error terminal*, which may be thought of as standing for any arbitrary string. The error production stands for a whole class of productions defining the form of erroneous sequences of symbols resembling something derivable from A, thus α and β will be chosen as a prefix and a suffix of the right hand side of some production for A.

When a grammar is augmented with error productions, a parser may be constructed in the usual way, by treating **?** as a terminal. A real parser will operate with a stack of states, so the recovery can be synchronized by the states with parsing actions for **?**. When such a parser detects an error it may recover by inserting the symbol **?** before the current symbol, popping the stack until it finds a state with some action defined on **?**, performing that action and then skipping input until it finds something for which an action is defined in the new state. After some further moves a reduction by the error production should be made, at which point a message describing the error can be issued, and any other necessary actions, such as stopping code generation, can be taken. The effect of this sequence corresponds to transforming $(\psi\rho, yz, \Pi)$ to $(\psi A, z, \Pi')$, but now $A \rightarrow \rho y$ is not a production in P, but there is an error production $A \rightarrow \alpha?\beta$ such that $\exists\omega : \rho y = \alpha\omega\beta$ and $\Pi' = A \rightarrow \alpha?\beta \cdot \Pi$. Parsing should be able to resume normally. However, if the error production has the form $A \rightarrow \alpha?\beta$ and there is a second error in the input derived from β the error reduction may never be made. For this reason, it is advisable to restrict error productions to one of the forms $A \rightarrow \alpha?$ or $A \rightarrow \alpha?a$ with $\alpha \in (N \cup T)^*$ and $a \in T$. Even with this restriction, since the **?** is inserted before the error symbol, it is possible for the mechanism to start looping under some circumstances (see below). For this reason, if a second error is detected before any shift moves are made the current token should be deleted before a second attempt at recovery.

Algorithm 8.1 shows how this sort of recovery may be added to the LR(1) parsing algorithm. Flags are used to control the recovery: *recovering* is set true when a move is made on **?**, so that the skipping of input will be performed afterwards; *recent.error* remains true until a successful shift takes place, in order to prevent looping.

Figure 8.2.1 shows part of the LALR(1) parser produced when the error productions $L \to ?$, $L \to L;?$ and $E \to E,?$ are added to G_1. When it is presented with the erroneous input **(aa)**, this parser will shift the prefix **(a** and enter state 12, with the stack holding $0 \cdot 6 \cdot 12$. State 12 has no action on **a**, so an error is announced and a recovery is started. The error state has no action on **?** so it is popped off the stack, exposing state 6, which has: a shift to state 13. This move is made, leaving the remaining input as **a)**⊣ and the state stack $0 \cdot 6 \cdot 13$. Here, there is no action on **a**, so it is discarded, leaving **)** as the lookahead symbol. The action in state 13 on **)** is to reduce by $L \to ?$. The semantic routine called during this reduction can issue a message including the words 'a badly formed list' to augment the message given when the error was first detected. After the reduction, parsing resumes in state 7 and continues successfully. If default reductions were being used, the error would not have been detected until an attempt to shift **a** from state 7 was made, following reductions by $P \to a$, $E \to P$ and $L \to E$. The recovery would have been identical though, since state 7 has no action for **?** and it would have been necessary to pop it, exposing state 6, as before. However, in the general case, making default reductions in states with some action on **?** can result in a poorer recovery, since such states might be popped off the stack during reductions made without consulting the lookahead symbol, and so not be available as starting points for the error recovery if an error is subsequently detected on that symbol. It is therefore advisable only to make default reductions in states with no action on **?**.

The recovery from this error is quite good; no spurious messages are produced, and the action, deleting the second **a**, corresponds to a feasible repair. If the input had been **(a(a,a))**, however, a much less satisfactory recovery would be made. It begins in the same way, but, in state 13 it is necessary to delete everything up to the first **)** before any action can be taken. Now, in effect, the string **a(a,a** is reduced, by $L \to ?$, as a malformed list; the significance of the left bracket is lost. The first closing bracket can be shifted, and a series of reductions takes place, as shown in Figure 8.2.2. A second error will then be detected in state 1, since the second **)** appears not to be legal. After reducing by the error

Algorithm 8.1. LR(1) parsing with error recovery using
  error productions

let $G = (N, T, P, S)$ be a CFG
let $LRA = (Q, N \cup T, P, q_0, \delta, \text{Reduce})$ be G's LR(1), LALR(1) or
                                          SLR(1) automaton

let $\gamma = input \cdot \dashv$
let $\sigma = q_0$ ‖ state stack
let $q, X = q_0, \gamma(1)$
let *recent.error*, *recovering* = **false**, **false**
let *accepted* = **false**
until *accepted* **do**
{   *recovering* := $X = ?$
    if $\text{Reduce}(q, X)$ is undefined
    then {   **if** $\delta(q, X)$ is undefined
            then {   *announce.error*
                    if *recent.error* **do** $\gamma := \gamma(2 \ldots)$ ‖ delete X
                    $X := ?$
                    while $no.action(q, X) \wedge \sigma \neq \Lambda$ **do**
                    { $\sigma := \sigma(1 \ldots |\sigma| - 1)$
                        if $\sigma = \Lambda$ **then** $\sigma, \gamma := S, \dashv$ ‖ give up
                                    else $q := \sigma(|\sigma|)$
                    }
                }
            else { $q := \delta(q, X)$; $\gamma := \gamma(2 \ldots)$
                    $\sigma := \sigma \cdot q$; $X := \gamma(1)$
                    recent.error := **false**
                }
        }
    else {   **let** $A \to \beta = \text{Reduce}(q, X)$
            ‖ perform semantic action
            $\sigma := \sigma(1 \ldots |\sigma| - |\beta|)$
            accepted := $A = S \wedge \gamma = \dashv \wedge \sigma = q_0$
            unless *accepted* **do**
            { $q := \delta(\sigma(|\sigma|), A)$; $\sigma := \sigma \cdot q$ }
        }
    if *recovering* **do**
    { **while** $no.action(q, X)$ **do**
        {   **if** $X = \dashv$ **then** $\sigma := S$ ‖ give up
                    else { $\gamma := \gamma(2 \ldots)$; $X := \gamma(1)$ }
        }
        recovering, *recent.error* := **false**, **true**
    }
}
where $no.action(q, X) = \text{Reduce}(q, X)$ is undefined $\wedge \delta(q, X)$ is undefined

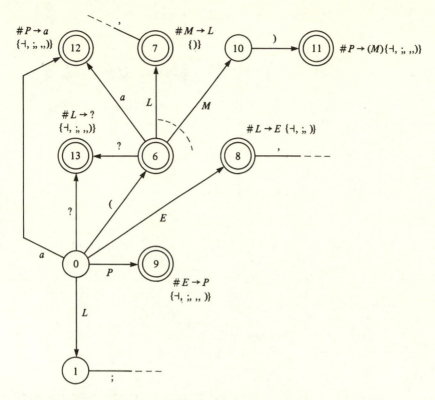

Figure 8.2.1. LALR(1) parser for G_1 with error productions

production, the parser immediately re-enters state 1 and detects the error again, so the) is deleted before the ? is inserted this time. Again the parser reduces by $L \rightarrow$?. Since the input is only ⊣, it now accepts.

This second example illustrates some pitfalls of error recovery. First, an arbitrary amount of input may be skipped, and any errors within it will therefore remain undetected. This means that if the original error is corrected, a subsequent run of the parser may produce a new crop of error messages; it is preferable if all the errors present can be detected at once. Second, because structural information is thrown away, the parser may get restarted in an inappropriate state, so that spurious and potentially misleading error messages may be produced later on. A crude way to deal with the second problem is not to issue any messages at all, unless a specified minimum number of shift moves has taken place since the last error. This may mean that some errors that could have been diagnosed will not be simply because they are too close to another

unscanned input	state stack	output
(a(a,a))⊣	0	
a(a,))⊣	0 6	
(a,a))⊣	0 6 12	error!
?(a,a))⊣	0 6	
(a,a))⊣	0 6 13	$L \rightarrow$? 'malformed list'
))⊣	0 6 7	$M \rightarrow L$
))⊣	0 6 10	
)⊣	0 6 10 11	$P \rightarrow (M)$
)⊣	0 9	$E \rightarrow P$
)⊣	0 8	$L \rightarrow E$
)⊣	0 1	error!
?)⊣	0	
)⊣	0 13	$L \rightarrow$? 'malformed list'
)⊣	0 1	(error!)
?⊣	0	
⊣	0 13	$L \rightarrow$?
		accept

Figure 8.2.2. Progress of Error Recovery

preceding one.

The quality of a recovery based on error productions is highly dependent on the particular productions added to the grammar. If $L \rightarrow L?E$ and $E \rightarrow E?P$ were used as error productions in G_1, then a much better recovery would be made for both the examples just described, having the same effect as the insertion of a missing operator. However, a phrase derived from E would have to be parsed successfully before a reduction by $L \rightarrow L?E$ could be made, so the recovery would be very vulnerable to clusters of errors. Furthermore, the resulting grammar would not be LR(1). In general, it is very difficult to add enough error productions to give a good recovery from all common errors without losing the LR(1) property. Largely for this reason, it is common to confine them to a few productions for 'important' nonterminals, representing major structural components. In a programming language this would include things such as statements, expressions and blocks. This means that obvious recoveries, such as the insertion of an operator in the examples just given, are not possible.

To overcome this problem, a two level recovery strategy is sometimes used: before invoking the phrase level mechanism, an attempt is made to patch up the input using primitive editing operations on the current symbol. That is, a symbol may be inserted before it, it may be replaced by another, or it may be deleted. This sort of *local correction* requires some way of selecting symbols to be inserted or used as a replacement, and some criteria for evaluating the success of the repair.

A 'short list' of candidates for insertion or replacement is provided by the set of terminals for which a parsing action is defined in the error state. Here, it does matter whether default reductions are made or not. By performing them and using only symbols that may be shifted, a smaller set of candidates is produced that is more likely to produce a successful repair in noncanonical parsers. As in the case of phrase level recovery, there is a danger of making too many reductions by default; the same heuristic can be used to decide when to stop (don't make default reductions if a state also has some action on ?), thus leaving the parser ready for phrase level recovery if local correction fails.

Consider again the example (a(a,a)), and assume that default reductions are taken. Then the error will be detected in state 7, with the current symbol (, so the suggested corrections are the insertion of ; or) before the (, its replacement by either of these symbols, or its deletion. Only the insertion of the semicolon, or replacement by it allows the parser to make any more moves using the actual input. The replacement is a less desirable repair, since it makes a bigger change to the input, so the insertion should be chosen.

For this example, the choice of repair was easy, and in fact produced the only correction that could lead to a successful parse, but in general the choice will be harder since more than one choice may allow parsing to continue. An obvious refinement of the method is to see how far it continues after each suggested edit is attempted, and select the most successful. This can be done roughly by buffering a limited number of input symbols, and for each possible local correction, running the parser over them and recording how many shifts were made before an error was detected. If no correction allows the parser to make more than a specified number of shifts, then the local correction is abandoned and a phrase level recovery can be attempted instead.

Other techniques may be used to supplement or replace the information obtained by running the parser forward on all attempted corrections. One uses a table of *a priori* costs associated with the insertion or deletion of each symbol to weight the number of successful shifts. Thus, taking examples from the syntax of programming languages, the cost of deleting keywords would be high (they are long, and unlikely to be inserted accidentally, unless there is a serious misunderstanding on the user's part) whereas the cost of deleting punctuation such as semicolons would be low (they might just be keyboard slips); the cost of inserting a keyword or operator would be low compared to the cost of inserting an identifier or constant, and so on. Usually, the cost of a replacement can be taken as the sum of deleting the old symbol and inserting a replacement, but a useful special case is the replacement of a name by a keyword, when the former is a feasible misspelling of the latter. In this case, the replacement cost would be very low.

One final source of information to help in selecting a local correction is semantics. Suppose for example that a Pascal compiler comes across two identifiers next to each other at the beginning of a statement, that is, at the point of error detection it has seen something like . . .; a b. Among the local corrections that would be considered for a recovery would be the insertion of a [, a (or an assignment operator, corresponding to feasible statements such as a[b] :=. . ., a(b) (a procedure call) or a := b. . .. In any of these cases, b may be the first symbol of an arbitrarily long expression, so a restricted forward move might never find the matching] or), if they were there, to select one of these alternatives. However, the symbol table will contain enough information for a choice to be made, since inserting [can only be correct if a has been declared as an array, (if it has been declared a procedure and := otherwise.

Systems performing local correction as part of their error recovery usually produce a message describing the action taken, such as 'a semicolon was inserted'. This has two main uses. First, even if the repair was not exactly what the user originally intended, it often suggests the true correction. Second, and more importantly, it informs the user of the parser's 'understanding' of the repaired text, so that any subsequent, possibly spurious, messages may be more easily understood.

Local correction uses the right context of the point where the error was detected to select a simple repair. This technique may be generalized to one where more radical changes, based on information extracted from the input following the error, are made.

In order to extract as much information as possible from the right context, recovery can begin by attempting to parse the input from the point of error detection, for as long as that is possible without altering the stack below what was its top at the time the error was detected. That is, if the error configuration was (ψ, axy, Π), the parser is restarted in some state p, such that $\delta(p, a)$ is defined, and parsing proceeds until another error is detected, suggesting that the choice of p was not appropriate, or some configuration $(\psi\gamma, y, \Pi)$ is reached, where a reduction by some production $A \to \beta\gamma$ is required, that would cause some of the symbols of ψ to be popped off the stack. There will, in general, be more than one state p from which this forward move may be started; each must be tried in turn, and each one that gets as far as an attempted reduction of this sort must be considered as a possibility for the next phase of the recovery, where an attempt is made to alter (ψ, axy, Π) into some configuration (ψ', axy, Π') such that $p = \delta^*(q_0, \psi')$, by simulating the insertion of some symbols before a and performing the corresponding parsing actions. If this is possible, then the recovery is successful. Otherwise, a must be deleted, and a new attempt made. If more than one recovery is successful, one must be selected, perhaps on the cost of inserting the particular symbols required. The local correction previously described now becomes a special case, when a single symbol repair is immediately successful.

Evidently, proceeding in exactly the manner described is very inefficient, and requires repeated parsing of portions of the right context. Practical forward move algorithms, such as those described in [MiMo78] or [PDeR78] retain information between attempts, or make them in parallel. Nevertheless, this sort of recovery is difficult to implement, and suffers from the serious drawback that it is inevitably thrown out if there are further syntax errors in the forward context.

An alternative is to base the recovery on left context, i.e., the stack in the error configuration. This leads to a type of phrase level recovery, similar to that made using error productions. Recall that a phrase level recovery transforms an error configuration $(\psi\rho, yz, \Pi)$ to $(\psi A, z, \Pi')$; the problem is to select A, the *reduction goal*, and ρy, the *error phrase*, when there are no error productions to guide the choice. In the case of real parsers, where the stack contains states, the problem is to find some A, such that there is a state q on the stack with an A-successor, p, and p has some parsing action on a terminal a, where the remaining input $yz = yaz'$, for some z'. This formulation is too general to allow an algorithm to identify unique reduction goals and error phrases, so it must be refined somehow.

The refinement suggested in [SiSS83] follows from assuming that the parse up to the error point is correct, so that the stack contents is an accurate representation of the structure of the left context of the error. In that case, if the stack holds $\psi\rho$, it only makes sense to consider reduction goals A such that $\exists w: A \Rightarrow^* \rho w$. For a given ρ these symbols may be computed, either from the grammar or from the transitions of the parser. (If the stack holds only states, ρ can easily be deduced from their accessing symbols.) An approximation may be obtained by considering all the nonterminals A such that $\exists w\colon A \Rightarrow^* Xw$ where $\rho = X\sigma$ for some $X \in N \cup T \cup \{\Lambda\}$ and $\sigma \in (N \cup T)^*$; this is easier to compute and includes all the reduction goals obtained by considering all of ρ. To make the set of reduction goals smaller, a nonterminal should be excluded from consideration if it can be derived from some other reduction goal by a chain of unit reductions. If $A \rightarrow B$ and $B \rightarrow C$, then if a successful recovery were made with B or C as the reduction goal, the unit reductions would follow, and the net result would be the same as if A had been used all along.

Given an error configuration (ψ, z, Π), it is necessary to find strings ρ and x and a terminal a such that $\psi = \psi'\rho$ and $z = xay$ for some ψ' and y so that there is a unique reduction goal A deriving ρw for some w and a phrase level recovery can be made to the configuration $(\psi' A, ay, \Pi')$ where the state $\delta^*(q_0, \psi' A)$ has some action on a. Of course, the stack will really contain states, so the recovery can be controlled by their transitions. The simplest strategy to find such strings is to begin with $\rho = x = \Lambda$. If the top stack state has a transition on any nonterminal, then that must be a reduction goal; if it is unique, the recovery is attempted on the basis that a complete string derivable from it has been missed out. In that case the successor will have an action on the first symbol of the remaining input, and parsing can recommence. If such an immediate recovery is not possible then the next state down the stack is considered; if $\psi = X_1 \ldots X_m$ this is equivalent to putting $\rho = X_m$. The reduction goals can be computed and an attempt to recover made if there is a unique one. If it fails, the next state down is tried ($\rho = X_{m-1} X_m$), and so on until $\rho = \psi$. If no state on the stack permits a recovery, then the first symbol of the remaining input is deleted and the process is repeated, with all of the stack being considered again. Thus, attempts to recover are made, varying ρ from Λ to ψ for each x, advancing x one symbol further into the input after each set of attempts fails.

Making attempts in this order may lead to excessive deletion of states from the stack. It is possible, by buffering input symbols, to try larger values of x for each ρ, and this may sometimes produce a better recovery; on the other hand, it may instead lead to excessive deletion of input. Choosing the best order for recovery attempts is not easy, so only the simplest strategy will be illustrated.

Consider again the example **(a(a,a))** and the LALR(1) parser for G_1

(Figure 5.1.2). The symbol stack in the error configuration will be $(P,$ the remaining input $(\mathbf{a,a}))$, and the state stack will be $0 \cdot 6 \cdot 9$. There are no reduction goals for $\rho = \Lambda$, since state 9 has no nonterminal transitions. With $\rho = P$, though, M is a possibility; L, E and P are not considered, since $M \Rightarrow L \Rightarrow E \Rightarrow P$. State 10, the M-successor to 9, has no action on (, so no recovery can be made. With $\rho = (P, L$ is the only possibility, but again, no recovery is possible, since state 1 has no action on (. The (is deleted and a new attempt is made, but with no success. Symbols must be deleted up to the first) before a recovery is possible, with reduction goal M in state 6. Just as in the recovery using error productions, a second error will be detected on the second), but this will be deleted and a second recovery will be made without special action.

The main weakness of this strategy is that reduction goals can only be nonterminals, so, unless a host of unit productions of the form $A \rightarrow a$ is added, there is no way to simulate single symbol repairs. The method is best suited to being used in a two level recovery, with a local repair being attempted first, as previously described.

Since recovery from errors is an essentially practical matter, the efficiency of any recovery scheme msut be considered important. It is generally considered unacceptable if a recovery mechanism imposes substantial extra overheads on the parsing of correct input. Using error productions inevitably leads to larger parsing tables, and, if a list-based implementation is used, this may slightly slow down parsing. Since there are unlikely to be very many error productions, this overhead is usually acceptable. (In [GHJ79], a figure of 16 error productions out of a total of 184 is given for a Pascal grammar, leading to 24 out of 337 states having shifts on ?.) Other mechanisms described impose no overheads.

The subject of error recovery has received a fair amount of attention in the literature. The most successful techniques seem to be those using a two level approach. [GHJ79] describes the use of local correction, assessed using weightings and semantics during a forward move over 5 tokens, augmented by a second level recovery based on error productions. The automatic selection of reduction goals for a second level strategy is taken from [SiSS83], where the local correction is based simply on a table of costs. Another approach, that deals specially with the tricky problem of unmatched scope delimiters (such as **begin**) is described in [BuFi82], while a more sophisticated approach to local repair is given in [MaFi82].

Finally, one more approach to recovery should be considered, namely handcrafting the recovery routines. A skilled programmer, who understands how an LR parser works, armed with the knowledge and experience of likely sorts of error can write specific recovery routines for each combination of error state and symbol, that make plausible corrections and adjust the stack accordingly. The designers of the PL/C compiler [CoWi73] took this approach (although it did not use an LR parser), and produced a system that could compile any syntactically incorrect program, and attempt to execute it. The PL/C recovery was not based on any general strategy, but on the special knowledge of the people writing it.

At the opposite extreme, it should be remembered that some parsers do not need to recover at all, and that in many environments, where only experienced users are concerned, a poor recovery may be perfectly adequate.

9

Extending the Technique

9.1 Use with non-LR grammars

It has been tacitly assumed in previous chapters that, if an LR parser is to be produced for a grammar, then the grammar must be LR(k). Indeed, if a useful parser is to be produced by practical methods it must be LR(1), LALR(1) or even SLR(1). If a parser constructor is presented with a grammar that does not fall into the class for which its algorithm produces a consistent parser it announces failure, and the grammar must be rewritten. It is sometimes the case, though, that conflicts can be resolved by using additional information.

As an example of how this may be done, consider what would happen if an attempt was made to construct an SLR(1) parser for the grammar G_2 exhibited in section 2.1. The grammar is ambiguous, so it certainly is not SLR(1). The item sets produced are shown in Figure 9.1.1, with the reductions annotated by the appropriate FOLLOW sets. The parsing conflicts in states 3 and 5 have not been resolved, and a parsing automaton constructed from these item sets would be nondeterministic.

If such a parser was presented with the input **a,a;a** after a few moves it would enter the configuration $(0145, ;a\dashv, L \rightarrow \mathbf{a} \cdot L \rightarrow \mathbf{a})$, the initial prefix of the input having been reduced to L,L. There is now a choice of moves to be made, either reduce this prefix using $L \rightarrow L,L$ or shift the ; and enter state 2, and thence state 3, where a reduction by $L \rightarrow L;L$ gives the sentential form L,L. In either case, the parse can then proceed successfully, in the first case giving a tree corresponding to the derivation tree on the left in Figure 2.1.6, in the second case, that on the right. These in turn correspond to the operator , being more binding than ; and vice versa, respectively. This interpretation can be used in the opposite direction: if it is asserted that , is more binding than ; then in state 5 a reduction should be performed, not a shift, if the next symbol is a ;.

In state 3 the opposite situation occurs: if , is the more binding operator then a reduction by $L \rightarrow L;L$ is wrong if , is the lookahead symbol,

$$L \to L;L \qquad L \to (M) \qquad M \to L$$
$$L \to L,L \qquad L \to \mathbf{a} \qquad M \to \Lambda$$

Item Set	Items	Successors
0	$L \to \cdot L;L$ $L \to \cdot L,L$ $L \to \cdot \mathbf{a}$ $L \to \cdot (M)$	$L \Rightarrow 1$ $\mathbf{a} \Rightarrow 10$ $(\Rightarrow 6$
1	$L \to L \cdot ;L$ $L \to L \cdot ,L$	$; \Rightarrow 2$ $, \Rightarrow 4$
2	$L \to L; \cdot L$ $L \to \cdot L;L$ $L \to \cdot L,L$ $L \to \cdot \mathbf{a}$ $L \to \cdot (M)$	$L \Rightarrow 3$ $\mathbf{a} \Rightarrow 10$ $(\Rightarrow 6$
3	$L \to L;L \cdot$ $L \to L \cdot ;L$ $L \to L \cdot ,L$	$\#L \to L;L\{\dashv,),;,,\}$ $; \Rightarrow 2$ $, \Rightarrow 4$
4	$L \to L, \cdot L$ $L \to \cdot L;L$ $L \to \cdot L,L$ $L \to \cdot \mathbf{a}$ $L \to \cdot (M)$	$L \Rightarrow 5$ $\mathbf{a} \Rightarrow 10$ $(\Rightarrow 6$
5	$L \to L,L \cdot$ $L \to L \cdot ;L$ $L \to L \cdot ,L$	$\#L \to L,L\{\dashv,),;,,\}$ $; \Rightarrow 2$ $, \Rightarrow 4$
6	$L \to (\cdot M)$ $M \to \cdot$ $M \to \cdot L$ $L \to \cdot L;L$ $L \to \cdot L,L$ $L \to \cdot \mathbf{a}$ $L \to \cdot (M)$	$M \Rightarrow 8$ $\#M \to \Lambda\{)\}$ $L \Rightarrow 7$ $\mathbf{a} \Rightarrow 10$ $(\Rightarrow 6$
7	$M \to L \cdot$ $L \to L \cdot ;L$ $L \to L \cdot ,L$	$\#M \to L\{)\}$ $; \Rightarrow 2$ $, \Rightarrow 4$
8	$L \to (M \cdot)$	$) \Rightarrow 9$
9	$L \to (M) \cdot$	$\#L \to (M)\{\dashv,),;,,\}$
10	$L \to \mathbf{a} \cdot$	$\#L \to \mathbf{a}\{\dashv,),;,,\}$

Figure 9.1.1. Construction of an SLR(1) parser for G_2.

the shift move should be made instead. In general, if expressions are defined by ambiguous grammars of this sort, wherever there is a parsing conflict between a reduction by $E \to Eo_iE$ and a shift of operator o_j it should be resolved in favour of the reduction if o_i is more binding than o_j, and the shift if it is less. This resolution can be done automatically if operator precedences are declared to the parser generator.

Operator precedence alone will not remove all the conflicts from this example. In state 5 there is a conflict between the reduction by $L \to L,L$ and a shift on the symbol , itself. It is easy to see that in this case reducing corresponds to the operator being left associative and shifting to its being right associative. In this case, it doesn't matter, because of the semantics to be associated with the operators, but in general, it might: arithmetic minus is a particularly important example where it matters a great deal whether $a - b - c$ is equivalent to $a - (b - c)$ or $(a - b) - c$. Here, associativity declarations can be used to resolve the conflict. If there is a parsing conflict between a reduction by $E \to Eo_iE$ and a shift of operator o_j, and the precedence of o_i is equal to the precedence of o_j (possibly $o_i = o_j$) then the reduction should be made if o_i is left associative and the shift if it is right associative. There is a possibility that o_i may be non-associative, that is, expressions of the form $e_1o_ie_2o_ie_3$ may be illegal (Fortran's .LT. is an example). In this case an error should be announced.

If the information that , is more binding than ; and they both associate to the left is added to G_2, then a deterministic parser may be produced by constructing the SLR(1) item sets and then resolving the remaining conflicts as described. The resulting parser will accept the same language as a parser for the unambiguous grammar G_1 and impose the same structure on it. It is slightly smaller, and, since G_2 has no unit productions except $L \to \mathbf{a}$ it will make few unit reductions, so the complex elimination procedures of section 6.3 will probably not be considered necessary or worthwhile.

A generalization of the precedence approach, to deal with other types of ambiguity is possible, by allowing precedences to be associated with productions, as well as with any terminal symbol. This makes it possible to deal with operator symbols having different priorities in different contexts. The best example of this is the symbol $-$ used in arithmetic expressions either as an infix subtraction operator or as a unary negation. In the latter case, it must have a higher priority than in the former if expressions are to be parsed in accordance with normal mathematical usage.

Giving precedences to productions can resolve most parsing conflicts. Reduce-reduce conflicts can be resolved as well as shift-reduce conflicts, by choosing the reduction by the production of higher precedence. However, such a facility should be used with discretion. Whereas the ideas of precedence and associativity of operators are widely understood, and have a long history, it is not clear that any comparable intuitive understanding is possible for the idea of precedence of productions, which only seems to have meaning in the context of shift-reduce parsers. If this sort of information is included in the input to a parser generator, then that input cannot provide an easily understood specification, in the way an unambiguous grammar can, and it is not easy to tell whether it describes the same language and structure as some other reference grammar. There would seem to be a particular danger in a system like Yacc that applies default conflict resolving rules based on the order in which operators are declared (see Chapter 10). A naive user could easily find their interpretation of the input grammar at variance with Yacc's.

Set against this disadvantage is the fact that for certain constructs, finding an unambiguous grammar may be difficult. A much quoted example is the following

$$C \rightarrow \textbf{if } b \textbf{ then } C \textbf{ else } C$$

$$C \rightarrow \textbf{if } b \textbf{ then } C$$

$$C \rightarrow s$$

where C stands for conditional statement, and b and s are boolean expression and statement respectively. The string **if** b **then if** b **then** s **else** s can be parsed in two distinct ways, matching the **else** with one or other of the **if**s. By giving **else** a higher priority than $C \rightarrow$ **if** b **then** C the conventional interpretation that the **else** goes with the nearest **then** is obtained. It is possible to write an unambiguous grammar for this construction – the reader is invited to try, but should bear in mind that most programming languages get round the difficulty by either outlawing it, using different keywords to introduce single and double branched conditionals, or using explicit terminating keywords, such as **fi**.

Another possible source of information for resolving conflicts is the semantics associated with the grammar. Semantics is what makes it possible for people to deal with the inherent ambiguity of natural languages. Although 'fruit flies like a banana' is an entertaining example of syntactical ambiguity in English, it never actually causes any difficulty, because everybody knows that bananas can't fly, so 'flies' cannot be the verb in the sentence. This use of semantics to disambiguate can be approximated in an LR parser by making use of constraints deduced from an attribute grammar to control the parsing decisions in inadequate states. This is potentially a very powerful technique.

Every parsing conflict involves at least one reduction. Where semantic actions are specified by an attribute grammar there may be predicates associated with the production concerned. If the AG is LR attributed, it will be possible to evaluate all the attributes of symbols on the left and right hand sides of the production by the time the inadequate state is entered, and thence to test whether the predicate is satisfied. If it is, the reduction should be made, otherwise, in the case of a reduce-reduce conflict further predicates may be tested, or, for a shift-reduce conflict the shift move will be made. Parsing tables will need a new type of entry, conflict n, where n identifies a list of possible actions and their associated predicates. The corresponding modification to the parsing functions is straightforward. If q is an inadequate state in an LR(1) parser, and, for every $t \in T$ no more than one of the predicates governing each production in $\text{Reduce}(q, t)$ can be true for any combination of attribute values, then using the predicates in this way will resolve the conflicts to give a deterministic parser.

This method is sufficient to deal with the problem of function and array names discussed in Chapter 7. An AG for these constructions could include productions

$$\textit{functiondecl} \downarrow \text{ENV} \uparrow \text{ENV} \cup \{(\text{NAME}, \text{ftype})\} \;\rightarrow$$
$$\textbf{function name} \uparrow \text{NAME}$$
$$\textit{arraydecl} \downarrow \text{ENV} \uparrow \text{ENV} \cup \{(\text{NAME}, \text{atype})\} \;\rightarrow$$
$$\textbf{array name} \uparrow \text{NAME}$$

for the declarations, and

$$\textit{arrayref} \downarrow \text{ENV} \ldots \;\rightarrow$$
$$\textit{identifier} \downarrow \text{ENV} \uparrow \text{atype} \;(\textit{subscripts} \downarrow \text{ENV} \ldots)$$
$$\textit{functioncall} \downarrow \text{ENV} \ldots \;\rightarrow$$
$$\textit{identifier} \downarrow \text{ENV} \uparrow \text{ftype} \;(\textit{subscripts} \downarrow \text{ENV} \ldots)$$
$$\textit{identifier} \downarrow \text{ENV} \uparrow \text{ENV}(\text{NAME}) \;\rightarrow \textbf{name} \uparrow \text{NAME}$$

for the references. A parser constructed from the CFG part of this grammar would include a state with a parsing conflict between *arrayref* → *identifier*(*subscripts*) and *functioncall* → *identifier*(*subscripts*) which could not be resolved by lookahead alone, if the grammar allowed the two to appear in the same context, as expressions. However, the AG stipulates that, for an array reference, the synthesized attribute of *identifier* must have the value atype, for a function reference, ftype. This is sufficient to resolve the conflict. (If it is neither of these values, an error should be reported.) Provided declarations precede the use of the names they declare, a grammar such as this will be LR attributed, so an LR parser could evaluate the necessary attributes during the parsing and use them to check this condition.

This example will be recognizable as the symbol table fix described in section 7.1, in a slightly different guise. Using attribute grammars here has some advantages, primarily that there is no need to introduce mysterious new terminals and thereby lose the connection between names in declarations and in expressions. The use of attributes can also be generalized to cope with other parsing conflicts; many examples of conflicts and ambiguities that can be resolved in this way are given in [Watt80]. Attributes can only be used automatically in a system incorporating an attribute evaluator, of course. Since the values are needed to direct the parse, this evaluator must work during it, and not need to build a tree and make multiple passes (at least not for the attributes involved in predicates used to resolve parsing conflicts). This means that the grammar must be LR attributed. The technique cannot therefore be used to parse an ambiguous grammar for arithmetic expressions, since this could only be done using inherited attributes dependent on the right context of the productions for expressions.

9.2   Regular Right Part Grammars

LR theory and parser construction methods are based on context free grammars, but context free grammars are rarely used nowadays as syntax definitions. Backus-Naur Form, or BNF, the metalanguage used in the Algol 60 report for describing the syntax of that language is just a cosmetic variant of the standard CFG notation, but subsequent descriptions of programming languages have introduced notational extensions to overcome some of its less convenient aspects. In particular, it is common to find special notations used for repetition, optional items and alternatives within the right part of a production. For example, the language generated by G_1 might be described in the following way.

$$L \to E\{\,;E\,\}$$
$$E \to P\{\,,P\,\}$$
$$P \to \mathbf{a} \mid (\,[L]\,)$$

Items enclosed between the metacharacters { and } may appear zero or more times, those between [and] are optional, | indicates alternatives. A production for arithmetic expressions using the operators + or − might take the form $E \rightarrow E(+|-)T$, where the brackets are metacharacters being used to delimit the alternative part of the right hand side. Notations such as this provide more compact, and arguably more readable, syntax descriptions than 'pure' CFGs or BNF. Quite a lot of research has been done into producing LR parsers directly from them, both because the resulting parser will often be smaller than one produced from an equivalent CFG, and because it is desirable to be able to go on using the same grammar as a language description and a parser specification despite the extensions.

The important difference between these extended notations and CFGs is that the right hand sides of productions denote entire sets of strings, infinite ones in the case of productions using repetition. For these particular extensions, these sets will always be regular languages over $N \cup T$. (Readers familiar with regular expressions should understand why this is so.)

Another form of syntax description, popularized by its use for Pascal, is the syntax diagram, as illustrated in Figure 9.2.1. Each diagram is a production, with its subject shown to the left. Nonterminals are drawn in rectangular boxes, terminals in round ones. The strings generated by the subject are those encountered in the boxes on any path leading from the left side of the diagram to its right; the path may have loops in it. A syntax diagram is really just an FSM transition diagram drawn 'inside out' – the states are shrunk to points and the labels are moved inside the arrows. Again, therefore, the language denoted by each diagram must be regular.

Regular right part grammars are a formal abstraction of notations using productions with right parts denoting regular languages. It turns out to be most convenient, for LR parser construction at least, to use FSMs as the right parts of the productions. This is achieved by the following definition.

A *(deterministic) regular right part grammar (RRPG)* G is a 7-tuple $(N, T, Q, \delta, F, P, S)$ where N and T are finite nonterminal and terminal alphabets, respectively, with $N \cap T = \emptyset$, Q is a finite set of right part states, $\delta: Q \times (N \cup T) \rightarrow Q$ is the transition function, $F \subseteq Q$ are the final states, $P \subseteq N \times Q$ is a set of productions, and S is the start symbol. The production (A, q) will be written $A \rightarrow q$.

For all $q \in Q$ define $L(q) = \{\, \alpha \mid \delta^*(q, \alpha) \in F \,\}$ and assume $L(q) \neq \emptyset$.

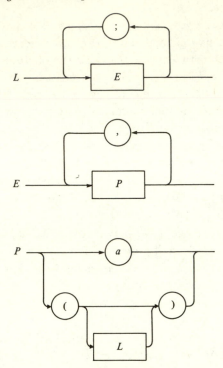

Figure 9.2.1. A syntax diagram.

A derives relation for RRPGs is defined by $\alpha A \gamma \Rightarrow \alpha \beta \gamma$ iff $\exists q \in Q : A \to q \in P \wedge \beta \in L(q)$; the language generated by G is $\{ w \in T^* \mid S \Rightarrow^* w \}$.

The class of languages that can be generated by RRPGs is no larger than the class of context free languages. If $G = (N, T, Q, \delta, F, P, S)$ is a RRPG, then for each $A \to q \in P$, the converse of Theorem 2.5 states that there is a right linear grammar $G_{A \to q} = (N_{A \to q}, N \cup T, P_{A \to q}, S_{A \to q})$ where $N_{A \to q} \cap N = \emptyset$ such that $L(G_{A \to q}) = L(q)$, so a CFG $G' = (N', T, P', S)$ may be constructed, with $N' = N \cup \bigcup_{A \to q \in P} N_{A \to q}$, and $P' = \{ A \to S_{A \to q} \mid A \to q \in P \} \cup \bigcup_{A \to q \in P} P_{A \to q}$, and $L(G')$ will obviously be equal to $L(G)$. G' is said to be a *representation* of G; it is not necessarily unique.

This demonstration suggests a way of constructing LR parsers from regular right part grammars, and an LR(k) definition for RRPGs. A parser can be built for an RRPG G by constructing a representation G' of G and then applying the item set construction. An RRPG is LR(k) iff this process produces a consistent parser, i.e., if G' is LR(k) in the context free sense. This way of defining the LR(k) property is given added credibility by the fact, shown in [Heil79], that if an RRPG has some LR(k) representation constructed using unambiguous right linear grammars, then every representation so constructed will be LR(k), so this seems to reflect an inherent property of the RRPG.

As a method of parser construction this transformation is not so satisfactory, because the original grammar's structure is not being directly used to control the parser, and no advantage is taken of the opportunities for producing smaller parsers offered by the more compact description given by RRPGs. These advantages can only be obtained by constructing the parser directly from the RRPG. This turns out to be more complicated than might at first be expected.

Considering the intuitive idea of an item, as corresponding to a particular stage in the recognition of a handle (see Chapter 3), it seems reasonable to identify the cores of items for a regular right part grammar with the right part states. Thus, an LR(k) item of an RRPG $G = (N, T, Q, \delta, F, P, S)$ is a pair, written $[q, u]$, in $Q \times T^k$. The item set construction is modified so that the nucleus of the X successor to an item set $\Im$ is

$$\mathrm{succ}(\Im, X) = \{\, [q, u] \mid \exists p \in Q : [p, u] \in \Im \wedge \delta(p, X) = q \,\}.$$

That is, it comprises all the right part states that could be reached via a transition under X from the states in $\Im$. The closure is computed from the relation $\downarrow$ defined by

$$[q, u] \downarrow [p, v] \text{ iff}$$
$$\exists A \in N : \delta(q, A) \neq \emptyset \wedge A \to p \in P \wedge v \in \mathrm{first}_k(L(\delta(q, A)) \cdot \{u\})$$

where the first_k function is defined using the $\Rightarrow$ relation for RRPGs and extended to sets of strings in the obvious way. The closure of a set of items $\Im$ is

$$\mathrm{closure}(\Im) = \{\, [q, u] \mid \exists [p, v] \in \Im : [p, v] \downarrow^* [q, u] \,\}$$

The reasoning behind this is similar to that justifying the closure computation in CFGs: if $\delta(q, A)$ is defined, then a string derived from A is expected on the input when the parser is in the state corresponding to this item set. Thus, all items with cores consisting of a state p such that $A \to p \in P$ must be added to the item set with lookaheads derived from the context of the item $[q, u]$.

The LR(k) automaton for G is $(\bar{Q}, N \cup T, P, \bar{q}_0, \bar{\delta}, \mathrm{Reduce})$ where $\bar{Q}$ is the set of item sets (bars are used to distinguish LR automaton components from grammar components), $\bar{q}_0 = \mathrm{closure}(\{\, [q, \perp] \mid S \to q \in P \,\})$,

$\bar{\delta}(\bar{q}, x) = \text{closure} \cdot \text{succ}(\bar{q}, X)$ for all $\bar{q} \in \bar{Q}$, $X \in N \cup T$, and

$\text{Reduce}(\bar{q}, u) = \{ A \to q \mid \exists p \in F, \alpha \in L(q) : p = \delta^*(q, \alpha) \wedge [p, u] \in \bar{q} \}$.

Example.

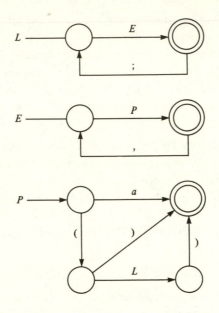

Figure 9.2.2. Productions for an RRPG

Figure 9.2.2 shows transition diagrams for a regular right part grammar generating $L(G_1)$. The item set construction for this grammar is shown in Figure 9.2.3; items' cores are shown as transition diagrams with a dot in the appropriate state; states with reductions are marked #. There are 14 item sets, compared with 23 in the LR(1) collection for G_1 (Figure 5.1.1).   □

The extensions to the theory of Chapter 4 needed to deal with RRPGs are quite complex[†] so only the practical difficulties of parsing will be discussed.

It is easy to see, given the way it is constructed, that the automaton built as described recognizes LR contexts, that is

$$A \to q \in \text{Reduce}(\bar{q}, u) \text{ iff } \exists \alpha, \beta, y : S \perp \Rightarrow^* \alpha A u y \Rightarrow \alpha \beta u y \wedge \beta \in L(q)$$
$$(9.2.1)$$

[†] LaLonde's thesis [LaLo75] gives some account of the relevant theory, using a different formulation from that of this book.

Item set	Items	Successors

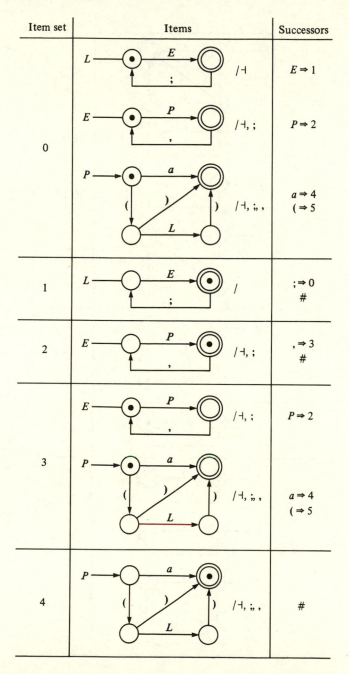

Figure 9.2.3. Example of the LR(1) item set construction for an RRPG

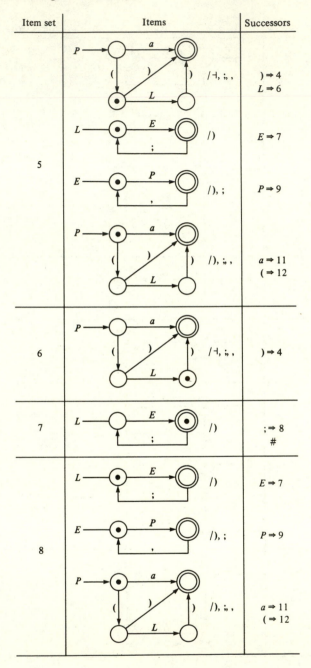

Figure 9.2.3. Example of the LR(1) item set construction for an RRPG (continued)

Item set	Items	Successors
9		, ⇒ 10 #
10		P ⇒ 9 a ⇒ 11 (⇒ 12
11		#
12		) ⇒ 11 L ⇒ 13 E ⇒ 7 P ⇒ 9 a ⇒ 11 (⇒ 12
13		) ⇒ 11

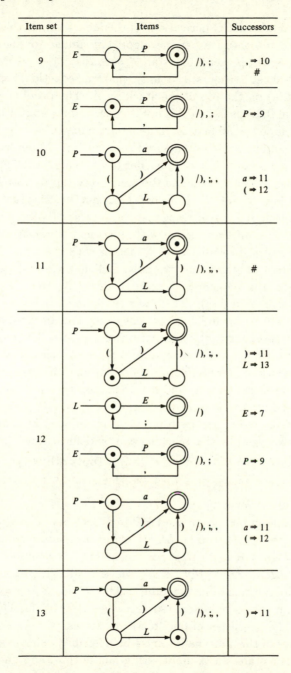

Figure 9.2.3. Example of the LR(1) item set construction for an RRPG (continued)

where $\Rightarrow$ denotes RRPG derivation (cf. Lemma 4.10). If this algorithm is to be used to control a parsing algorithm similar to Algorithm 3.3, then, whenever the parser is in a state $\bar{q}$, such that $A \to q \in \text{Reduce}(\bar{q}, u)$ and the lookahead string is u, it must make a reduction, replacing the string $\beta \in L(q)$ on the top of the stack by A. The peculiar problem of LR parsing of RRPGs is that β is not unique, and its length, the number of stack items to be popped, is, in general, unknown.

Several solutions have been devised (see [PuBr81, MaKr76, NaSa86]); the most general, and elaborate, is that of LaLonde [LaLo79]. The idea is to construct FSMs to examine the stack from top to bottom in order to find the left end of β. It is not sufficient to construct FSMs for each production $A \to q$ to recognize the reverse of $L(q)$ (consider the productions $S \to aaA$ and $A \to \{a\}$). Instead, the *readback machines*, as they are called, are used in conjunction with the usual LR parsers that use a stack of states, not symbols, and they are built to recognize the reverse of the sequences of states entered by the LR automaton as it reads strings in $L(q)$. These states distinguish between different contexts in which a symbol appears, so they can be used to find the context corresponding to the first symbol of a handle. The required state sequences must start with some state $\bar{p}$ where q was added by closure (and from which A can therefore be shifted) and must end in the state with the reduction. That is, for each reduction by a production $A \to q$ in a state $\bar{q}$ a readback machine $B(\bar{q}, A \to q) = (Q^B, \bar{Q}, \delta^B, q_0{}^B, F^B)$ is constructed. Using the path notation introduced in chapter 4, the language recognized by this machine can be defined thus:

$$L(B(\bar{q}, A \to q)) = \{ \, [\bar{p} : \beta]^R \mid \beta \in L(q) \wedge \text{Top}(\bar{p} : \beta]) = \bar{q}$$
$$\wedge \exists v : [q, v] \in \bar{p} \wedge \exists [q', v'] \in \bar{p} : [q', v'] \downarrow [q, v] \, \} \qquad (9.2.2)$$

(x^R means the reverse of x).

The automaton built from the RRP item sets can be augmented with these machines to produce an *LR(k) automaton with readback* $LRB = (\bar{Q}, N \cup T, P, \bar{q}_0, \bar{\delta}, \text{Reduce}, R, \rho, I, \bar{F})$. The first six components are the same as in LRA. $R = \bigcup Q^B$ is the set of readback states, $\rho = \bigcup \delta^B$ is the readback transition function, $I : \bar{Q} \times P \to R$ selects an initial readback state for a reduction, so $I(\bar{q}, A \to q) = q_0^B$ for $B(\bar{q}, A \to q)$, $\bar{F} \subseteq R = \bigcup F^B$ is the set of final readback states.

The moves of this automaton must be described using configurations consisting of a state stack, input string and output, and an extra component, the current state, a member of $\bar{Q} \cup R$, since during readback this will no longer be on top of the stack. The moves are as follows:

Algorithm 9.1. LR(1) parsing for regular right part grammars.

let $G = (N, T, Q, \delta, F, P, S)$ be a RRPG
let $LRB = (\bar{Q}, N \cup T, P, \bar{q}_0, \bar{\delta}, \text{Reduce}, R, \rho, I, \bar{F})$ be G's
       LR(1) automaton with readback
let $\gamma = input \cdot \dashv$
let $\sigma = \bar{q}_0$
let $\bar{q}, X = \bar{q}_0, \gamma(1)$
let $accepted = $ **false**
until $accepted$ **do**
{   **while** $\text{Reduce}(\bar{q}, X)$ is undefined **do**
     { $\gamma := \gamma(2\ldots)$
        if $\bar{\delta}(\bar{q}, X) = \emptyset$ **then** error
                    else { $\bar{q} := \bar{\delta}(\bar{q}, X)$; $X := \gamma(1)$ }
       $\sigma := \sigma \cdot q$
     }
     let $A \to q = \text{Reduce}(\bar{q}, X)$
     let $r = I(\bar{q}, A \to q)$
     until $r \in \bar{F}$ **do**
     { $r := \rho(r, \sigma(|\sigma|))$; $\sigma := \sigma(1 \ldots |\sigma| - 1)$ }
     $accepted := A = S \land \gamma = \dashv \land \sigma = \bar{q}_0$
     unless $accepted$ **do** { $\bar{q} := \bar{\delta}(\sigma(|\sigma|), A)$; $\sigma := \sigma \cdot \bar{q}$ }
}

$([\bar{q} : \alpha], tz, \Pi, \bar{p}) \vdash ([\bar{q} : \alpha t], z, \Pi, \bar{r})$ iff
$$\exists [q, v] \in \bar{p} : \delta(q, a) \neq \emptyset \land k : aw \in \text{first}_k(L(q) \cdot \{v\})$$
$([\bar{q} : \alpha], uw, \Pi, \bar{p}) \vdash ([\bar{q} : \alpha], uw, (A \to q) \cdot \Pi, I(\bar{q}, A \to q))$ iff
$$A \to q \in \text{Reduce}(\bar{p}, u)$$
$([\bar{q} : \alpha X], z, \Pi, r) \vdash ([\bar{q} : \alpha], z, \Pi, r')$ iff
$$r' = \rho(r, \text{Top}([\bar{q} : \alpha X])) \text{ is defined}$$
$([\bar{q} : \alpha], z, (A \to q) \cdot \Pi, r)$
$$\vdash ([\bar{q} : \alpha A], z, (A \to q) \cdot \Pi, \bar{\delta}(\text{Top}([\bar{q} : \alpha]), A)) \text{ iff } r \in \bar{F}$$

Whenever the current state is in $\bar{Q}$, it is equal to the stack top. Algorithm 9.1 shows how these moves may be implemented for $k = 1$.

The operation of the readback machine is linear, so the parser operating in this way is efficient. There is one pitfall, however, and that is that the stack may grow excessively. For example, if a grammar for a programming language included the production

$$program \rightarrow statement\{\ ;\ statement\ \}$$

then the parse stack would grow until it had as many entries as there were statements in the program being parsed. Care must be taken to avoid overflow, and it may be necessary to define lists of things recursively when it is known that they may become very long.

The readback machines can be constructed by identifying R with the subset of $\bar{Q} \times (Q \times T^k)$, the set of state-item pairs, such that, for all $(\bar{q}, [q, u]) \in R$, $[q, u] \in \bar{q}$. Then $I(\bar{q}, A \rightarrow q)$ is $(\bar{q}, [p, u])$ where $\exists \alpha : \delta^*(q, \alpha) = p \in F$, i.e., $[p, u]$ is the item triggering the reduction. $\bar{F}$ consists of the pairs $(\bar{p}, [p, u])$ such that, for some $[q, v] \in \bar{p}$, $[q, v] \downarrow [p, u]$ (cf. 9.2.2). Finally, ρ is obtained by putting $\rho((\bar{p}, [p, u]), \bar{q}) = (\bar{q}, [q, u])$ where $\exists X : \bar{\delta}(\bar{q}, X) = \bar{p}$ and $\delta(q, X) = p$, so ρ is tracing backwards through the items corresponding to shift moves and successor computations.

The construction as described is based on $LR(k)$ items and is thus unsuitable for generating practical parsers. A method of building $LALR(1)$ parsers for RRPGs, based on the lookahead algorithm of DeRemer and Pennello described in chapter 5, is given in [Chap84]. The computation is made more complex for RRPGs because parser states do not have unique accessing symbols, and so the computation of both lookback states and the includes relation requires the recognition of regular sets, instead of simply strings matching production right hand sides.

A readback machine can never detect an error, since the top states on the stack necessarily form a path. This means that many readback states can be merged and the part of the parser concerned with readback can be very compact. Further optimizations can be made by introducing new actions that simply pop the stack a fixed number of times when the readback action is independent of the state exposed – a common occurrence caused by successive right part transitions involving no alternatives. These optimizations do impose a considerable overhead during parser construction but are usually worthwhile.

To avoid backtracking, the LR automaton with readback must be deterministic. This means both that all the states in $\bar{Q}$ must be consistent and that the readback must be deterministic. Deterministic $LR(k)$ automata with readback provide another way of defining the $LR(k)$ regular right part grammars, as those grammars for which a deterministic machine can be built. It is not clear whether this class is the same as that defined by representations using $LR(k)$ CFGs.

10

LR Parser Generators

10.1 Some Examples

All LR parser generators do the same basic job of taking a grammar and producing a parser from it. They differ in the class of grammars they accept, the support for adding semantic actions and error handling to the parser, their ease of use and portability, and the efficiency of the parser construction process and of the parsers produced. A few representative examples will be described briefly, to illustrate the range of currently available systems.

In most respects **LR** [WeSh81] represents the crudest type, in that it does little more than parser generation; there is no automatic error recovery mechanism in the parsers produced, a lexical analyser must be supplied by the user, and the interface with semantic actions consists simply of a call to a routine, made just before each reduction is performed. Unlike most other parser generators, though, **LR** will accept any LR(1) grammar, since it uses Pager's algorithm. It was designed to be highly portable, to which end it is entirely written in Ansi Standard Fortran 66. This causes some inefficiencies, because of the limited support for data structuring and the poor text handling, but has allowed **LR** to be ported to at least nine systems; only two subroutines need to be changed when it is moved, provided a compiler conforming to the standard is available.

The input is a grammar written in a notation resembling BNF. The names of nonterminals and of basic symbol classes are enclosed between < and >; all symbols that do not appear as the subject of a production are taken to be terminals; the start symbol is deduced from context. All productions with the same subject must be grouped together. A group of productions consists of a nonterminal (the subject) immediately followed by the right hand sides, separated by the sequence **&a** if there is more than one. The group is terminated by **&p** and the whole grammar by **&g**. Comments may be added, extending from the sequence **&c** to the end of the line. Directives controlling the form of output and the amount of

information produced may be inserted in the form of flags, preceded by
&. This form of input is unattractive, but it does overcome some of the
portability problems presented by differing character sets. Figure 10.1.1
shows the input corresponding to the typed list grammar of section 7.2.

```
&c
&c  This is the grammar for typed lists, given in
&c  Figure 7.2.1.
&c
&j &k &c  flags to generate Fortran 66 tables
&c
<prog> type <decls> in <list> &p
<decls> <decls> <decl> &a
        <decl> &p
<decl> <name> = <typespec> &p
<typespec> * <typespec> &a
          <stype> &p
<stype> i &a c &p
<list> <list> ; <element> &a
       <element> &p
<element> <element> , <prim> &a
          <prim> &p
<prim> <name> &a <number> &a <character> &a
       ( <list> ) &p
&g
```

Figure 10.1.1. An example of input to **LR**.

LR will produce a lot of informative output if it is required: a pret-
typrinted listing of the grammar, a vocabulary and cross-reference listing, a list of nullable nonterminals, and various sets which are used
internally and can be helpful for debugging grammars which are not
LR(1). It will also produce a fairly readable listing of all the item sets
and the transitions of the parser it builds.

Parser tables may be produced as either Fortran DATA statements or
raw data tables. The latter format may be processed by some program
provided by the user in order to produce a representation such as those
described in Chapter 6, to be used with parsing routines written in any
language. The Fortran tables may be inserted straight into a standard
skeleton to create a complete parser. The data stucture employed is
not efficient in its use of space, but it is portable, because it makes no
assumptions about how values may be packed into a machine word. The
format appears to be list based, with default reductions.

LR is reported as being widely used in constructing system utilities, such as a debugger, and front ends for data analysis programs. It has also been used by students to build compilers, and for research into programming languages.

The next example is a system that provides more facilities for specifying semantic actions, and an automatic error recovery scheme. Yacc [Joh78] is probably the most widely available LR parser generator. It was developed under the Unix† operating system, and is distributed as one of its standard utilities; it has now become more widely available and versions for a variety of operating systems and machines, including personal computers, now exist.

A Yacc specification consists of three parts: declarations, productions and programs, the parts separated by the sequence %%. The productions correspond to the input grammar; productions with the same subject may be grouped together, but this is not required. If they are, the different right hand sides are separated by vertical bars (|) and the group is terminated by a semicolon. A colon separates the subject from the right hand sides. The symbols used may be either single character literals, enclosed in single quotes, representing terminals, or names, made up of letters, underscores, dots and digits (a name may not begin with a digit). These are taken to be nonterminals, unless they are declared as 'tokens' among the declarations.

Actions may be associated with each production. They take the form of arbitrary statements in the programming language C, enclosed in braces. They may call procedures and alter the values of global variables declared in the specification. Additionally, pseudovariables $1, $2 and so on may be used to access values on the action stack, and $$ may be used to store values on it, as described in section 7.2. If no action is associated with a production, the default $$=$1 is performed. Actions are normally specified at the end of a right hand side, but may be placed anywhere within a production. Yacc transforms a production with actions anywhere except at the end by inserting a nullable nonterminal. For example

```
    X:   A { do_something() } B C ;
```
is transformed into

```
    X:   A Y B C ;
```

---

† Unix is a registered trade mark of Bell Laboratories, who get very annoyed with people who don't mention the fact.

```
Y:   { do_something() } ;
```

The action must therefore appear in a free position, unless a parsing conflict is to result. All actions are performed during reduce moves in the transformed grammar.

The declarations section must include definitions of all global variables accessed by the actions. These take the from of ordinary C declarations, enclosed in special brackets %{ and %}. Type definitions for any structures used by the actions may also appear, as may a definition of the type of values appearing on the action stack; this will typically be the union of several basic types, and is introduced by the keyword %union. There must also be declarations of any names used as terminals; these are introduced by the keyword %token. Optionally, the start symbol may be declared using the keyword %start. If it is not, it is taken to be the subject of the first production.

Additionally, there may be declarations of the associativity and precedence of terminals, usually operators. The keywords %left, %right and %nonassoc may appear at the beginning of a line, followed by a list of terminals; they signify associativity in the obvious way. All symbols on the same line are given the same precedence, and the lines are in order of increasing precedence. These declarations are used in the way described in section 9.1 to resolve parsing conflicts, and they allow Yacc to produce parsers from ambiguous grammars.

The definitions of any procedures called by the actions appear in the programs section. These are simply C code, but may access the global variables used by the actions. Also in the programs section may be the definition of a lexical analysis function. This must return a token value, an integer, to be used by the parsing routines, and may assign a value to a special variable yylval, to be used by the actions (cf. section 7.1). Yacc automatically assigns token values to each name declared by %token, and the lexical analyser can use the token name as if it had been declared a constant, thus ensuring that parser and lexical analyser use the same values. Literals are returned as themselves. Another utility, called Lex, is available, which can produce analysers from a lexical specification using regular expressions; these are compatible with parsers produced by Yacc.

The essential parts of a Yacc specification for typed lists, using an ambiguous grammar, are shown in Figure 10.1.2, which should be compared with Figure 7.2.3. Text between /* and */ is a comment; the use of upper case letters for terminal names follows convention. The typedef declaration is the way, in C, the type LIST must be declared as a list header; in actions, the operator '.' is used with values of this type, to select fields from the structure pointed to. In C, = is the assignment operator, and semicolons are mandatory statement terminators.

The output consists of a C function, with the parsing tables embedded in it in the form of declarations of arrays that constitute a compressed list representation (see [AhUl77]). Additionally, a listing of the item sets and the parsing actions for each state may be obtained. Yacc reports the number of parsing conflicts, but will use precedence and associativity to resolve most of them. If no relevant declarations have been given, all shift-reduce conflicts are resolved in favour of shift, and reduce-reduce ones in favour of whichever of the productions involved appears first in the specification. Because of its conflict resolving mechanism, Yacc will produce parsers from a large class of grammars, even though its constructor algorithm is only LALR(1).

Error recovery is based on error productions, as described in section 8.2. When an error is detected, a procedure **yyerror** is called to print a message. By default, this is simply 'syntax error', but the user may supply a definition of **yyerror** in the programs section of the specification, to give a more helpful message. If there are no error productions, the parser stops after printing the message, otherwise the recovery will lead to a reduction by an error production, and the action associated with it can issue further information and perform any other necessary action. Yacc will not attempt a full recovery unless at least three successful shift moves have been made. If they have not, the error symbol is simply deleted. This prevents the recovery mechanism looping, and helps reduce the possibility of a cascade of spurious messages. A version of Yacc is available under some Unix systems that incorporates an improved, two level, recovery scheme described in [GHJ79].

Yacc has been used in the construction of production compilers for languages including C, Pascal, APL and Sasl. It has also been used to provide the input handling routines of a number of diverse system utilities on Unix, including a preprocessor for a typesetting system and a desk calculator simulator. It is very fast, and produces efficient parsers. Despite its recent more widespread availability, it remains very much a part of the Unix environment, embracing many of its conventions and shortcomings, most notably the paucity of informative messages and the lack of support for any programming language but C.

Yacc's weakness is that its specifications are a rather unhappy mixture of a grammar, at a fairly high level of abstraction, and actions written at a much lower level in a poorly designed and somewhat old-fashioned sys-

```
%token   TYPE IN NAME NUMBER CHARACTER
%start   list

%{
/*   type declarations for nodes   */

    struct listnode {
                .
                .
        }

    typedef struct listhead {
        int type ;
        struct listnode *head, *tail
        } LIST /*    LIST is the type of the header   */

    /*   other declarations   */
                .
                .
%}

%union   {    /*   types that may end up on action stack   */
    LIST lval ;
    int ival ;
    /*   any other types   */
                .
                .
        }

%left    ';'
%left    ','

%%
```

Figure 10.1.2. A Yacc Specification

```
/*  Productions  */

prog:    TYPE decls IN list  {  $$ = $4 ;  }
    ;
decls:   decls decl
    |    decl
    ;  /* no action required */
decl:    NAME '=' typespec  {  $1.type = $3 ;  }
    ;
typespec:    '*' typespec    {  $$ = $2 << 1 ;  }
        |    stype           /* default action  */
        ;
stype:   'i' | 'c'           /* default returns the char  */
    ;
list:    list ';' list       {  if ($1.type != $3.type)
                                    type_error () ;
                                 $$ = append($1, $3) ;
                              }
    |    list ',' list       {  if ($1.type != $3.type)
                                    type_error () ;
                                 $$ = append($1, $3) ;
                              }
    |    NAME    {  $$ = node(eval(&$1), $1.type) ;  }
    |    NUMBER              {  $$ = node($1, 'i') ;  }
    |    CHARACTER          {  $$ = node($1, 'c') ;  }
    |    '(' list ')'  {  $$ = node($2, ($2.type)<<1); }
    ;

%%

/*  Definitions of node, append etc.

    Definition of yylex (lexical analyser) and
    yyerror (error reporter).

*/
```

Figure 10.1.2. A Yacc Specification (continued)

tems programming language. The problem is neatly described in [Joh78], where a description of recommended formating conventions for Yacc specifications is followed by the comment: '... the central problem ... is to make the rules visible through the morass of action code'. The mixed metaphor seems entirely appropriate.

Mixed levels of specification are less of a problem if attribute grammars are used to specify both syntax and semantics, when much low level detail can be taken over by the attribute evaluator. A good example of a system accepting such specifications is HLP (the Helsinki Language Processor) [Rai83]. This system is primarily aimed at the implementation of programming languages, and can produce complete compilers. The input to HLP may comprise a lexical specification, describing the basic symbols, an attribute grammar, describing syntax and semantics, and a set of translation rules, describing the output to be produced by the resulting compiler.

The details of the lexical specification will not be described; it is turned into a lexical analyser by HLP, so the interface between lexical and syntax analysis is dealt with automatically. Since the semantic actions are also produced automatically, the details of how values associated with tokens are passed around can also be handled by the system, the user need only specify how the values are to be computed, and may subsequently use them as attributes. The use of translation rules will not be described either. They simply specify output to be produced on a final traversal of the derivation tree, after all attributes have been evaluated. This is a practical alternative to making the output be a synthesized attribute of the start symbol.

The format used for productions in HLP is similar to that used by Yacc, except that = is used to separate subject and right parts. In attribute grammars, each production with semantics must be given separately, but, for those without, alternative right hand sides may be grouped together, separated by !. Names are used for nonterminals and basic symbol classes; other basic symbols, referred to as 'proper terminals' are written enclosed in single quotes. Nonterminals must be declared explicitly and each name used for a basic symbol class must have an entry in the lexical specification describing the form of its members.

HLP does not support the extended attribute grammar notation used in section 7.3, but instead uses an older notation, more closely resembling a programming language. Each nonterminal has a collection of attribute names associated with it (by declaration); each production may be followed by evaluation rules showing how the value of some attributes may be computed from others. The rules take one of two forms: either a simple rule, assigning the value of an arithmetic or Boolean expression to one attribute of a symbol, or a compound rule, when a procedure is called to perform a more elaborate computation, and assign values to one or more attributes. In rules, the attribute A of a symbol S is written as A(S), if there is only one occurrence of S in the production. Otherwise, A(S) refers to the leftmost occurrence, the next is referred to as A(S*), then A(S**), and so on. A curious syntax is used for the procedure calls in compound rules. The expressions passed as parameters to the procedure are preceded by the keyword IN:, the attributes receiving values by OUT:. This conveys information to the system, allowing it to devise an evaluation order for attributes. The order in which evaluation rules are written is not important. There are no predicates, as such, in HLP specifications, but conditional expressions are available, and these may be used to achieve a vaguely similar effect.

A complete specification requires a fair amount of declarative information in addition to the actual attribute grammar. The names and types of all attribute names must be declared; their types may be integer, real or Boolean only, but an attribute may be an array, of up to seven dimensions, of one of these types. Each nonterminal must be declared with a list of the names of its attributes. The start symbol must be declared explicitly, and declarations of any procedures called in the evaluation rules must be given; these are written in the language Burroughs Extended Algol. Other procedures used, but not called directly from a rule, must also be declared; the ones called directly are distinguished by preceding their declaration by an &. There is also a facility for giving mnemonic names to constants used in evaluation rules.

Figure 10.1.3 shows a final version of the grammar for typed lists, based on the AG of Figure 7.3.1, in a form suitable for input to HLP. The example illustrates the details of the syntax, which is quite straightforward; lines beginning % are comments. Because of the restricted types allowed for attributes in HLP, the lists have to be represented as integers, which can be taken to be indices for some large array, in which space allocation is handled by routines supplied by the user. It will be noticed that some productions have no rules attached. This is because HLP implements a default copy rule, that performs a copy of attributes with the same name. (There are technical details about what is copied, depending on whether inherited or synthesized attributes are involved, and whether they are on the right or left of the production. Essentially, it does what you would expect.) The use of exclusively upper case letters is a regrettable HLP restriction.

The parser produced by HLP consists of a single procedure in Burroughs Extended Algol. The tables are embedded in the code as case statements, in the manner described in section 6.2. They are optimized by removing LR(0) reduce states; the use of default reductions can be selected as an option. During reduce moves of the parser, a derivation tree is built for the input, with space in its nodes for the values of attributes. The attributes will be evaluated by alternating left-to-right and right-to-left, depth-first traversals of the tree; the code for performing the evaluation rules at each node is also produced as Extended Algol procedures. The evaluation process and the allocation of space for attribute values are carefully and extensively optimized. In particular, large attributes, such as symbol tables, are not copied unless necessary, instead pointers to them are used.

HLP will produce listings and detailed diagnostic information, if desired. It also has options to control whether it produces a complete system, with lexical analyser, parser and attribute evaluator, or just a parser. It may also just check whether its input grammar is $LR(k)$ or $SLR(k)$ for some given value of k.

The treatment of syntax errors is completely automatic. Both the messages issued when an error is detected and the recovery routines are produced from the input grammar; no extra information, such as error productions, is required. The recovery is a two level one, as described in section 8.2., with automatic selection of reduction goals for the phrase level part.

The parser construction algorithm is LALR(1), based on the merger of LR(1) item sets rather than the addition of lookahead to an LR(0) automaton. The particular attribute evaluation strategy used does not work for all non-circular AGs, so it is possible for semantic conflicts to arise, as well as parsing conflicts. The user must therefore know something about attribute evaluation to understand such conflicts, but the necessary knowledge is little more than an understanding of the way attribute values may depend on each other.

HLP was designed specifically as a compiler writing tool, and has been applied to the production of compilers for programming languages including Pascal, Simula and Euclid. Its designers also envisage it being used for application-oriented, special-purpose languages. It has been heavily used as an educational tool in compiler writing courses. Because its output is produced in a language supported only on the machines of

ATTRIBUTE GRAMMAR TLISTS

%   The AG would be preceded by a lexical specification
%   describing the classes name, number and character.

MNEMONICS ARE
    EMPTYLIST = -1   %   illegal pointer index
    ENVSIZE = 100   %   max number of entries
    ENTRYSIZE = 2   %   number of fields in an entry
    E_NAME = 1   %   name field
    E_TYPE = 2   %   type field
END OF MNEMONICS

SYNTHESIZED ATTRIBUTES ARE
    INTEGER
        LISTVAL,   %   used as pointers
        TYPE;
    INTEGER ARRAY
        ENVIRON [1:ENVSIZE, 1:ENTRYSIZE],
        ENTRY [1:ENTRYSIZE]
END OF SYNTHESIZED ATTRIBUTES

INHERITED ATTRIBUTES ARE
    INTEGER ARRAY
        ENVIRONMENT [1:ENVSIZE, 1:ENTRYSIZE]
END OF INHERITED ATTRIBUTES

NONTERMINALS ARE
    DECL   HAS ENTRY ;
    DECLS   HAS ENVIRON ;
    ELEMENT, LIST, PRIM
            HAVE LISTVAL, TYPE, ENVIRONMENT ;
    PROG   HAS LISTVAL ;
    STYPE, TYPESPEC
            HAVE TYPE
END OF NONTERMINALS

START SYMBOL IS LIST

Figure 10.1.3. Example HLP specification

```
PROCEDURES ARE

&PROCEDURE APPEND ...
%  declaration of a procedure called from a rule

    PROCEDURE GETNODE ...
%   declaration of a procedure not called directly

%   other procedure declarations

&END OF PROCEDURES

PRODUCTIONS ARE

PROG = 'TYPE' DECLS 'IN' LIST ;
DO
    LISTVAL(PROG) := LISTVAL(LIST) ;
    ENVIRONMENT(LIST) := ENVIRON(DECLS)
END

DECLS = DECLS DECL ;
DO
    ADD(OUT: ENVIRON(DECLS) ;
        IN:  ENVIRON(DECLS*), ENTRY(DECL))
END

DECLS = DECL ;
DO
    NEWENVIRONMENT(OUT: ENVIRON(DECLS) ;
                   IN:  ENTRY(DECL))
END

DECL = NAME '=' TYPESPEC ;
DO
    ENTRY(DECL)[E_NAME] := VAL(NAME) ;
    ENTRY(DECL)[E_TYPE] := TYPE(TYPESPEC)
END

TYPESPEC = '*' TYPESPEC ;
DO
    TYPE(TYPESPEC) = 2*TYPE(TYPESPEC*)
END
```

Figure 10.1.3. Example HLP specification (continued)

```
TYPESPEC = STYPE ;
% default copying rule

STYPE = 'i' ;
DO
    TYPE(STYPE) := INT
END

STYPE = 'c' ;
DO
    TYPE(STYPE) := CHAR
END

LIST = LIST ';' ELEMENT ;
DO
    APPEND(OUT: LISTVAL(LIST) ;
            IN:  LISTVAL(LIST*), LISTVAL(ELEMENT)) ;
    TYPE(LIST) := IF TYPE(LIST*) = TYPE(ELEMENT)
                    THEN TYPE(LIST*)
                    ELSE ERRORTYPE
    % environments inherited by default
END

LIST = ELEMENT ;

ELEMENT = ELEMENT ';' PRIM ;
DO
    APPEND(OUT: LISTVAL(ELEMENT) ;
            IN:  LISTVAL(ELEMENT*), LISTVAL(PRIM)) ;
    TYPE(ELEMENT) := IF TYPE(ELEMENT*) = TYPE(PRIM)
                        THEN TYPE(ELEMENT*)
                        ELSE ERRORTYPE
    % environments inherited by default
END

ELEMENT = PRIM ;

PRIM = NAME ;
DO
    NODE(OUT: LISTVAL(PRIM); IN: EVAL(VAL(NAME))) ;
    LOOKUP(OUT: TYPE(PRIM) ;
            IN:  VAL(NAME), ENVIRONMENT(PRIM))
END
```

Figure 10.1.3. Example HLP specification (continued)

```
PRIM = NUMBER ;
DO
    NODE(OUT: LISTVAL(PRIM); IN; VAL(NUMBER)) ;
    TYPE(PRIM) := INT
END

PRIM = CHARACTER ;
DO
    NODE(OUT: LISTVAL(PRIM); IN; VAL(CHARACTER)) ;
    TYPE(PRIM) := CHAR
END

PRIM = '(' LIST ')' ;
DO
    TYPE(PRIM) := 2*TYPE(BLIST) ;
    NODE(OUT: LISTVAL(PRIM); IN: LISTVAL(BLIST))
END

END OF PRODUCTIONS
END OF ATTRIBUTE GRAMMAR TLIST
```

Figure 10.1.3. Example HLP specification (continued)

one manufacturer, HLP is not portable. Its input format seems rather old-fashioned, and the restriction of the types of attributes to numeric and Boolean can make manipulation of data structures awkward. Despite these shortcomings, HLP is a fine demonstration of how much can be achieved by combining LR parsing with attribute grammars.[†]

10.2   Using LR Parser Generators

An LR parser generator can be an extremely useful tool; any program that reads data possessing some structure should verify that its input is correctly formed, and analyse it accordingly. The parser generator needs only a specification of the structure, in the form of a grammar, to produce a program to do exactly this. As the systems described in the previous section illustrate, they may also produce error handling procedures and provide a convenient syntax directed interface

---

[†] A successor system is under construction, but details are not yet available to me.

to the rest of the system being constructed. Because of the convenience they offer, parser generators have become popular in recent years; they can, however, present some problems to the naive user.

Logically, the very first question that should be asked when it is proposed to use any software tool is: 'Is this the right tool for the job?' Regrettably, this question is sometimes overlooked. Because LR parser generators will produce analysers for a large class of grammars, it is easy to assume that they should be used for any grammar. Often, however, grammars are sufficiently simple for less complex methods of analysis, such as finite state machines, to be suitable. Indeed, in many applications, the input is of such a restricted form, for example, a list of keywords followed by parameters, that a hand-built, special-purpose analyser, based on no particular parsing algorithm, is the best solution. In general, it is a good rule that simple methods are to be preferred to complex ones, and it must be acknowledged that LR parser generators are complex.

Once the decision to use an LR parser generator has been made, the user's task is to write a grammar that describes the form of input and is acceptable to the constructor algorithm used by whatever system is available. This will usually mean that the grammar must be LALR(1). If it is not, and most first attempts are not, then some rewriting will be necessary. A parser generator should produce at least a listing of the item sets involved in any parsing conflicts, and this can be used to identify the productions and symbols immediately involved in the conflict. Unfortunately, no algorithm for removing all sources of parsing conflicts from a grammar is available, but there are a few simple methods that work in common cases.

The most common reason for parsing conflicts is that the grammar is ambiguous, and thus not LR(k) for any k. (This is an observation about the sort of grammars people write, there is no apparent theoretical reason for it.) Certain patterns of ambiguity are quite common. One involves nonterminals that are both left and right recursive. Thus, the grammar with the two productions $L \rightarrow L,L$ and $L \rightarrow$ **a** is ambiguous. The two derivation trees for the string **a,a,a** correspond to left and right associativity for the comma, so there is a genuine structural ambiguity. The information about associativity can be incorporated in the grammar by adding an extra nonterminal and using either a left recursive production, for left associativity, or a right recursive one, for right. Thus, if the latter were chosen, the grammar would become

$$L \to E,L$$
$$L \to E$$
$$E \to \mathbf{a}$$

A similar ambiguity concerns precedence; this has been seen in G_2, in section 2.1, and the solution again lies in the introduction of new non-terminals and productions, this time to provide levels of precedence, as in G_1. As previously described, this sort of ambiguity may, in some systems, be resolved by the parser generator instead, using precedence and associativity declarations.

Another common type of ambiguity can occur when an attempt is made to include semantic information (in the sense used in Chapter 7) in the grammar. A typical example is the grammar given in section 7.2.

$$exp \to fncall \mid arrayref \mid \mathbf{name}$$
$$fncall \to fnname \ (\ explist \ )$$
$$arrayref \to arrayname \ (\ explist \ )$$
$$explist \to exp \mid explist \ , \ exp$$
$$fnname \to \mathbf{name}$$
$$arrayname \to \mathbf{name}$$

As explained there, this can be disambiguated by removing the nonter-minals *fncall* and *arrayref*, replacing them by *subsexp*, and using symbol table information to select the appropriate semantics for any particular subscripted expression, depending on the type of the name. Again, there is an alternative to rewriting the grammar, namely resolving the parsing conflict using predicates derived from an attribute grammar (see section 9.1). This facility is rarely available, though.

Some ambiguities should be taken as an indication that the proposed structure is not perspicuous. The 'dangling else' (see section 9.1) is an example of this type, where rewriting the grammar is difficult, and imposes an arbitrary choice of interpretation. For cases such as this, the best thing to do is redesign the language construct.

Grammars that are not LR(1) are not necessarily ambiguous. Some-times, a grammar is LR(k), for some $k > 1$; the case $k = 2$ is quite common, but LR(2) parser generators are rarely found. The language generated by such a grammar can always be generated by some LR(1) grammar (Theorem 4.15). It is possible to devise a procedure for sys-tematically transforming any LR(k) grammar, for $k > 1$, into an LR(1) grammar generating the same language and imposing a similar struc-ture. Such a procedure is described in [MiLS76], but the ideas behind it can often be applied heuristically.

Consider a grammar that is LR(2) but not LR(1). If there is an LR(1) shift-reduce conflict, say between items $[A \rightarrow \alpha \cdot a\beta, b]$ and $[B \rightarrow \gamma\cdot, a]$, but there is no corresponding conflict in the LR(2) parser, then adding a new nonterminal, designated $[Ba]$ and replacing the production $B \rightarrow \gamma$ by $[Ba] \rightarrow \gamma a$ will remove the conflict by forcing a shift of the a before a reduction is needed, when the lookahead symbol will be the second of the LR(2) lookahead string that was able to resolve the conflict. Similarly, a reduce-reduce conflict between $[A \rightarrow \alpha\cdot, a]$ and $[B \rightarrow \beta\cdot, a]$ can be removed by introducing $[Aa] \rightarrow \alpha a$ and $[Ba] \rightarrow \beta a$. Of course, productions with A and B occurring on their right hand sides must be replaced by new ones with $[Aa]$ and $[Ba]$ instead, and any other productions for A and B must be replaced, in such a way that the language generated by the original grammar is preserved. (So $[Aa] \Rightarrow^* \alpha a$ if and only if $A \Rightarrow^* \alpha$.)

The transformation can obviously be carried out if, whenever nonterminals that must be replaced occur on the right hand side of a production, they are followed by a terminal (unless they are also its subject). The grammar

$$S \rightarrow Abb \qquad A \rightarrow aA \qquad B \rightarrow aB$$
$$S \rightarrow Bbc \qquad A \rightarrow a \qquad B \rightarrow a$$

is LR(2). Its LR(1) parser will have a reduce-reduce conflict between $[A \rightarrow a, b]$ and $[B \rightarrow a, b]$. It can be transformed by adding nonterminals $[Ab]$ and $[Bb]$ and productions that derive from them the right hand sides of productions for A and B, followed by a b. Thus, the new grammar is

$$S \rightarrow [Ab]b \qquad [Ab] \rightarrow a[Ab] \qquad [Bb] \rightarrow a[Bb]$$
$$S \rightarrow [Bb]c \qquad [Ab] \rightarrow ab \qquad [Bb] \rightarrow ab$$

which is LR(1). This transformation is called *premature scanning*.

If a nonterminal involved in a conflict occurs in the right hand side of a production followed by another nonterminal, an additional transformation must be carried out first. If the production in question is $D \rightarrow AC$, a new nonterminal, designated $[a/C]$ must be introduced, that derives the strings $\{\alpha \mid C \Rightarrow^* a\alpha\}$, for each a such that this set is not empty. In the simplest case that there is a production $C \rightarrow a\alpha$, it is replaced by $[a/C] \rightarrow \alpha$ and $D \rightarrow AC$ can be replaced by $D \rightarrow Aa[a/C]$. Premature scanning can now be applied.

These two transformations will turn the LR(2) grammar G_5 given in section 4.2 into an LR(1) grammar. The original productions are

$$S \to AB \qquad B \to aCb$$
$$A \to a \qquad C \to \Lambda$$
$$A \to aa \qquad C \to c$$

and there is a shift-reduce conflict between $A \to a$ and $A \to aa$ in the LR(1) parser for G_5. It is necessary to introduce a nonterminal $[a/B]$ so that the production $S \to AB$ can be replaced by $S \to Aa[a/B]$. This means that $B \to aCb$ must be replaced by $[a/B] \to Cb$. This leaves the grammar suitable for premature scanning, which gives

$$S \to [Aa][a/B] \qquad [a/B] \to Cb$$
$$[Aa] \to aa \qquad C \to \Lambda$$
$$[Aa] \to aaa \qquad C \to c$$

which is LR(1).

In more complex cases, unless an implementation of the systematic transformation procedure is available, it may be easier to redesign the language, or to use the lexical analyser to perform extra lookahead in an *ad hoc* way. For example, the following grammar fragment might be used to define labelled statements and assignments in an Algol-like language.

$$statement \to lhs : = expression \,|\, labeller \; statement$$
$$lhs \to \textbf{name} \,|\, \ldots$$
$$labeller \to \textbf{name} :$$

An LR(1) shift-reduce conflict on the colon would result. The grammar is LR(2), so it could be transformed into LR(1) form, but not easily, if the remaining alternatives for *lhs* were many and complex. The usual solution adopted is to treat := as a single symbol for syntactical purposes. The lexical analyser can use one character lookahead to distinguish it from an isolated colon.

Since most LR parser generators are based on LALR(1) algorithms, reduce-reduce conflicts may arise for grammars that are LR(1) but not LALR(1). If there is no full LR(1) parser generator available, the premature scanning transformation can often be used to rewrite the grammar and remove the conflict. The grammar of Figure 5.3, with productions

$$S \to aAc \qquad S \to bAd \qquad A \to e$$
$$S \to bBc \qquad S \to aBd \qquad B \to e$$

is LR(1) but not LALR(1). It can be transformed to the LALR(1) grammar

$$S \rightarrow a[Ac] \qquad S \rightarrow b[Ad]$$
$$S \rightarrow b[Bc] \qquad S \rightarrow a[Bd]$$
$$[Ac] \rightarrow ec \qquad [Bc] \rightarrow ec$$
$$[Ad] \rightarrow ed \qquad [Bd] \rightarrow ed$$

In this case there is a simpler solution: remove the offending nonterminals and productions entirely, giving

$$S \rightarrow aec \qquad S \rightarrow bed$$
$$S \rightarrow bec \qquad S \rightarrow aed$$

This only works here because the grammar is a toy one, designed to illustrate a specific point, but the trick can sometimes be used, even with real grammars.

Two different sorts of problem can arise from the use of right recursive productions. The first is typified by the following grammar.

$$prog \rightarrow decls ; statements$$
$$decls \rightarrow decl| decl ; decls$$
$$statements \rightarrow statement| statement ; statements$$

Since the semicolon both separates declarations and terminates the list of declarations, a shift-reduce conflict occurs between items [*decls* → *decl* ; *decls*, ;] and [*decls* → *decl*, ;]. This disappears if left recursive productions are used to define *decls*. More insidiously, if a program contained many statements, a parser based on a grammar with right recursive production for *statements* might overflow its parse stack. This is because reductions by *statements* → *statement* ; *statements* only begin to occur after the last statement has been read, so the parse stack will have approximately twice as many entries as there are statements. If a left recursive production is used instead, then reductions take place as each statement is read, so the stack never has more than three entries corresponding to these productions. Left recursion should always be used in preference to right if at all possible, therefore. The only common situations when right recursion is necessary are for defining expressions with right associative operators, or when it results from the application of a premature scanning transformation.

10.3 Conclusion

The examples described in section 10.1 show that LR parser generators have been developed into useful practical tools. They are widely available and have been used extensively for a variety of applications. There remain some areas in which one would expect or hope to see further development in coming years. These include continued research into automatic diagnosis of and recovery from errors, better methods for removing the sources of parsing conflicts from grammars, and the investigation of efficient representations of parsing automata to be used with the next generation of programming languages, especially functional languages. It is to be hoped that more systems will be based on the algorithms of section 5.3, accepting all LR(1) grammars.

Finally, it seems likely that simple parser generators, such as **LR** or Yacc will disappear, to be replaced by systems producing executable programs from specifications in the form of attribute grammars. An LR parser generator will be an essential part of such a system, but its presence will become transparent to the users.

Appendix

Relations and the Computation of Reflexive Transitive Closure

A.1 Relations and their Reflexive Transitive Closure

Statements such as '7 is less than 9', 'London is the capital of England' and 'R is a subset of S' express *relationships* or associations between things. Many pairs of objects may be associated in the same way, thus '5 is less than 9' and '5 is less than 7', and so on; 'is less than' is a relationship that can hold between pairs of numbers. This is a common, intuitively understandable, idea but it is quite difficult to give a definition of relationship which corresponds to this intuitive understanding and makes it possible to talk about and manipulate the relationship independently of any particular objects that are related. The mathematical analogue of a relationship is called a *relation*, which is defined to be a set of ordered pairs. That is, if R is a relation, then $\forall z \in R: \exists a, b: z = (a, b)$. This captures the idea of a relationship by identifying it with the set of pairs of objects between which the relationship holds. Thus 'less than' is simply the set $\{(a, b) \mid a < b\}$. Relation defines a very general concept of association, which certainly encompasses the examples 'less than', 'capital of' and 'subset'.

If R is a relation, then it is possible to identify a pair of sets X and Y such that, if $(a, b) \in R$, $a \in X$ and $b \in Y$. X is called the domain of R, Dom(R) and Y its range, Rng(R), and $R \subseteq X \times Y$. Identifying the domain and range of a relation makes it possible to specify the sorts of things between which the relationship can hold. Thus if C is the relation $\{(a, b) \mid a$ is the capital of $b\}$, then Dom$(C) =$ cities and Rng$(C) =$ countries. Following colloquial usage, if $(a, b) \in R$ it is usual to write aRb. Also $R(a)$ is used to denote $\{b \mid aRb\}$.

An idea closely associated with relations is that of a *graph*. A graph is a pair (V, E) comprising a set V of *vertices* and a set E of *edges*, where $E \subseteq V \times V$. It is usual to draw graphs as diagrams, with dots representing vertices, and arrows representing edges: if $(v_1, v_2) \in E$ there is an arrow from v_1 to v_2. A sequence of edges leading from v_1 to v_k is called a *path*; its length is equal to the number of edges. Every relation has a graph associated with it in an obvious way: if $R \subseteq X \times Y$ is a relation, the graph induced by R is $G_R = (X \cup Y, \{ (a,b) \mid aRb \}) = (X \cup Y, R)$.

Example. In section 3.3 the relation 'can immediately start with' is defined. If $G = (N, T, P, S)$ then for all $X, Y \in N \cup T$, $X \ll Y$ iff $\exists \beta, \gamma \in (N \cup T)^*: \gamma \Rightarrow^* \Lambda \wedge X \to \gamma Y \beta \in P$. If G has the following productions

$$
\begin{array}{lll}
S \to Ax & & \\
 & C \to AE & F \to Fz \\
A \to B & & \\
 & E \to F & F \to yD \\
A \to C & & \\
 & E \to z & D \to A \\
B \to x & &
\end{array}
$$

then the graph induced by $\ll$ is as shown in Figure A.1. There are paths of length $3i$ for $i \geq 1$ from D to x, and one of length 1 from F to itself. $\square$

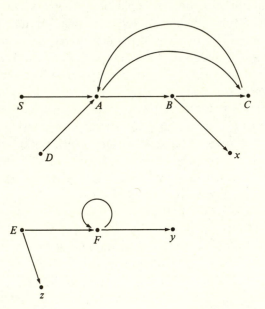

Figure A.1. Example of the Graph Induced by a Relation

If $R \subseteq X \times Y$ and $S \subseteq Y \times Z$ are relations, their *composition* is $RS = \{ (a, c) \mid \exists b: aRb \wedge bRc \}$; this is only defined if $\mathrm{Rng}(R) = \mathrm{Dom}(S)$. In the quite common case that $\mathrm{Rng}(R) = \mathrm{Dom}(R)$ it is possible to compose a relation with itself, and this leads to the idea of powers of a relation. If $R \subseteq A \times A$, let $I_A = \{ (a, a) \mid a \in A \}$; I_A is the identity

Algorithm A1. Iterative Computation of RTC

let $R \subseteq A \times A$ be a relation
let $R^* = I_A$, the identity relation in A
for $a \in A$ **do**
{   **let** $R' = R(a)$
    until $R' = \emptyset$ **do**
    {   **let** $R'' = R'$
            $R^*(a) := R^*(a) \cup R'$
            $R' := \emptyset$
            for $b \in R''$ **do**
                for $c \in R(b)$ **do**
                    if $c \notin R^*(a)$ **then** $R' := R' \cup R^*(c)$
    }
}

relation in A. Define $R^0 = I_A$ and, for $i \geq 1$, $R^i = R^{i-1}R$. In the graph induced by R, if aR^ib there is a path from a to b of length i. In the example $D \ll^3 x$.

The *transitive closure* of a relation $R \subseteq A \times A$, written R^+ is $\{ (a,b) \mid \exists j > 0 : aR^jb \}$. Graphically, if aR^+b then there is a a path of some length ≥ 1 between a and b. The *reflexive transitive closure*, or *RTC*, of R, written R^* is $R^+ \cup I_A$. (So, for all a, aR^*a.)

A note on the terminology is in order. A relation $R \subseteq A \times A$ is *reflexive* iff aRa for all $a \in A$; it is *transitive* iff $\forall a, b, c \in A : aRb \wedge bRc$ implies aRc. It can be shown that R^+ is the smallest transitive relation such that $R \subseteq R^+$. R^* is reflexive, as just noted, and R^* is the smallest reflexive and transitive relation which includes R. (In fact, this is an alternative way of defining RTC.)

There are many examples of RTCs in this book. Perhaps the most important is the derives relation $\Rightarrow^*$, which is the RTC of $\Rightarrow$, the immediately derives relation. More examples can be found in the item set construction, and in lookahead computations. It is only feasible to carry out the computation of reflexive transitive closure on a computer if the relations are finite; for these, a number of good algorithms exist.

A.2   Algorithms for RTC Computation.

The methods for computing the RTC of a relation can most easily be understood by thinking about the graphical representation, in which case the problem becomes that of finding all vertices reachable by a path of any length from each vertex in the graph. If $R \subseteq A \times A$, a simple strategy for computing R^* is, for each member a of A, to add first those elements directly reachable from a, then to proceed iteratively, adding at each stage the elements directly reachable from those added in the previous step. In order to ensure the algorithm terminates, it is necessary to check whether an element is already present before adding it; the algorithm will terminate when nothing new is added during one iteration.

This algorithm can be improved slightly, by making use of information that may be available from elements which have already been dealt with. If R^* is initialized to I_A then on each iteration, instead of adding elements that are directly reachable from those added in the previous step, their R^* values can be added. If these have already been computed, this will immediately add all reachable elements, if not, just the directly reachable ones, as before. This algorithm is shown as Algorithm A1.

This is not a very clever way of computing R^*, since the extent to which information already computed can be re-used depends on the order in which elements are considered. For example, if the algorithm was applied to compute $\ll^*$ for the example given earlier, if $R^*(S)$ and $R^*(D)$ were computed before $R^*(A)$ then $R^*(A)$ would actually be computed three times. This suggests a better way of computing the closure would be to use a recursive procedure RTC as shown in Algorithm A2, to compute each RTC value as it is required. The intention is to compute $R^*(a) = \{a\} \cup \bigcup_{b|aRb} R^*(b)$, by considering each b reachable from a, in turn. If b has already been considered, so $R^*(b) \neq \emptyset$, the procedure immediately returns and the value already computed is used, otherwise RTC is called recursively to compute $R^*(b)$ from all the elements reachable from b. Unfortunately this algorithm gives the wrong answer for relations whose graphs include loops.

For the example relation, if the computation starts with $RTC(S)$, this will call $RTC(A)$, which sets $R^*(A)$ to A then calls $RTC(B)$, which calls $RTC(C)$, which calls $RTC(A)$; this returns immediately, so $R^*(C)$ is set incorrectly to $\{A, C\}$. Clearly, a value for $R^*(A)$ should not be allowed to percolate back until all the recursive calls made from A have returned.

This may be achieved by using an auxiliary stack to hold elements whose R^* values have not yet been computed. When RTC is called to consider an element $a \in A$, a is pushed on the stack, and the current stack depth is recorded in an array, as $N(a)$. After each recursive call of RTC has considered an element $B \in R(a)$, $N(a)$ is set to the minimum

Algorithm A2. Recursive, Incorrect Computation of RTC

let $R \subseteq A \times A$ be a relation
let $R^* = \emptyset$
proc $RTC(a)$
{   **if** $R^*(a) = \emptyset$ **do**
    { $R^*(a) := \{a\}$
      for $b \in R(a)$ **do**
      { $RTC(b)$; $R^*(a) := R^*(a) \cup R^*(b)$ }
    }
}
for $a \in A$ **do** $RTC(a)$

of its current value and $N(b)$. This will have no effect unless a takes part in a loop in G_R. After all the recursive calls have been made, $N(a)$ is compared with its original value. If they are the same, either a is not involved in a loop, or it is the first element of a loop that was encountered. In that case, each element of the loop will be in the stack on top of a, and they should be popped and all have their R^* values set to that computed for a. Since all the elements reachable from a have been considered this will be correct. As elements are popped off the stack, their N values should be set to infinity, so that they will not interfere with the subsequent computation.

A version of this algorithm (which is based on a well-known method of topological sorting) was first proposed for the computation of the RTC of a relation by Eve and Kurki-Suonio, who show in [EvKS77] that the algorithm deals correctly with loops within loops and short-circuits across loops. Algorithm A3 shows how RTCs may be computed in this way; the parameter k to RTC will be the stack depth. The algorithm may be improved slightly by not computing values of R^* for elements inside a loop until they are popped off the stack. The optimization is left as an exercise.

The presentation so far has not considered how relations are to be represented in a computer's memory. There are a number of suitable data structures; perhaps the best to use in Algorithm A3 is a vector of lists, one per element a of A, holding the values of $R(a)$. These can be kept sorted, in order to facilitate the set union operations. Elements of a can be mapped to integers to index the vector. Variations on this structure are possible; the precise structure to be chosen will depend on the number of elements of A and R.

There is one way of representing relations that is quite different, and

Algorithm A3. Eve and Kurki-Suonio's Algorithm

let $R \subseteq A \times A$ be a relation
let $R^* = \emptyset$
let $N: A \to$ int be an array of 0, indexed by elements of A
let S be a stack
proc $RTC(a, k)$
{   push(S, a)
     $N(a) := k$; $R^*(a) := \{a\}$
     for all $b \in R(a)$ **do**
     {   **if** $N(b) = 0$ **then** $RTC(b, k + 1)$
       $N(a) := \min(N(a), N(b))$
       $R^*(a) := R^*(a) \cup R^*(b)$
     }
     if $N(a) = k$ **then** **until** top$(S) = a$ **do**
     { $N(\text{top}(S)), R^*(\text{top}(S)) := \infty, R^*(a)$
       pop(S)
     }
     pop(S) ‖ this pops a, in any case
}
for all $a \in A$: $N(a) = 0$ **do** $RTC(a, 1)$

	S	A	B	C	D	E	F	x	y	z
S	F	T	F	F	F	F	F	F	F	F
A	F	F	T	T	F	F	F	F	F	F
B	F	F	F	T	F	F	F	T	F	F
C	F	T	F	F	F	F	F	F	F	F
D	F	T	F	F	F	F	F	F	F	F
E	F	F	F	F	F	F	T	F	F	T
F	F	F	F	F	F	F	T	F	T	F
x	F	F	F	F	F	F	F	F	F	F
y	F	F	F	F	F	F	F	F	F	F
z	F	F	F	F	F	F	F	F	F	F

Figure A2. Matrix Representation of a Relation

permits an alternative approach to computing the closure. A relation $R \subseteq A \times A$ can be held as an $n \times n$ matrix, M, of Boolean values, where $n = |A|$, and $M_{ij} =$ true iff $a_i R a_j$ for any pair of elements $a_i, a_j \in A$. (A must be ordered in some manner.) Figure A2 shows the matrix for the example relation given earlier. It should be obvious that if the

Algorithm A4. Simple Computation by Boolean Matrix

let $R \subseteq A \times A$ be a relation
let $M = R$'s matrix representation
let $M^+ = M$
let $n = |A|$
for $m = 1$ **to** n **do**
    for $i = 1$ **to** n **do**
        for $j = 1$ **to** n **do**
            for $k = 1$ **to** n **do**
                $M^+(i,j) := M^+(i,j) \vee (M^+(i,k) \wedge M(k,j))$

Algorithm A5. Warshall's Algorithm

let $R \subseteq A \times A$ be a relation
let $M = R$'s matrix representation
let $M^+ = M$
let $n = |A|$
for $i = 1$ **to** n **do**
    for $j = 1$ **to** n **do**
        if $M^+(j,i)$ **do**
            for $k = 1$ **to** n **do** $M^+(j,k) := M^+(j,k) \vee M^+(i,k)$

product P of two such matrices R and S is computed by setting $P_{ij} = \bigvee_{k=1}^{n} R_{ik} \wedge S_{kj}$, then P will represent the composition of the relations represented by R and S. By noting that, for a finite relation $R \subseteq A \times A$, if $|A| = n$, then $R^n = R^*$ (in graphical terms, if there is a path from a to b, it can have length at most $n - 1$, otherwise it will run out of vertices), and that $\forall 1 \leq i < n\colon R^i \subseteq R^{i+1}$, a method of computing R^+ by matrix multiplication, as in Algorithm A4, is suggested.

R^* can be obtained by inserting true on the leading diagonal of M^+ after this computation.

Algorithm A4 requires $O(n^4)$ Boolean operations. A little thought and juggling with the loops shows that this can be improved to $O(n^3)$, as shown in Algorithm A5, Warshall's Algorithm [Wars62].

Algorithm A5 has another advantage. Since the innermost loop variable iterates along rows of the matrix, if the Boolean elements are represented by a single bit and these are packed into machine words, the computation can be carried out on whole words at a time, in parallel. Although this only produces a linear improvement in performance, for many relations the size of n is only 2 or 3 times the wordlength of many computers, so the effect is noticeable.

Warshall's algorithm is often the most efficient way of computing RTC, although Eve and Kurki-Suonio's method is superior for sparse relations (ones whose graphs have relatively few edges). If bit matrix techniques are to be used, the overhead of setting up the initial bit matrix representation and extracting values from it must be considered. On most machines, this will involve shift and masking operations.

Bibliography

[AhJo74] Aho, A.V. and Johnson, S.C., "LR parsing", *ACM Computing Surveys*, **6**, 99–124 (1974).

[AhJU75] Aho, A.V., Johnson, S.C. and Ullman, J.D., "Deterministic parsing of ambiguous grammars", *Communications of the ACM*, **18**, 441–452 (1975).

[AhUl72] Aho, A.V. and Ullman, J.D., *The Theory of Parsing, Translation and Compiling, Volume 1: Parsing*, Prentice-Hall, Englewood Cliffs, N.J. (1972).

[AhUl72a] Aho, A.V. and Ullman, J.D., "Optimization of LR(k) parsers", *Journal of Computer and System Sciences*, **6**, 573–602 (1972).

[AhUl73] Aho, A.V. and Ullman, J.D., "A technique for speeding up LR(k) parsers", *SIAM Journal on Computing*, **2**, 106–127 (1973).

[AhUl77] Aho, A.V. and Ullman, J.D., *Principles of Compiler Design*, Addison-Wesley, Reading, Mass. (1977).

[AHSt86] Al-Hussainin, A.M.M. and Stone, R.G., "Yet another storage technique for LR parsing tables", *Software – Practice and Experience*, **16**, 389–401 (1986).

[AnEH73] Anderson, T., Eve, J. and Horning, J.J., "Efficient LR(1) parsers", *Acta Informatica*, **2**, 12–39 (1973).

[Back76] Backhouse, R.C., "An alternative approach to the improvement of LR(k) parsers", *Acta Informatica*, **6**, 277–296 (1976).

[Back79] Backhouse, R.C., *Syntax of Programming Languages – Theory and Practice*, Prentice-Hall, Englewood Cliffs, N.J. (1979).

[Back57] Backus, J.W. and others, "The FORTRAN automatic coding system" in *Proceedings of the Western Joint Computer Conference* (1957), pp188–198.

[Baue76] Bauer, F.L., "Historical remarks on compiler construction" in Bauer, F.L. and Eickel, J., *Compiler Construction – An Advanced Course (2nd ed.)*, Springer Verlag, Berlin (1976), pp603–621.

[Beat82] Beatty, J.C., "On the relationship between the LL(1) and LR(1) grammars", *Journal of the ACM*, **29**, 1007–1022 (1982).

[Boch76] Bochmann, G.V., "Semantic evaluation from left to right", *Communications of the ACM*, **19**, 55–62 (1976).

[BuJa81] Burgess, C. and James, L., "An indexed bibliography for LR grammars and parsers", *Sigplan Notices*, **16,8**, 14–26 (1981).

[BuFi82] Burke, M. and Fisher, G.A., "A practical method for syntactic error diagnosis and recovery" in *Proceedings of Sigplan 82 Conference on Compiler Construction* (1982), pp67–78.

[Cele78] Celentano, A., "Incremental LR parsers", *Acta Informatica*, **10**, 307–321 (1978).

[Chap84] Chapman, N.P., "LALR(1, 1) parser generation for regular right part grammars", *Acta Informatica*, **21**, 29–45 (1984).

[Chom59] Chomsky, N., "On certain formal properties of grammars", *Information and Control*, **2**, 137–167 (1959).

[CoMo82] Cole, A.J. and Morrison, R., *An Introduction to Programming with S-Algol*, Cambridge University Press, Cambridge (1982).

[CoWi73] Conway, R.W. and Wilcox, T.R., "Design and implementation of a diagnostic compiler for PL/I", *Communications of the ACM*, **16**, 169–179 (1973).

[Deme75] Demers, A.J., "Elimination of single productions and merging nonterminal symbols of LR(1) grammars", *Computer Languages*, **1**, 105–119 (1975).

[DeRe69] DeRemer, F.L., *Practical Translators for LR(k) Languages*, Ph.D. Thesis, MIT, Harvard, Mass. (1969).

[DeRe71] DeRemer, F.L., "Simple LR(k) grammars", *Communications of the ACM*, **14**, 453–460 (1971).

[DePe79] DeRemer, F.L. and Pennello, T.J., "Efficient computation of LALR(1) lookahead sets", *Sigplan Notices*, **8**, 176–187 (1979).

[DePe82] DeRemer, F.L. and Pennello, T.J., "Efficient computation of LALR(1) lookahead sets", *ACM Transactions on Programming Languages and Systems*, **4**, 615–649 (1982).

[EvKS77] Eve, J. and Kurki-Suonio, R., "On computing the transitive closure of a relation", *Acta Informatica*, **8**, 303–314 (1977).

[Farr82] Farrow, R., "LINGUIST-86, yet another translator writing system based on attribute grammars" in *Proceedings of Sigplan 82 Conference on Compiler Construction* (1982), pp160–171.

[FiMa80] Fischer, C.N. and Mauney, J., "On the role of error productions in syntactic error correction", *Computer Languages*, **5**, 131–139 (1980).

[FiWe79] Fisher, G.A., Jr. and Weber, M., "LALR(1) parsing for languages without reserved words", *Sigplan Notices*, **14,11**, 26–30 (1979).

[Floy64] Floyd, R.W., "Bounded context syntactic analysis", *Communications of the ACM*, **7**, 62–67 (1964).

[Fu82] Fu, K.S., *Syntactic Pattern Recognition and Applications*, Prentice-Hall, Englewood Cliffs, N.J. (1982).

[GhMa79] Ghezzi, G. and Mandrioli, D., "Incremental parsing", *ACM Transactions on Programming Languages and Systems*, **1**, 58–70 (1979).

[GiLe78] Gillett, W.D. and Leach, S., "Embedding semantics in LR parser tables", *Software – Practice and Experience*, **8**, 731–753 (1978).

[GiGr66] Ginsburg, S. and Greibach, S., "Deterministic context-free languages", *Information and Control*, **9**, 602–648 (1966).

[GHJ79] Graham, S.L., Haley, C.B. and Joy, W.N., "Practical LR error recovery", *Sigplan Notices*, **8**, 168–175 (1979).

[Groe84] Groening, K., "Combined actions to reduce LR parser tables (experimental results)", *Sigplan Notices*, **19,3**, 42–45 (1984).

[Harr78] Harrison, M.A., *Introduction to Formal Language Theory*, Addison-Wesley, Reading, Mass. (1978).

[Heil77] Heilbrunner, S., *Using item grammars to prove LR(k) theorems, Bericht Nr. 7701*, Fachbereich Informatik, Hochschüle der Bundeswehr, Munich (1977).

[Heil79] Heilbrunner, S., "On the definition of ELR(k) and ELL(k) grammars", *Acta Informatica*, **11**, 169–176 (1979).

[Heil81] Heilbrunner, S., "A parsing automata approach to LR theory", *Theoretical Computer Science*, **15**, 117–157 (1981).

[Heil83] Heilbrunner, S., "A metatheorem for undecidable properties of formal languages and its application to LRR and LLR grammars and languages", *Theoretical Computer Science*, **23**, 49–68 (1983).

[Heil85] Heilbrunner, S., "Truly prefix-correct chain-free LR(1) parsers", *Acta Informatica*, **22**, 499–536 (1985).

[HoUl79] Hopcroft, J.E. and Ullman, J.D., *Introduction to Automata Theory, Languages and Computation*, Addison-Wesley, Reading, Mass. (1979).

[Horn76] Horning, J.J., "LR grammars and analysers" in Bauer, F.L. and Eickel, J., *Compiler Construction – an Advanced Course (2nd ed.)*, Springer Verlag, Berlin (1976), pp85–108.

[Horn76a] Horning, J.J., "What the compiler should tell the user" in Bauer, F.L. and Eickel, J., *Compiler Construction – An Advanced Course (2nd ed.)*, Springer Verlag, Berlin (1976), pp525–548.

[HuSz78] Hunt, H.B.,III and Szymanski, T.G., "Corrigendum to 'Lower bounds and reductions between grammar problems'", *Journal of the ACM*, **25**, 687–688 (1978).

[HuSU75] Hunt, H.B.,III, Szymanski, T.G. and Ullman, J.D., "On the complexity of LR(k) testing", *Communications of the ACM*, **18**, 707–716 (1975).

[Joh78] Johnson, S.C., *Yacc: Yet Another Compiler-Compiler, Computing Science Report 32*, Bell Laboratories, Murray Hill, N.J. (1978).

[John86] Johnsson, T., "Attribute grammars and functional programming", to appear (draft, 1986).

[Joli74] Joliat, M.L., "Practical minimisation of LR(k) parser tables" in *Proceedings of the IFIP Congress* (1974), pp376–380.

[Joli76] Joliat, M.L., "A simple technique for partial elimination of unit productions from LR(k) parsers", *IEEE Transactions on Computers*, **C-25**, 763–764 (1976).

[JoMa80] Jones, N.D. and Madsen, C.M., "Attribute-influenced LR parsing" in N.D. Jones, *Semantics-Directed Compiler Generation, LNCS94*, Springer Verlag, Berlin (1980), pp393–407.

[JoLe82] Joshi, A.K. and Levy, L.S., "Phrase structure trees bear more fruit than you would have thought", *American Journal of Computational Linguistics*, **8**, 1–11 (1982).

[Kemp73] Kemp, R., "An estimation of the set of states of the minimal LR(0) acceptor" in Nivat, M., *Automata, Languages and Programming*, North-Holland, Amsterdam (1973), pp563–574.

[Knu65] Knuth, D.E., "On the translation of languages from left to right", *Information and Control*, **8**, 607–639 (1965).

[Knu68] Knuth, D.E., "Semantics of context-free languages", *Mathematical Systems Theory*, **2**, 127–145 (1968).

[Knu73] Knuth, D.E., *The Art of Computer Programming, Volume 1: Fundamental Algorithms (2nd ed.)*, Addison-Wesley, Reading, Mass. (1973).

[Kore69] Korenjak, A.J., "A practical method for constructing LR(k) processors", *Communications of the ACM*, **12**, 613–623 (1969).

[KoSS79] Koskimies, K. and Soisalon-Soininen, E., "On a method for optimizing LR parsers", *International Journal of Computer Mathematics*, **7**, 287–295 (1979).

[KoRS82] Koskimies, K., Räihä, K-J. and Sarjakoski, M., "Compiler construction using attribute grammars" in *Proceedings of Sigplan82 Conference on Compiler Construction* (1982), pp153–159.

[KrDe73] Kral, J. and Demner, J., "A note on the number of states of the DeRemer recognizer", *Information Processing Letters*, **2**, 22–23 (1973).

[KrMa81] Kristensen, B.B. and Madsen, O.L., "Methods for computing LALR(k) lookahead", *ACM Transactions on Programming Languages and Systems*, **3**, 60–82 (1981).

[LaLo75] LaLonde, W.R., *Practical LR analysis of regular right part grammars*, Ph.D. thesis, University of Waterloo, Waterloo, Ontario (1975).

[LaLo77] LaLonde, W.R., "Regular right part grammars and their parsers", *Communications of the ACM*, **20**, 731–741 (1977).

[LaLo79] LaLonde, W.R., "Constructing LR parsers for regular right part grammars", *Acta Informatica*, **11**, 177–193 (1979).

[LaLo81] LaLonde, W.R., "The construction of stack-controlling LR parsers for regular right part grammars", *ACM Transactions on Programming Languages and Systems*, **3**, 168–206 (1981).

[LaLH72] LaLonde, W.R., Lee, L.S. and Horning, J.J., "An LALR(k) parser generator" in *Proceedings of the IFIP Congress 1971* (1972), pp513–519.

[LaBS78] Lawson, H.W., Jr., Bertran, M. and Sanagustin, J., "The formal definition of human/machine communications", *Software – Practice and Experience*, **8**, 51–58 (1978).

[Levi78] Levinson, L.E., "The effects of syntactic analysis on word recognition accuracy", *Bell Systems Technical Journal*, **57**, 1627–1644 (1978).

[Mads80] Madsen, O.L., "On defining semantics by means of extended attribute grammars" in Jones, N.D., *Semantics-Directed Compiler Generation, LNCS94*, Springer Verlag, Berlin (1980), pp259–299.

[MaKr76] Madsen, O.L. and Kristensen, B.B., "LR parsing of extended context free grammars", *Acta Informatica*, **7**, 61–73 (1976).

[MaFi82] Mauney, J. and Fischer, C., "A forward move algorithm for LL and LR parsers" in *Proceedings of Sigplan82 Conference on Compiler Construction* (1982), pp67–78.

[MiLS76] Mickunas, M.D., Lancaster, R.L. and Schneider, V.B., "Transforming LR(k) grammars to LR(1), SLR(1) and (1, 1) bounded right-context grammars", *Journal of the ACM*, **23**, 511–533 (1976).

[MiMo78] Mickunas, M.D. and Modry, J.A., "Automatic error recovery for LR parsers", *Communications of the ACM*, **21**, 459–465 (1978).

[MoSc81] Morris, J.M. and Schwartz, M.D., "The design of a language-directed editor for block-structured languages", *Sigplan Notices*, **16,6**, 28–33 (1981).

[NaSa86] Nakata, I. and Sassa, M., "Generation of efficient LALR parsers for regular right part grammars", *Acta Informatica*, **23**, 149–162 (1986).

[Page77] Pager, D., "A practical general method for constructing LR(k) parsers", *Acta Informatica*, **7**, 249–268 (1977).

[Page77a] Pager, D., "The lane tracing algorithm for constructing LR(k) parsers and ways of enhancing its efficiency", *Information Science*, **12**, 19–42 (1977).

[Page79] Pager, D., "Eliminating unit productions from LR parsers", *Acta Informatica*, **9**, 31–59 (1979).

[PaCC85] Park, J.C.H., Choe, K.M. and Chang, C.H., "A new analysis of LALR formalisms", *ACM Transactions on Programming Languages and Systems*, **7**, 159–175 (1985).

[Pavl77] Pavlidis, T., *Structural Pattern Recognition*, Springer Verlag, Berlin (1977).

[PDeR78] Pennello, T.J. and DeRemer, F., "A forward move algorithm for LR error recovery" in *Conference Record of the 5th Annual ACM Symposium on Principles of Programming Languages* (1978), pp241–254.

[PeyJ85] Peyton-Jones, S.L., "Yacc in Sasl – an exercise in functional programming", *Software – Practice and Experience*, **15**, 807–820 (1985).

[PeyJ87] Peyton-Jones, S.L., *The Implementation of Functional Programming Languages*, Prentice-Hall, Englewood Cliffs, N.J. (to appear, 1987).

[Pitt81] Pittl, J., "Negative results on the size of deterministic right parsers" in Gruska, J. and Chytil, M., *Mathematical Foundations of Computer Science 1981, LNCS118*, Springer Verlag, Berlin (1981), pp442–451.

[Pur74] Purdom, P., "The size of LALR(1) parsers", *BIT*, **14**, 326–337 (1974).

[PuBr80] Purdom, P. and Brown, C.A., "Semantic routines and LR(k) parsers", *Acta Informatica*, **14**, 299–315 (1980).

[PuBr81] Purdom, P.W. and Brown, C.A., "Parsing extended LR(k) grammars", *Acta Informatica*, **15**, 115–127 (1981).

[Rai80] Räihä, K-J., "Experiences with the compiler writing system HLP" in Jones, N.D., *Semantics-Directed Compiler Generation, LNCS94*, Springer Verlag, Berlin (1980), pp350–362.

[Rai80a] Räihä, K-J., "Bibliography on attribute grammars", *Sigplan Notices*, **15,3**, 35–44 (1980).

[Rai83] Räihä, K-J., Saarinen, M., Sarjakoski, M., Sippu, S., Soisalon-Soininen, E. and Tienari, M., *Revised Report on the Compiler Writing System HLP, Department of Computer Science Report A-1983-1*, University of Helsinki, Helsinki (1983).

[RayS83] Rayward-Smith, V.J., *A First Course in Formal Language Theory*, Blackwell Scientific, Oxford (1983).

[Reis81] Reisner, P., "Formal grammar and human factors design of an interactive graphics system", *IEEE Transactions on Software Engineering*, **SE-7**, 229–240 (1981).

[RiWS79] Richards, M. and Whitby-Strevens, C., *BCPL – the Language and its Compiler*, Cambridge University Press, Cambridge (1979).

[Schm84] Schmitz, L., "On the correct elimination of chain productions from LR parsers", *International Journal of Computer Mathematics*, **15**, 99–116 (1984).

[SiSS83] Sippu, S. and Soisalon-Soininen, E., "A syntax-error-handling technique and its experimental analysis", *ACM Transactions on Programming Languages and Systems*, **5**, 656–679 (1983).

[SoiS77] Soisalon-Soininen, E., "Elimination of single productions from LR parsers in conjunction with the use of default reductions" in *Proceedings of the 4th ACM Symposium on Principles of Programming Languages* (1977), pp183–193.

[SoiS80] Soisalon-Soininen, E., "On the space optimizing effect of eliminating single productions from LR parsers", *Acta Informatica*, **14**, 157–174 (1980).

[SoiS82] Soisalon-Soininen, E., "Inessential error entries and their use in LR parser optimization", *ACM Transactions on Programming Languages and Systems*, **4**, 179–195 (1982).

[Spec81] Spector, D., "Full LR(1) parser generation", *Sigplan Notices*, **16,8**, 58–66 (1981).

[Tai78] Tai, K.C., "On the implementation of parsing tables", *Sigplan Notices*, **14**, 100–101 (1979).

[Toku81] Tokuda, T., "Eliminating unit reductions from LR(k) parsers using minimum contexts", *Acta Informatica*, **15**, 447–470 (1981).

[Turn79] Turner, D.A., *Sasl Language Manual (Revised edition), CS/79/3*, St. Andrews University Department of Computational Science, St. Andrews (1979).

[Ukko83] Ukkonen, E., "Lower bounds on the size of deterministic parsers", *Journal of Computer and System Sciences*, **26**, 153–170 (1983).

[Ukko85] Ukkonen, E., "Upper bounds on the size of LR(k) parsers", *Information Processing Letters*, **20**, 99–103 (1985).

[Wars62] Warshall, S., "A theorem on Boolean matrices", *Journal of the ACM*, **9**, 11–12 (1962).

[Watt74] Watt, D.A., *LR Parsing of Affix Grammars, Report no. 7*, University of Glasgow Computing Department, Glasgow (1974).

[Watt80] Watt, D.A., "Rule-splitting and attribute-directed parsing" in Jones, N.D., *Semantics-Directed Compiler Generation*, Springer Verlag, Berlin (1980), pp363–392.

[WaMa83] Watt, D.A. and Madsen, O.L., "Extended attribute grammars", *The Computer Journal*, **26**, 142–153 (1983).

[Weth78] Wetherell, C., "Why automatic error correctors fail", *Computer Languages*, **2**, 179–186 (1977).

[WeSh81] Wetherell, C. and Shannon, A., "LR – automatic parser generator and LR(1) parser", *IEEE Transactions on Software Engineering*, **SE-7**, 274–278 (1981).

Index

accept state, 54
accessing symbol, 109, 161
action stack, 141, 144, 152, 154
ad hoc techniques, 3, 98, 99, 139, 208
AGs, *see attribute grammars*
alphabet, 9, 23
ambiguous grammars, 17, 175, 194, 205
ambiguous languages, 17
Anderson, T., 88
applied positions, 150
arrays, 100
associativity, 177, 194
attribute evaluators, 154
attribute expressions, 151
attribute grammars, 149–157, 179–181, 198–204
   circular, 154, 157
   LR attributed, 155, 179
attributed symbol forms, 150
attributes, 150
augmented grammars, 54

backtracking, 21, 25, 31
Backus Naur Form, 5, 191
   extensions, 180
basic symbol classes, 136–137, 198
basic symbols, 135–136
BCPL, 6, 7–8, 102, 112–115
bit matrices, 92, 216
BNF, *see Backus Naur Form*
bottom up parsing, 3, 4, 18–23
bounded context grammars, 5
Brown, C.A., 149
Burroughs Extended Algol, 199

C programming language, 193
canonical LR(0) parser, 158
canonical LR(k) parser, 61, 84, 95
case statements, 112

CFG, 10
chains of unit reductions, 124
characteristic FSM, 34, 37, 40
Chomsky, N., 5, 10
closure items, 41, 42–45, 63
clusters of errors, 168
combined table, 105
comments, 7
compilers, 3, 135, 198
   multi-pass, 149, 154
complexity results, 75–77, 154, 163
composition of relations, 212
concatenation, 9
configurations
   of a PDA, 31
   of an LR(k) automaton, 39
   of an LR(k) automaton with readback, 188
consistent, 68
construction of FSMs from RL grammars, 27
context free grammars, 3, 5, 10
context free languages, 2, 11
contingent items, 148
core function, 79, 87, 159
correct prefix parsers, 158
correct prefix property, 158

dangling else, 178
data structures, 43, 88
DCFLs, *see deterministic context free languages*
declarations, 138, 142, 194
default actions, 107, 117
default reductions, 159, 200
defining positions, 150
DeRemer, F.L., 6, 88
DeRemer/Pennello lookahead set, 89
derivations, 11–12
   leftmost, 12, 16, 73

rightmost, 12, 16
  in an RRPG, 182
derivation tree, 12, 14–16, 141
derives relation, 11
deterministic context free languages, 32, 69, *see also es-DCFLs
  and fs-DCFLs*
discrimated union, 151
domain, 211

editing operations, 162, 169
efficiency, 119, 173
empty stack, 69
empty string, 9
endmarker symbol, 36, 54–55, 57,
  71
error configuration, 160
error correction, 162
error corrector, 162
error distance, 162
error entries, 105
error messages, 22, 160–161
  in HLP, 200
  spurious, 167
error phrase, 171
error productions, 164
error recovery, 163–174
  handcrafted, 173
  in HLP, 200
  in Yacc, 195
error state, 160
error symbol, 160
error terminal, 164
errors, 35, 139, 158–174
es-DCFLs, 70
evaluation rules, 199
exception items, 133

final states of a PDA, 31
FINISH, 50
finite state machines, 23–27, 136
  deterministic, 25
  nondeterministic, 25
first$_k$, 62, 64
FOLLOW, 49, 78, 94
Follow sets, 90
  computation of, 93
forbidden items, 148
Fortran, 191
forward move, 169, 171
free items, 147
frontier, 14

fs-DCFLs, 70
FSMs, *see finite state machines*
functional languages, 113, *see also
  Sasl*
  and attribute grammars, 155
global attributes, 155
graph, 211
Groening, K., 120

handle, 5, 22, 34, 48
Heilbrunner, S., vii, 74
Helsinki Language Processor
  (HLP), 198
human-computer interaction, 4

identification of nullable nonterminals, 18
identity relation, 212
inadequate states, 54
includes relation, 92
inherently ambiguous languages,
  17
inherited attributes, 150, 154–155
initial configuration, 39
initial item set, 40, 43, 63
item grammar, 65
item set construction
  LR(0), 40–46
  LR(k), 62–64
  for RRPGs, 183
item sets, 40, 63
items, 40

Knuth, D.E., 5, 149
Korenjak, A.J., 5
Kristensen, B.B., 88

labelled tree, 14
LaLonde, W.R., 6, 188
LALR(k) automaton, 79
LALR(k) grammars, 6, 78, 86
language, 10
  accepted by an FSM, 24
  generated by a CFG, 11
lazy evaluation, 156
leaf, 14
left recursion, 148, 209
left recursive, 17, 73
leftmost sentential forms, 12
Lex, 194
lexical analysis, 135–139, 194
linearity, 75

lists, 105–111, 113
LL(1) grammars, 87
LL(k) grammars, 73, 147
local correction, 169
look states, 112
lookahead completion, 79, 86, 88
lookahead LR(k) grammars, *see*
    LALR(k) grammars
lookahead sets, 78, 88–90
lookahead symbol, 48
lookback states, 90
LR languages, 69–71
LR (parser generator), 191–193
LR(0) automaton, 38–39, 43
LR(0) collection of item sets, 41
LR(0) contexts, 33
LR(0) grammars, 34, 46, 72
LR(0) parsers, 33–39, 78
LR(0) reduce states, 120–121, 133,
    200
LR(1) contexts, 46
LR(k) automaton, 63
LR(k) contexts, 59, 66
LR(k) grammars, 5, 58, 61, 68, 74
LR(k) item set construction, 63
LR(k) parsers, 33, 56–62

Madsen, O.L., 88
minimum distance error corrector,
    162
moves relation of a PDA, 31, 57

natural languages, 4
nonterminal alphabet, 10
nonterminal columns, 108
nontextual applications, 135, 139–
    140
notational conventions, 56
nucleus, 41
nullable nonterminals, 18, 52, 147,
    155, 193

operator precedence, 177

Pager, D., 95
Pager's algorithm, 95, 191
parser defined errors, 160
parser generators, 98, 191–204
parser tables, 100
parsing conflicts, 33, 54, 78, 84,
    178, 205, *see also reduce-reduce*
    conflicts and shift-reduce conflicts
parsing relation, 57, 60

partial derivation tree, 14
path, 68, 90
    in a graph, 211
pattern matching, 117
pattern recognition, 4, 140
PDA, *see pushdown automaton*
Pennello, T.J., 88
phrase level recovery, 163, 171
phrase structure grammar, 10
powers of a language, 10
powers of a relation, 212
precedence, 194, 206
precedence techniques, 77, 160
p-reduced grammars, 87
prefix, 10
prefix correct parsers, 123, 133
prefix property, 70
premature scanning, 207
presentation of algorithms, 6–8
productions, 10
pseudovariables, 144, 193
Pumping Lemma, 30n
Purdom, P.A., 149
pushdown automaton, 30, 57, 70

range, 211
readback machines, 188
reads relation, 91
recursive descent, 87, 99
reduce states, 34
reduce-reduce conflicts, 46, 61, 86,
    195, 207
reductions, 20, 31, 39, 48, 103,
    110, 114, 117
reduction goals, 171, 200
reflexive transitive closure, 45, 52,
    92, 97, 213
regular languages, 27, 34
regular right part grammars, 180–
    190
    representation of, 182
relations, 211–213
reserved words, 137
right hand side, 11
right linear grammars, 27, 65, 183
right recursive nonterminals, 17,
    209
rightmost sentential forms, 12
RL grammars, *see right linear gram-*
    mars
RRPGs, *see regular right part gram-*
    mars

RTC, *see reflexive transitive closure*

S-Algol, 6
Sasl, 7, 113–120
self embedding, 17
semantic actions, 140–149
semantic domains, 150
semantic routines, 140
sentences, 11
sentential forms, 11
shared lists, 108
shift moves, 21, 31, 39, 103, 104–105, 107, 117
shift-reduce conflicts, 46, 61, 195, 207
shift-reduce optimization, 120–121
shift-reduce parsing, 20–22, 31, 35
size of LR parsers, 120
size of LR(k) automata, 76
size of parser tables, 105
size of a grammar, 76
SLR(1) contexts, 49–50
SLR(1) parsers, 48
sparse matrix techniques, 105
START, 50, 64
start symbol, 10
strings, 7, 9
strong compatibility, 96
structured domains, 151
subject, 10
successor, 41, 43, 63, 87
successor symbol, 41, 44
suffix, 10
symbol tables, 137, 144, 151, 180
syntax, 1
syntax analysis, 1–4, 14
syntax diagram, 181
syntax directed schemes, 141
synthesized attributes, 150, 152–153

table driven parsers, 98
table initializing, 102
terminal alphabet, 10
terminal columns, 106
textual applications, 135
token classes, 137
tokens, 135, 194
Top, 68
top down parsing, 3, 19, 73
topological sorting, 215
transition diagrams, 24
transition function
    of a FSM, 23
    of a PDA, 31
transitive closure, 213
two level recovery, 168, 173
typing of states, 112

unambiguous grammars, 58
undecidability results, 17, 62, 87, 160, 162
unit productions, 122, 144
unit reduction elimination, 122–134, 159
    by modifying the parser construction process, 129–130
    from LALR(1) automata, 126–127
    from SLR(1) automata, 127, 131–132
unit reductions, 122, 177
useless nonterminals, 18, 59
useless productions, 18
user defined operators, 139

valof/resultis, 7

Warshall's Algorithm, 217
weak compatibility, 95

Yacc, 88, 144, 178, 193–198